IMAGES
of America

HUNTINGTON PARK

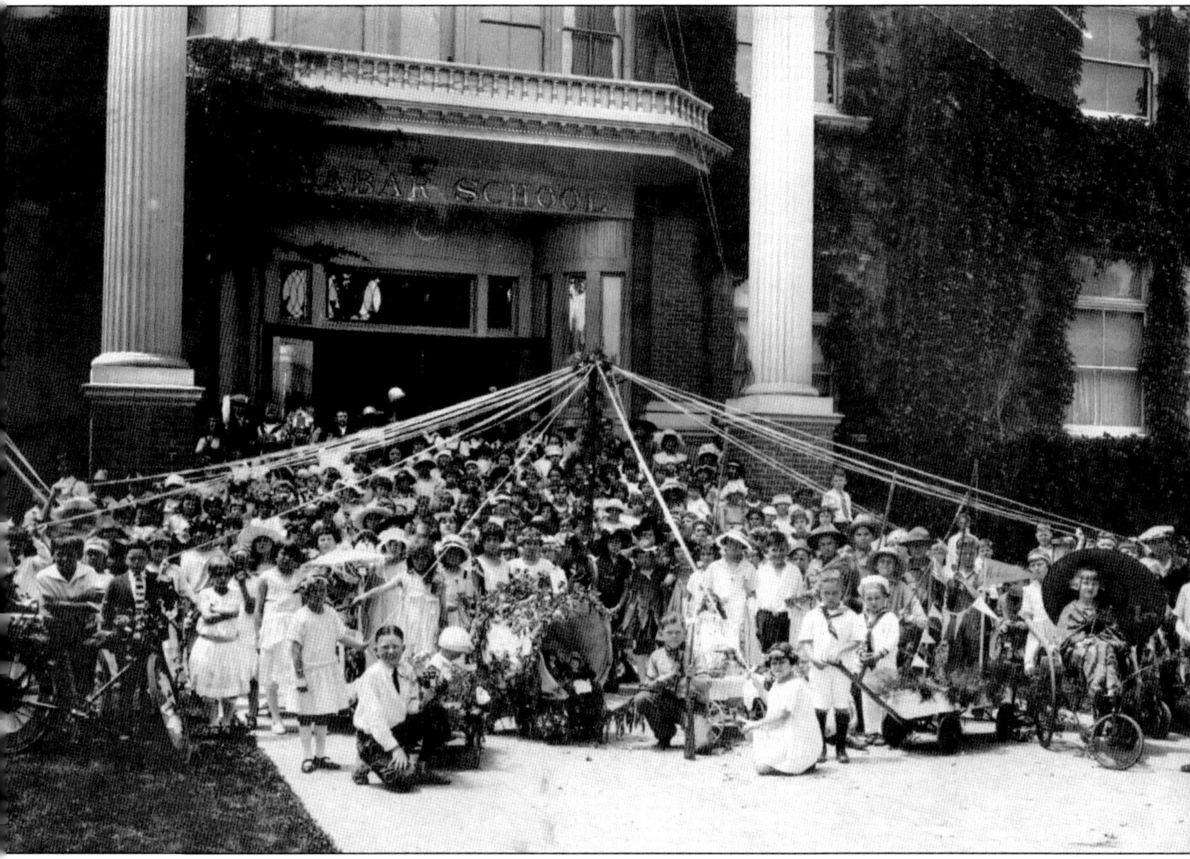

ON THE COVER. Students from Malabar Street School celebrate May Day with a Maypole Dance in 1925. May Day, as celebrated in Europe and the United States, has Pagan origins like some other modern holidays do, but this one is not associated with labor or communism. It celebrates fertility and the beginning of the spring/summer season. This holiday lost most of its popularity in the United States in the second half of the 20th century, although many remember dancing around the Maypole as children. (Courtesy of the City of Huntington Park.)

IMAGES
of America

HUNTINGTON PARK

James M. Kinsey

ARCADIA
PUBLISHING

ISBN 978-0-7385-4711-4

Published by Arcadia Publishing
Charleston SC, Chicago IL, Portsmouth NH, San Francisco CA

Printed in the United States of America

Library of Congress Catalog Card Number: 2006934435

For all general information contact Arcadia Publishing at:
Telephone 843-853-2070
Fax 843-853-0044
E-mail sales@arcadiapublishing.com
For customer service and orders:
Toll-Free 1-888-313-2665

Visit us on the Internet at www.arcadiapublishing.com

Dedicated to all of my fellow city employees with whom I've had the honor to serve the citizens of Huntington Park for nearly 25 years.

Contents

Acknowledgments

The task of researching and compiling information and photographs for a 100-year-old city is daunting to say the least and required the efforts and assistance of many.

Thanks to Wally Shidler, a local southeast area historian whose wealth of information made this project possible. Wally is a native of Walnut Park and attended Huntington Park High School. Thanks to Huntington Park retired police captain Michael Gwaltney for his historical insights on the police department. I would also like to thank chief of police Mike Trevis; city manager Greg Kordner; city clerk Rosanna Ramirez; Mayor Elba Gurerrero; mayor pro-tem Mario Gomez; city council members Juan Noguez, Ofelia Hernandez, and Elba Roma; and the Centennial Celebration Committee for their support and assistance in the production of this publication. All images in this volume are courtesy of the City of Huntington Park.

I would especially like to thank my wife, Kim Kinsey, and my son, Devin Kinsey, for their assistance, patience, and support during this long project.

INTRODUCTION

On September 1, 2006, the City of Huntington Park celebrated its 100th birthday. The city engaged in a yearlong celebration emphasizing its rich and entertaining history with roots back to the early 19th century. This fascinating collection of photographs from the city's archives depicts the birth and growth of an American city.

Much of Southern California was explored by Francisco Salvatore Lugo, sometimes known as Don Jose Maria Lugo. Lugo claimed the land himself in the name of the king of Spain. At that time, the area now known as Huntington Park was vast, fertile prairie land.

In 1810, Don Antonio Maria Lugo, son of Francisco, was granted 29,514 acres by the king of Spain in a show of gratitude for services rendered as a distinguished soldier, explorer, and loyal follower. He called this property Rancho San Antonio, possibly after the city in Spain where he was born in 1775. He developed this huge estate into a cattle and horse ranch of more than 46 square miles, extending from the present-day Monterey Park south to North Long Beach, encompassing all or parts of the communities of Vernon, Bell, Maywood, Cudahy, Bell Gardens, Commerce, Compton, South Gate, Lynwood, and Montebello among others. During this same time period, Don Antonio Lugo also purchased a large tract of land in what is now San Bernardino. The Lugo family was also involved in the development of the city of Los Angeles.

Throughout the 19th century, the early history of Huntington Park revolved around the Lugo family, who witnessed and survived the rise of the missions, the independence of Mexico, the Gold Rush, and American statehood. The road from the Lugo ranch house to the city of Los Angeles was well traveled by a steady stream of visitors. With the growth of the population and expansion of farms, businesses essential to farming began to appear, such as blacksmiths, feed suppliers, and brokers. They settled sometimes along the wide stretch of road near the watering trough that civic leaders had placed in the center of the street, thus establishing a pattern for the subsequent development of Pacific Boulevard as a broad thoroughfare.

In the middle and latter part of the 19th century, many of the old ranchos began breaking up as Lugo family members sold portions. Farmers and land developers descended on the area following statehood. The land changed ownership many times, and much of the area became farmland.

In the years between 1900 and 1906, the real estate firm of Burbank and Baker purchased a large area south of what is now Randolph Street, which was briefly called La Park. Business and residential lots were offered for sale from $75 to $350 on the promise of electricity and that the railway would soon be extended to the new development with a 5¢ fare for the ride to and from downtown Los Angeles. In 1902, as part of their efforts to entice Henry Huntington to extend a line of his Pacific Electric Railway through their development, Burbank and Baker named the tract Huntington Park. When Henry Huntington built his Whittier line in 1903, he extended it through Huntington Park along Randolph Street.

By 1906, the population had awakened to the importance of incorporation. George A. Garlow, D. B. Lyons, William Lindsay, and A. A. Weber joined forces to obtain from the county board of supervisors a permit to incorporate and, in a series of mass meetings in the streets of the town, aroused citizens to the need for action. A population of 500 persons was legally necessary for incorporation as a sixth-class city, and Huntington Park had exactly 526 residents.

An election was held August 20, 1906, with a total of 94 votes cast—77 were in favor of incorporation and 17 votes were against. The results were certified by the California secretary of state on August 30, and the city was officially incorporated on September 1, 1906. The first city council meetings were held at the home of the first mayor, Dr. Louis Weber, near the corner of Pacific Boulevard and Randolph Street.

The first city motto of "Beautiful City of Homes" later became "The City of Perfect Balance" for its planned balance of residential, business, and manufacturing sections, and thus Huntington Park grew up with the mushrooming expansion of industry. The city's transportation resources were outstanding, and the abundance of job opportunities in almost every type of business brought in many new residents. As homes sprang up, there was a great demand for community improvements. Schools, churches, recreation facilities, and civic institutions developed rapidly.

This pictorial history will take the reader from the days of the Lugo family through the city's growth, development, redevelopment, and rebirth into the vibrant culturally diverse city it has become today.

One

The City of Perfect Balance

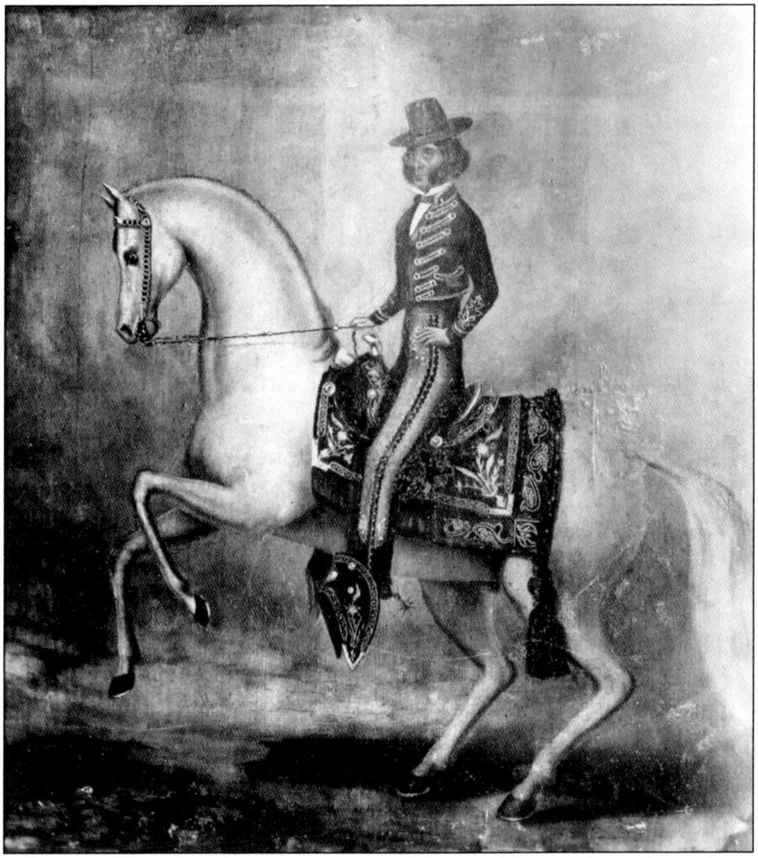

Soldier and Explorer. In 1810, for service to the king of Spain, Don Antonio Maria Lugo was granted 29,514 acres of land. It was said of the Lugo holdings, "No horses so fast, No cattle so fine, No land so fertile, No Rancho more fertile than the Rancho San Antonio."

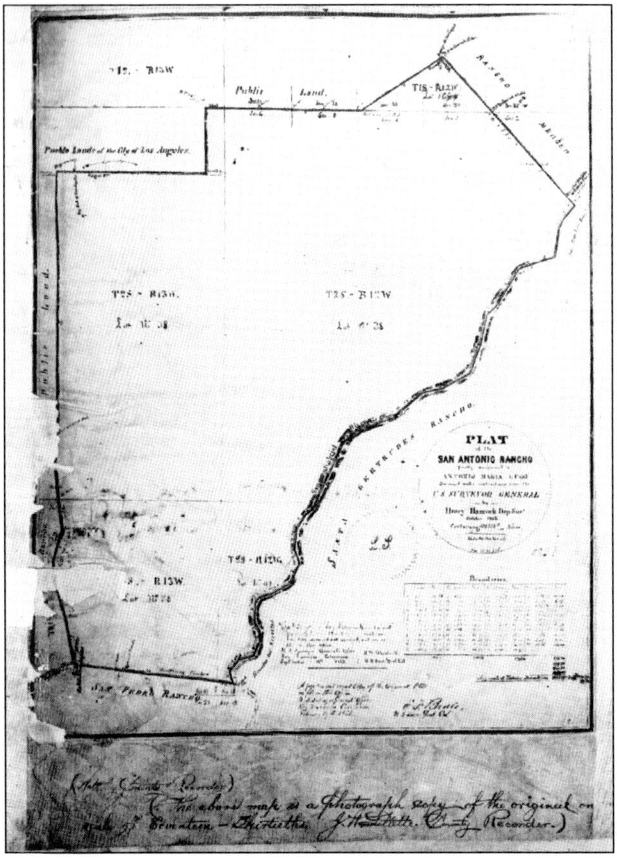

RANCHO SAN ANTONIO. Bordering "Pueblo Lands of the City of Los Angeles" on the north and the San Pedro rancho on the south, cities such as Huntington Park, Bell, Bell Gardens, Compton, Lynwood, Vernon, and South Gate, among others, rest on this 47-square-mile area.

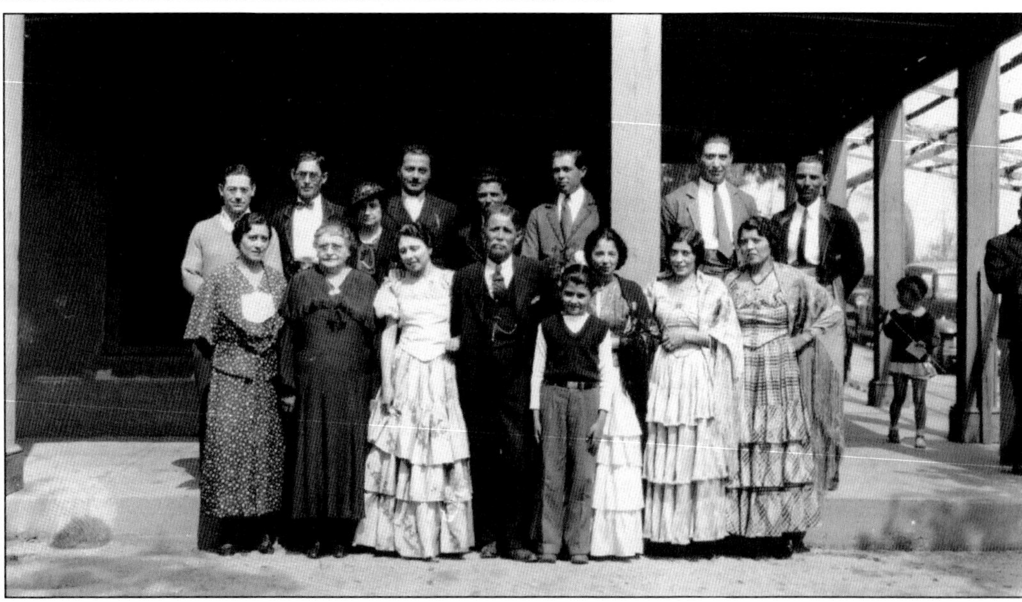

THE LUGO FAMILY HOME. The Lugo family is pictured in front of the Lugo adobe on Gage Avenue in Bell Gardens in March 1936. The structure burned down in the 1980s before it could be moved, as planned, to Huntington Park.

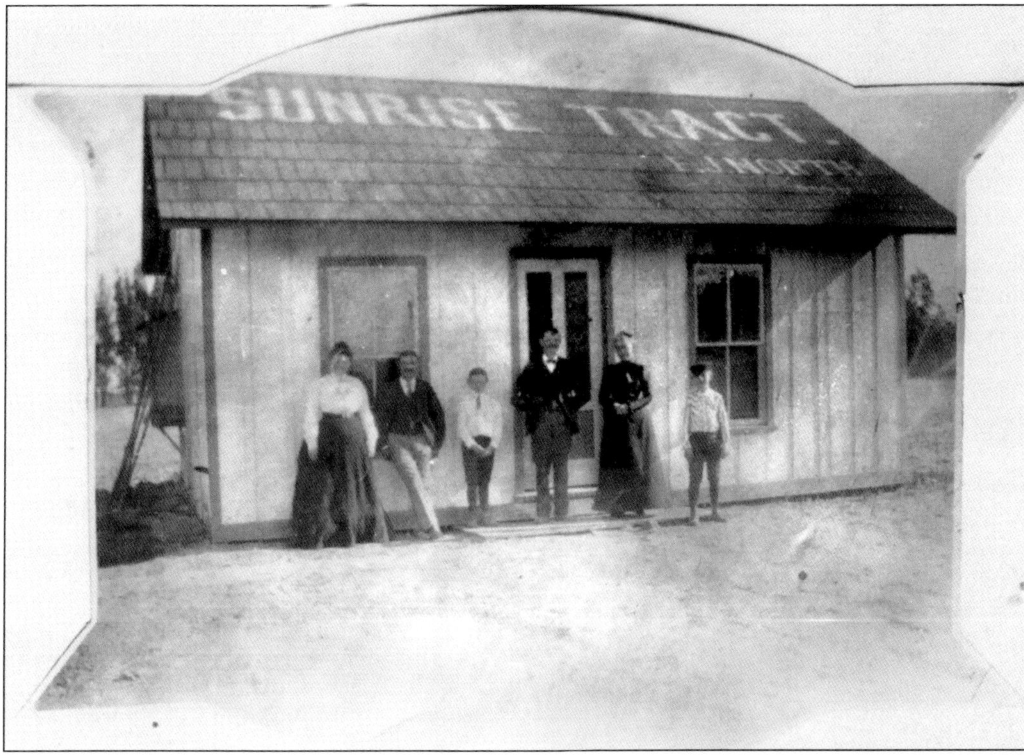

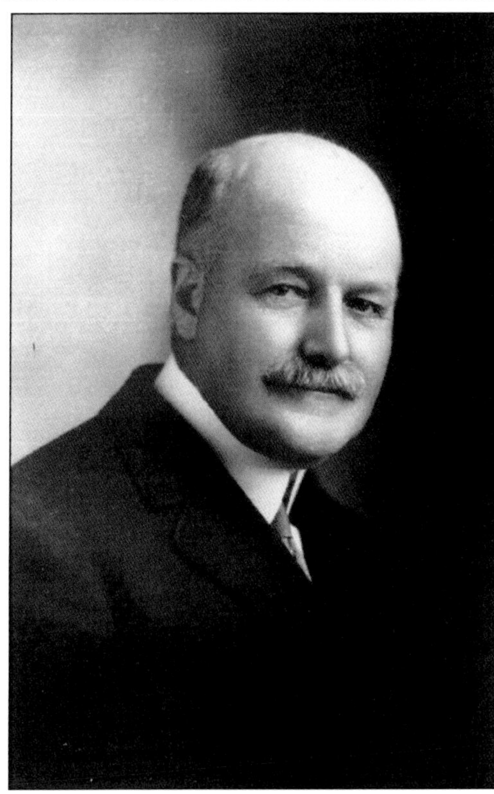

THE SUNRISE TRACT. In 1901, Floyd J. North (right) started a real estate business at Middleton Street and Clarendon Avenue called the Sunrise Tract. He erected a small California-style building and put the tract's name on the roof (above). During this same time period, Burbank and Baker, a firm of real estate subdividers, offered lots of their 100-acre tract of land south of Randolph Street for sale at $75 to $350. North was the first city treasurer from 1906 to 1908 and was succeeded by W. H. Boss. He recruited groups from his native state of New York to see the tract he had purchased from the Lugos.

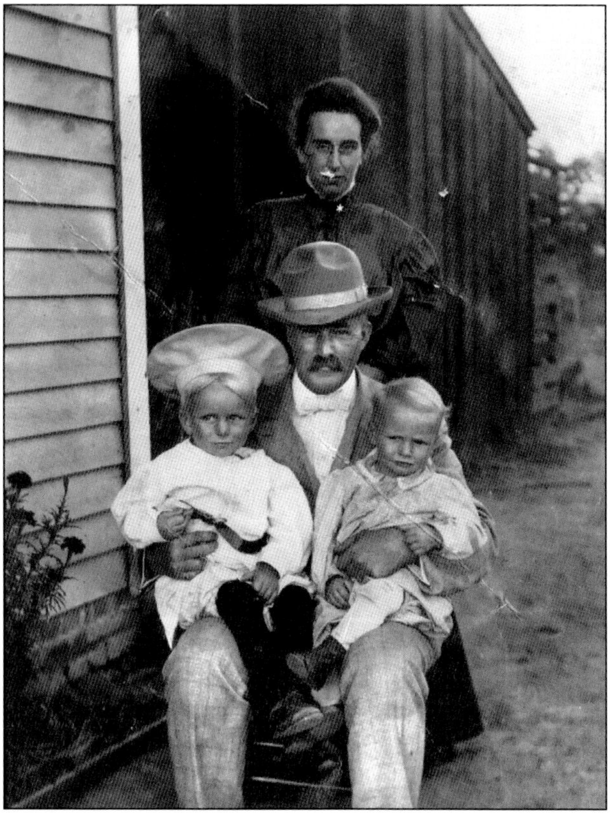

The North Family. North and his wife were married in 1903. There were six homes on the tract at that time, and North believed Santa Fe Avenue would have a city built around it. The Norths were the victims of the city's first fire on April 16, 1904, when their home burned to the ground. Florence C. North escaped from the house with only two kitchen chairs and a pet parrot she had thrown out a kitchen window. A longtime resident, Floyd North (below, left) built a new home at 6301 Middleton Street around 1923, where he lived for many years. He saw his dreams come true, with his kids and wife (left), as Huntington Park developed.

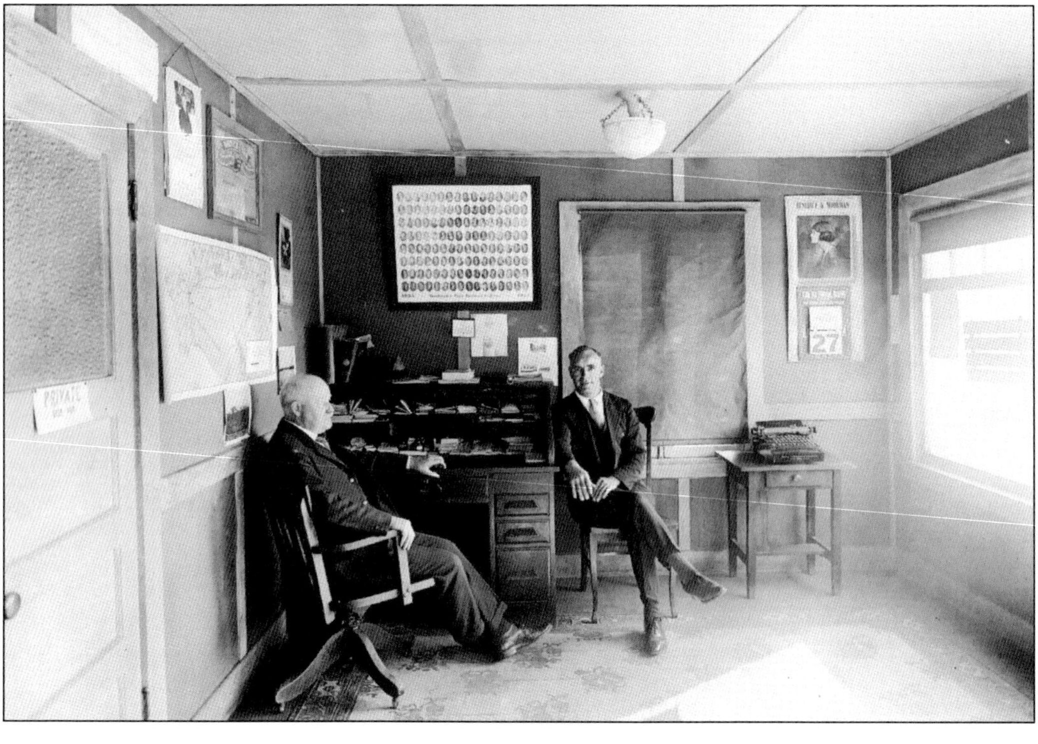

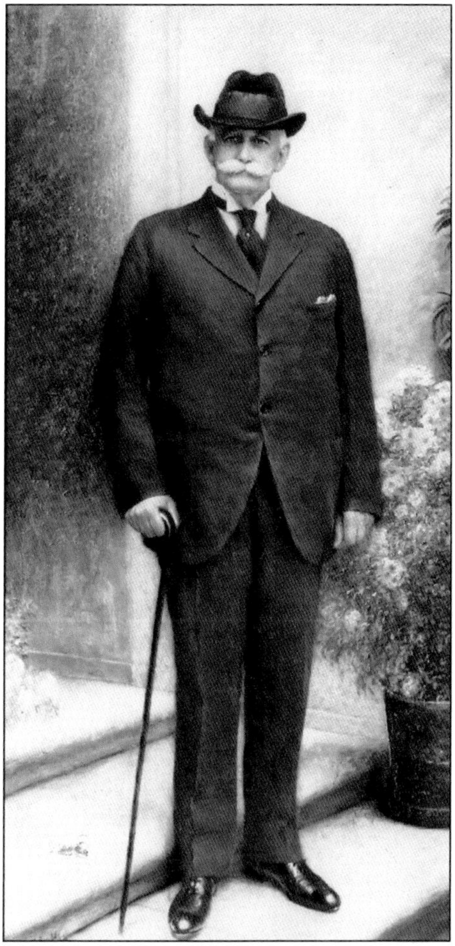

HENRY HUNTINGTON. In an effort to lure a railway through their development, Burbank and Baker called their tract Huntington Park in order to convince railroad tycoon Henry Huntington (right) to run his Red Line through the city. Known as the Pacific Electric Red Cars, a railroad line ran through Huntington Park on Randolph Street to the city of Whittier (below). The original fare was advertised as 5¢, and early residents were outraged when the fare was found to be 10¢.

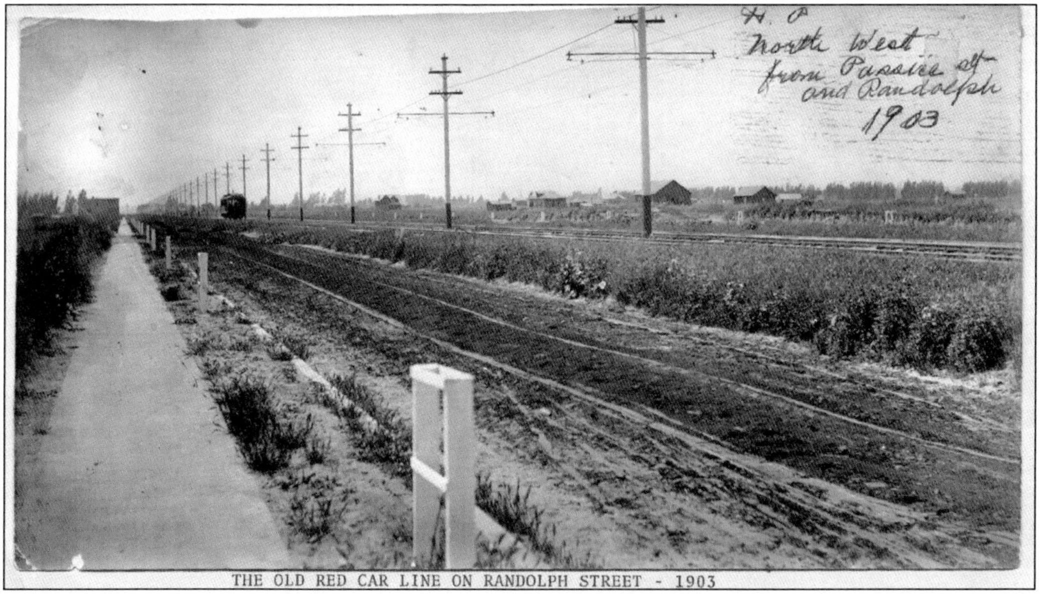

THE OLD RED CAR LINE ON RANDOLPH STREET - 1903

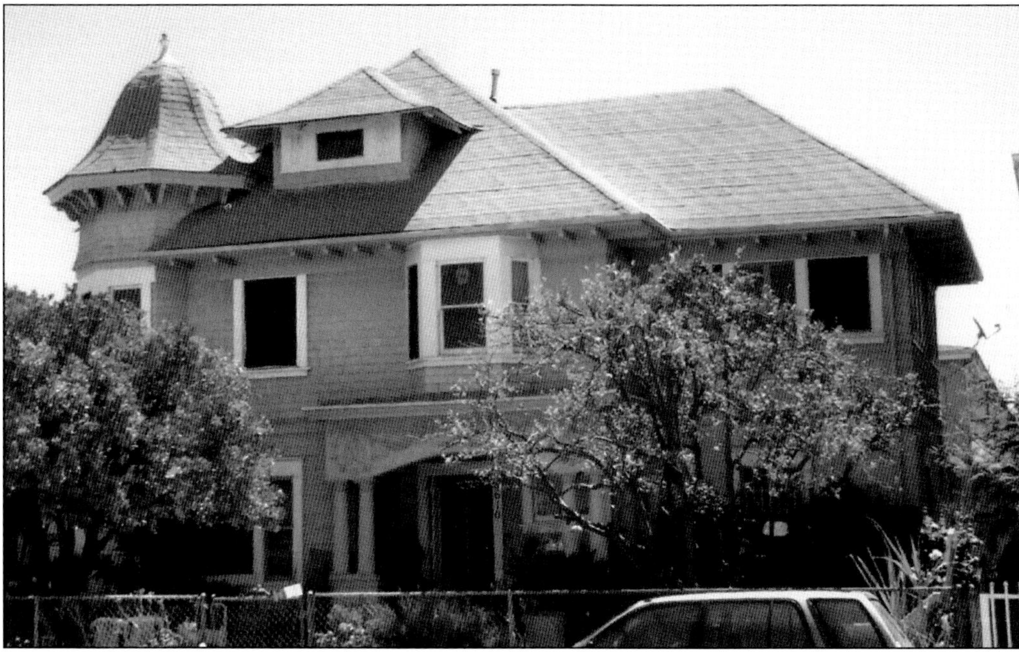

First Large Home in Huntington Park. Built in 1903 and pictured as it appears today, this was the home of George A. Garlow, a consulting hair and scalp specialist who settled in Huntington Park. He became a farmer of fowl with more than 3,000 chickens and 3,000 pigeons. He was also very involved in the incorporation of the city, the development of its schools, and the acquisition of the streetcar line. The house was later used as the city health department. For many years, a large cobblestone arch that Garlow built near his home was a city landmark.

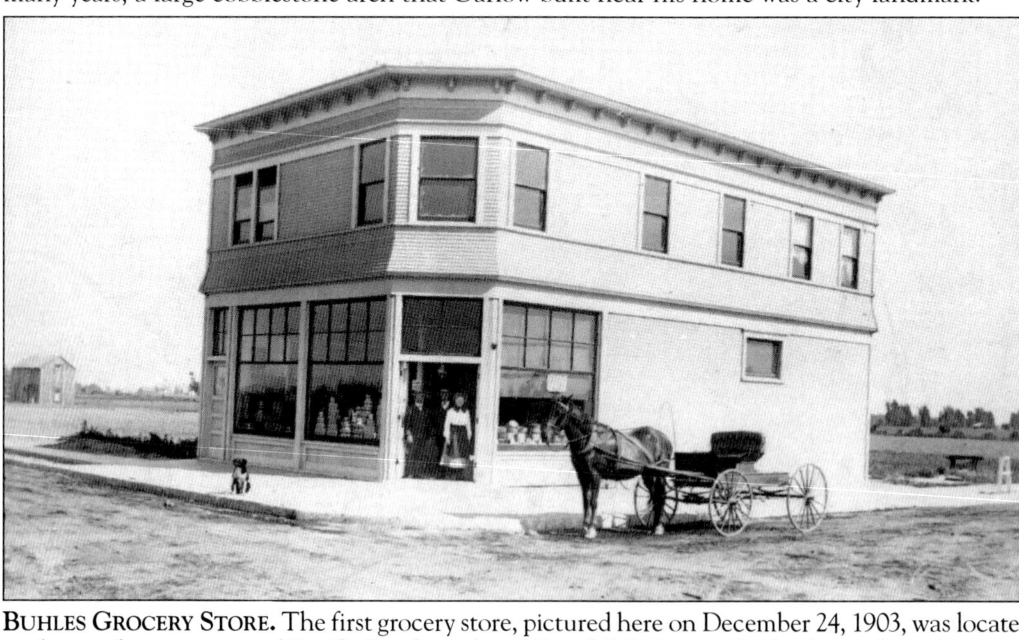

Buhles Grocery Store. The first grocery store, pictured here on December 24, 1903, was located at the southeast corner of Pacific Boulevard and Randolph Street. It also housed the first post office. The horse and wagon seen here were for deliveries. The first office of the *Huntington Park Daily Signal*, first published August 13, 1904, was later attached to the structure.

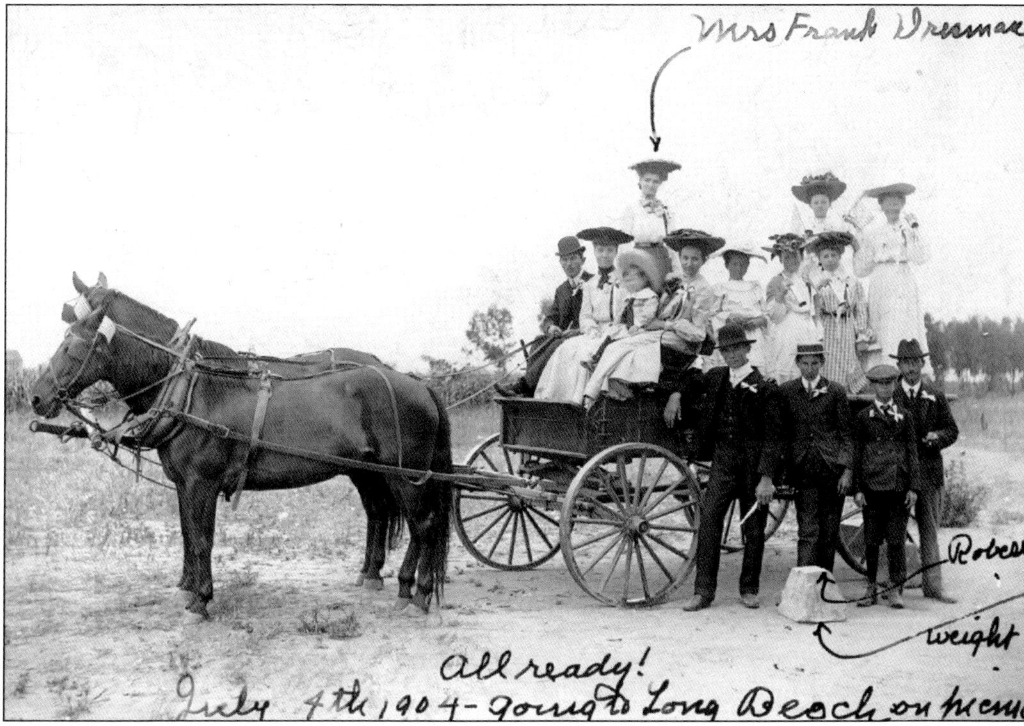

HUNTINGTON PARK PIONEERS. Pictured are the Buhles family and friends, including a woman identified as Mrs. Frank Dressman, on their way to Long Beach to celebrate the Fourth of July in 1904. Frank Dressman, a native of Kentucky, moved to Huntington Park in 1906. The 1935 history of Huntington Park identifies Mrs. Dressman as Mary A. Cobler, who later married Frank.

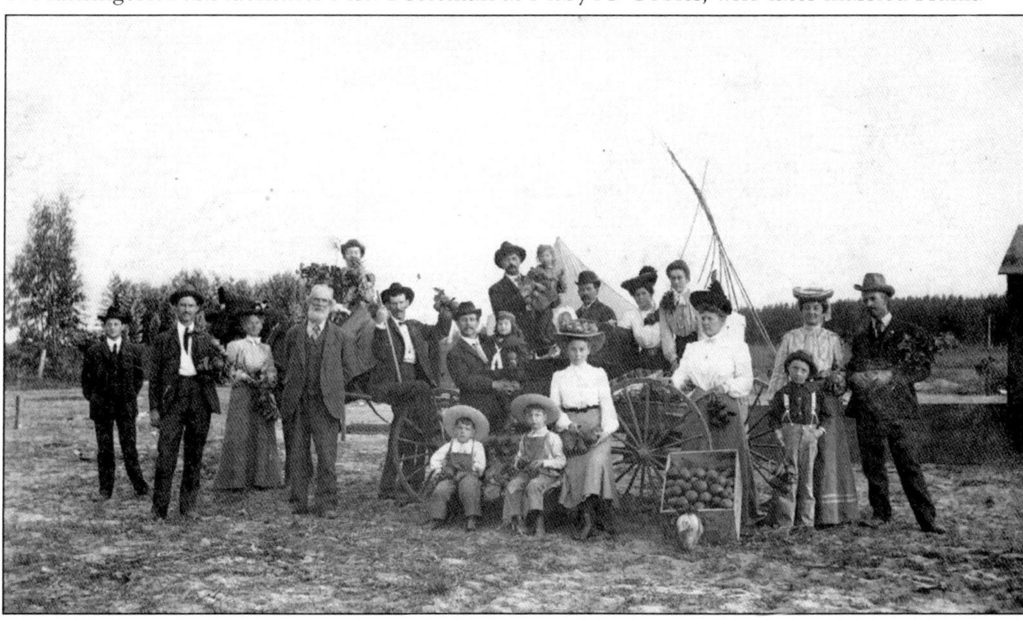

FACES FROM HUNTINGTON PARK HISTORY. Pictured are several members of the Buhles family, the owners of the grocery store, and several other local farmers, including the Haights and the Chapmans. They appear to be showing off their fresh fruit.

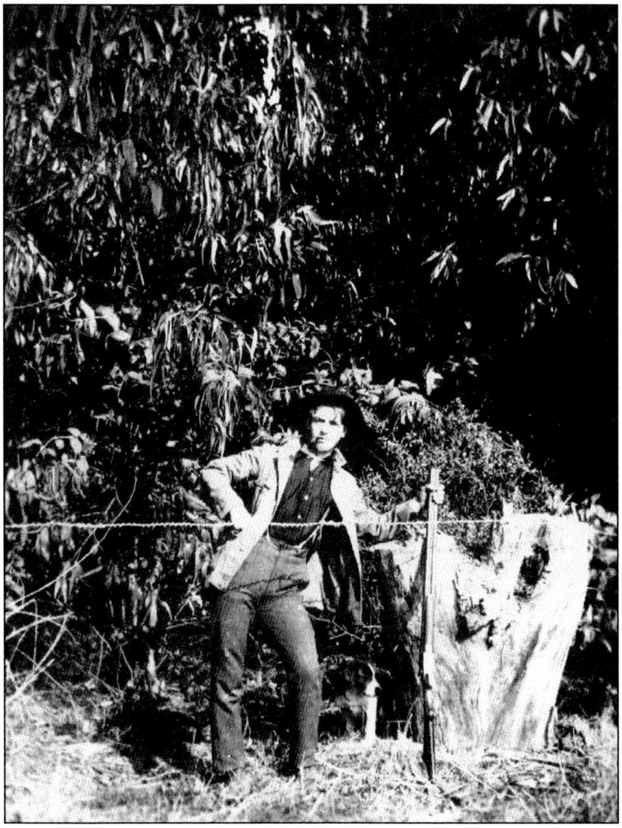

A Huntington Park Hunter. When Huntington Park was incorporated in 1906, much of the area was farmland and wilderness. This photograph was taken at Miles and Florence Avenues and depicts a local hunter and his dog.

Founded with Spirituality. The first church founded in Huntington Park was a Methodist Episcopal congregation. At one time, services were held in a tent at Rugby Avenue and Clarendon Avenues with William "Dad" Lusk as pastor. This 1905 Easter photograph is possibly that church.

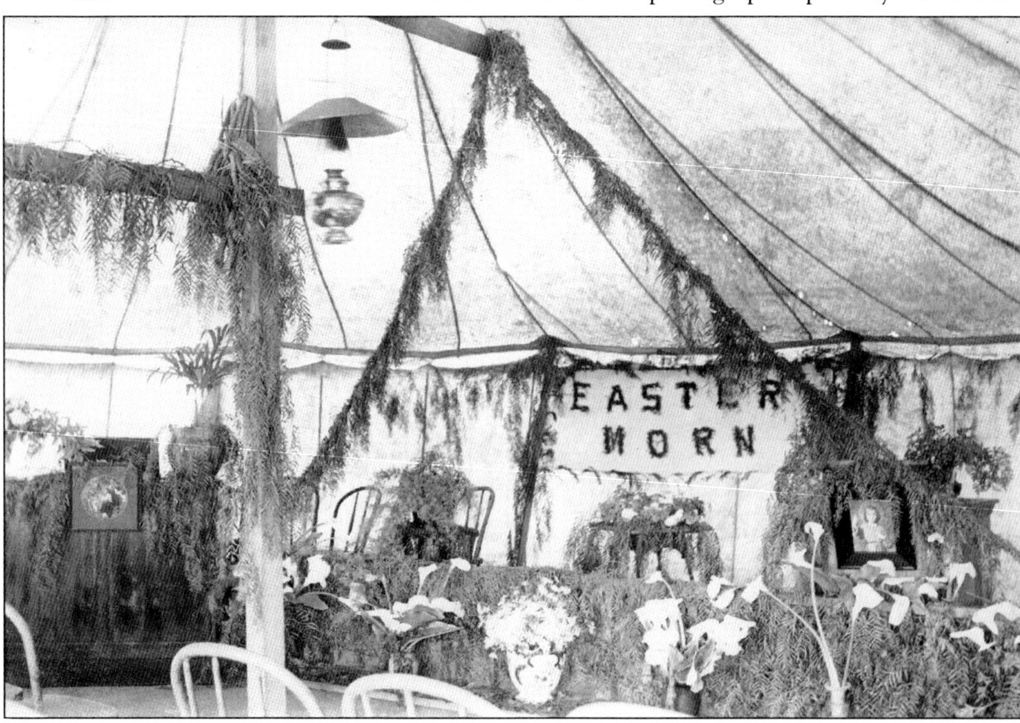

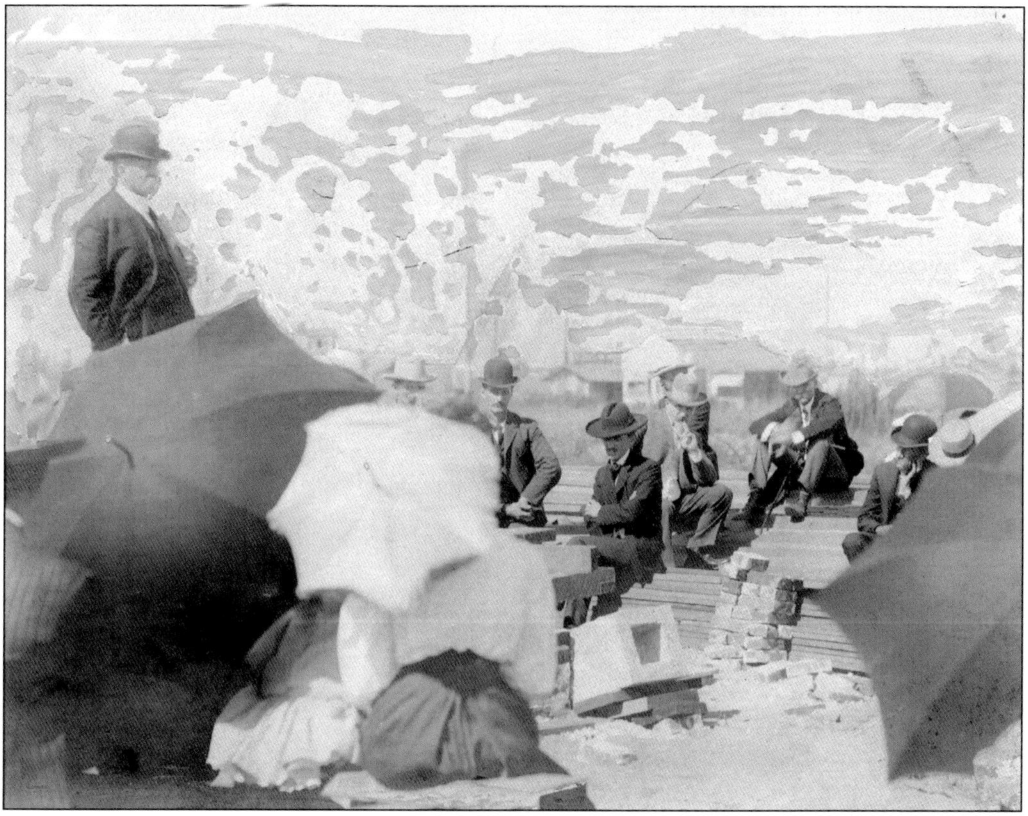

FIRST METHODIST EPISCOPAL CHURCH. Pictured (above) is the 1905 laying of the cornerstone of the Methodist Episcopal Church at Gage and Rita Avenues. As Huntington Park began to grow rapidly, other denominations appeared, including the Baptists, who built the first church edifice in 1905 (below) at Rita and Clarendon Avenues.

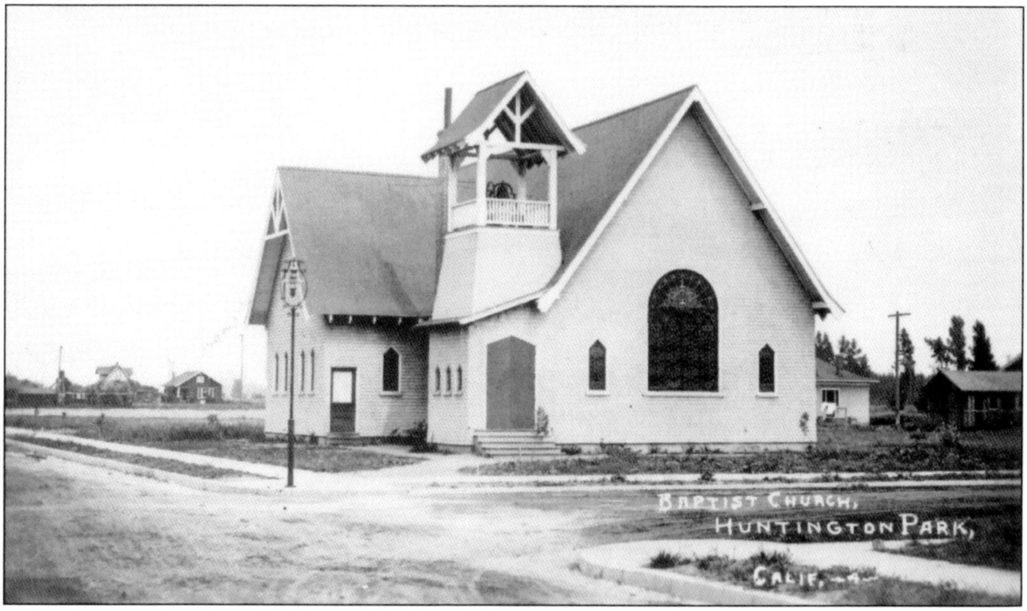

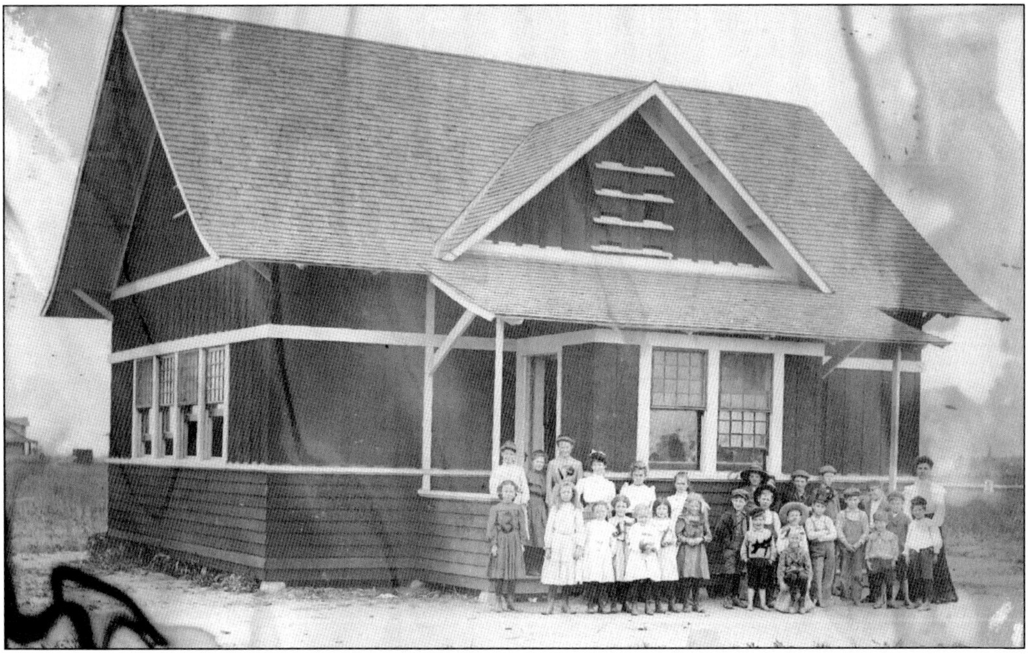

First School in Huntington Park. The first schoolhouse was built by developers Burbank and Baker, seen here in 1905, in response to pressures from the residents. The structure was also used for church services and city meetings. The families of the first 13 students hired a teacher for $50 a month. It was located at the southeast corner of Gage Avenue and Pacific where city hall later stood.

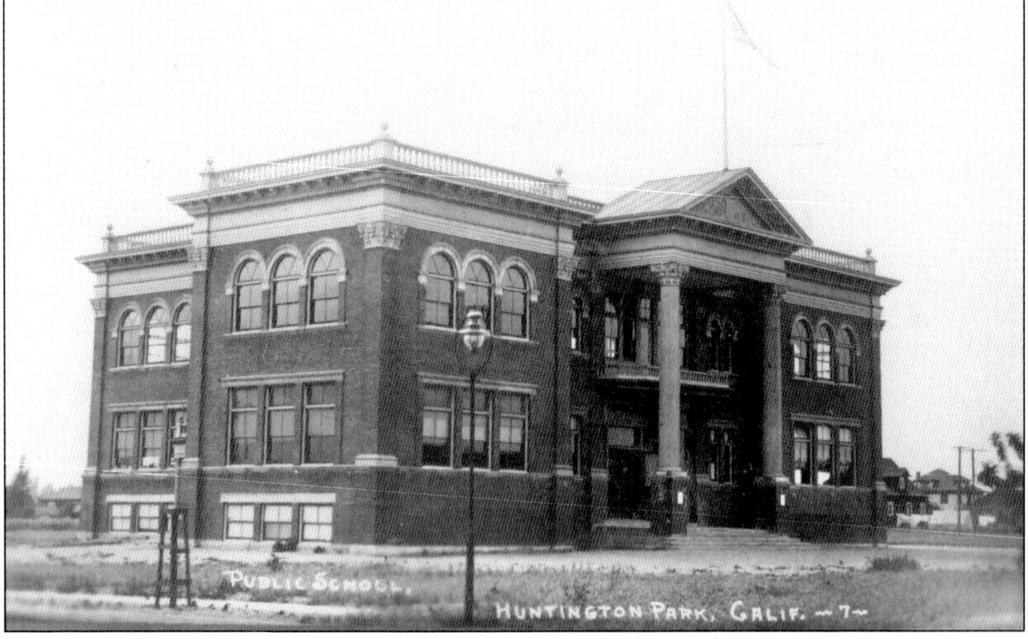

Malabar Street School. City pioneer George Garlow paid $6,000 of his own money to purchase a school site at Malabar Street and Zoe Avenue. There was opposition by developers Burbank and Baker, so at 3:00 a.m. he hitched his horse and buggy and drove to Los Angeles to file the deed. The school was subsequently built.

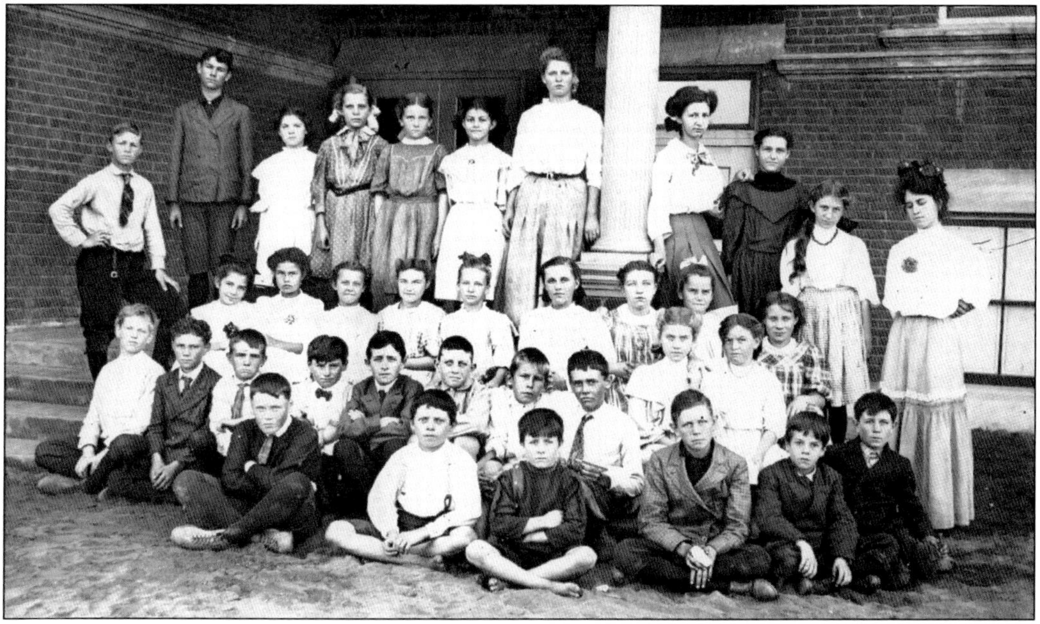

FIFTH AND SIXTH GRADE, 1907. This photograph has a notation referring to it as Middleton Street School in 1907. Malabar Street School was later changed to Middleton Street when the school was rebuilt. The front of the school is now back at Malabar Street, but the school name did not change back. Middleton Street was the first road paved in the city.

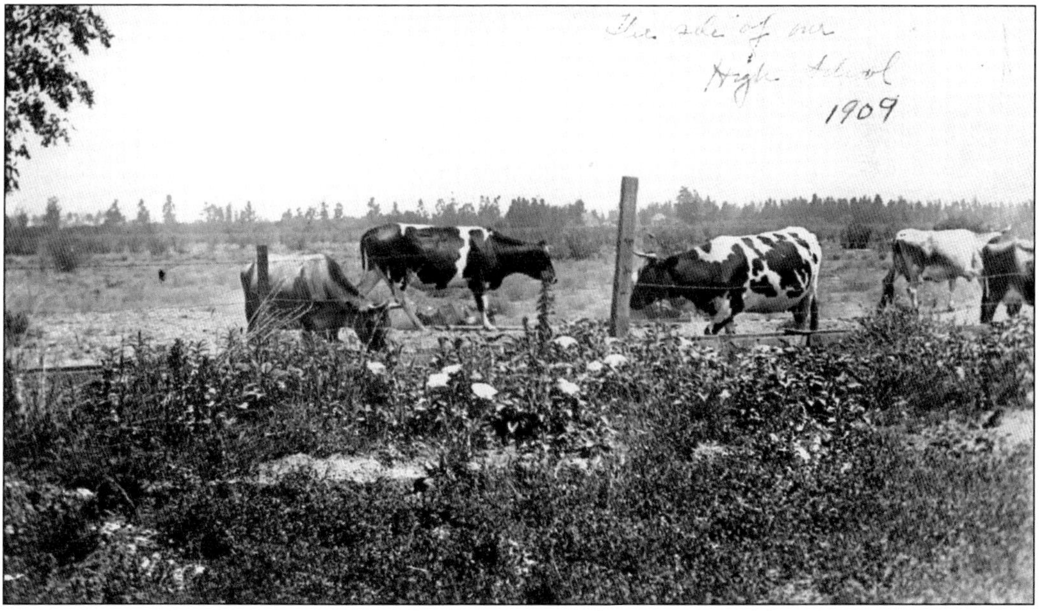

HUNTINGTON PARK HIGH SCHOOL SITE. In 1909, a $65,000 school bond issue was passed to purchase this 5.72-acre tract located on the east side of Miles Avenue, between Slauson Avenue and Randolph Street, for a high school. Classes started in 1909 in a structure at Pacific Boulevard and Randolph Street known as the Weber Building.

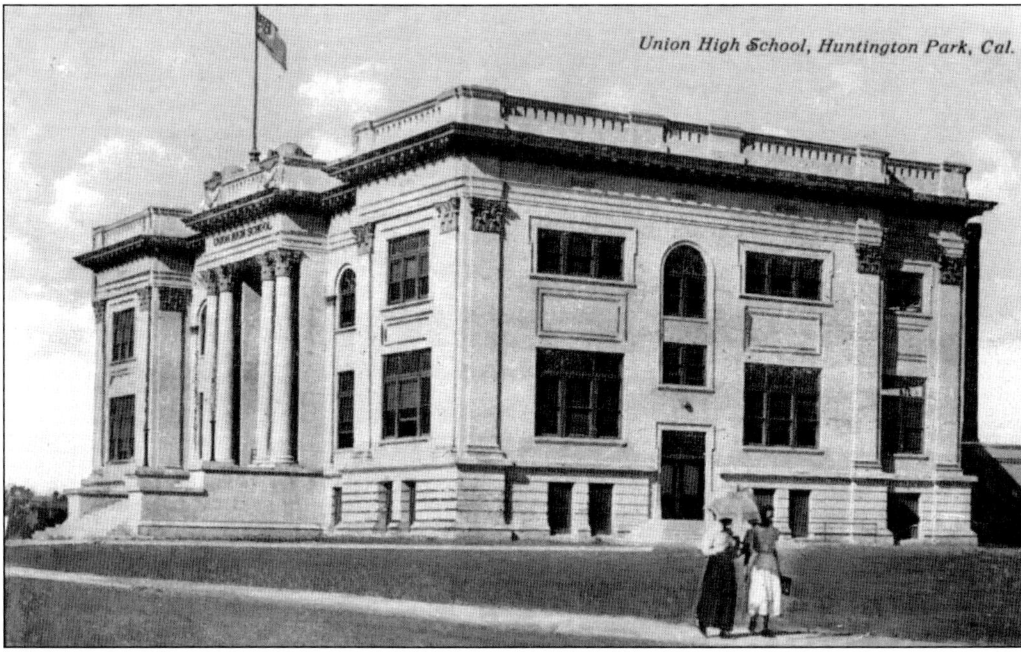

UNION HIGH SCHOOL. The cornerstone for the beautiful Huntington Park High School was laid on December 2, 1909. Miss Olive Pettus was the first graduate in June 1910. A fire destroyed the school in 1911, and classes were held in the gymnasium until 1914.

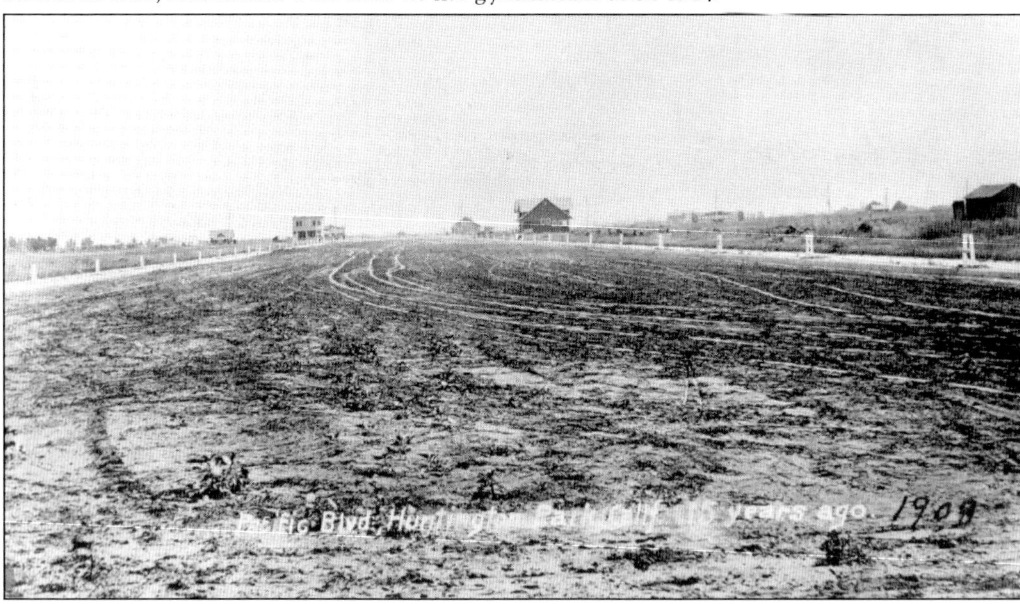

PACIFIC BOULEVARD, 1908. Looking south from Belgrave Avenue, Buhles Grocery Store is on the left. Pacific Boulevard started as little more than a wide place in the road between Los Angeles and Long Beach. Early settlers placed a horse-watering trough in the middle of the street, resulting in the city becoming a rest stop and gathering place. In 1909, the Woman's Improvement Club raised money and built a new cement horse trough and drinking fountain on Pacific Boulevard. The fountain served to divert horse-drawn vehicles from other cities through Huntington Park. One accounting had 127 animals and thirsty travelers using the trough and fountain in one day.

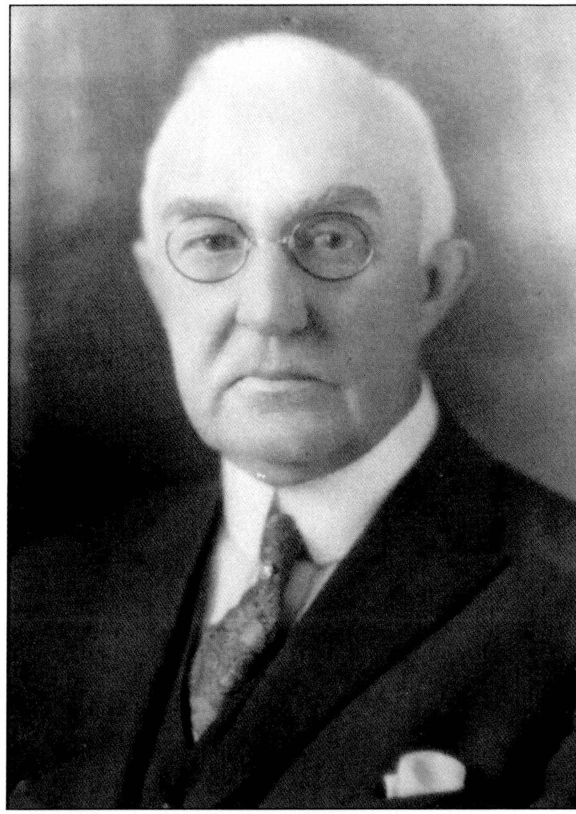

FIRST MAYOR OF HUNTINGTON PARK. In 1906, Doctor A. A. Weber received a permit from the county board of supervisors to incorporate. On August 31, 1906, Huntington Park was incorporated as a sixth-class city of one square mile and just over 500 residents. The Weber home was the site of the first city council meeting before moving to the Weber Building at Pacific Boulevard and Randolph Street for two years. It then moved to the Bank Building at Pacific Boulevard and Park Place.

FIRST HUNTINGTON PARK CITY HALL. In this photograph, the first dedicated Huntington Park City Hall nears completion in 1914. City hall at that time was located at the southeast corner of Pacific Boulevard and Irvington Avenue (Gage Avenue.) The structure was built by Huntington Park resident W. D. Geck, the husband of historian Anna Geck, at a cost of $15,780. A three-day carnival celebrated the building's dedication.

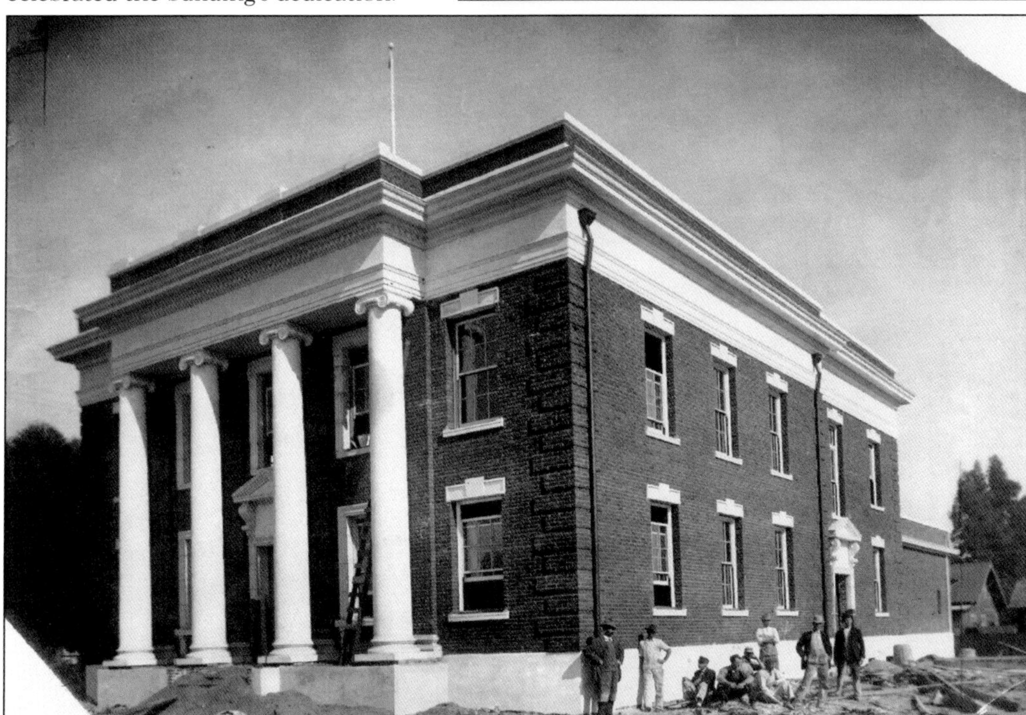

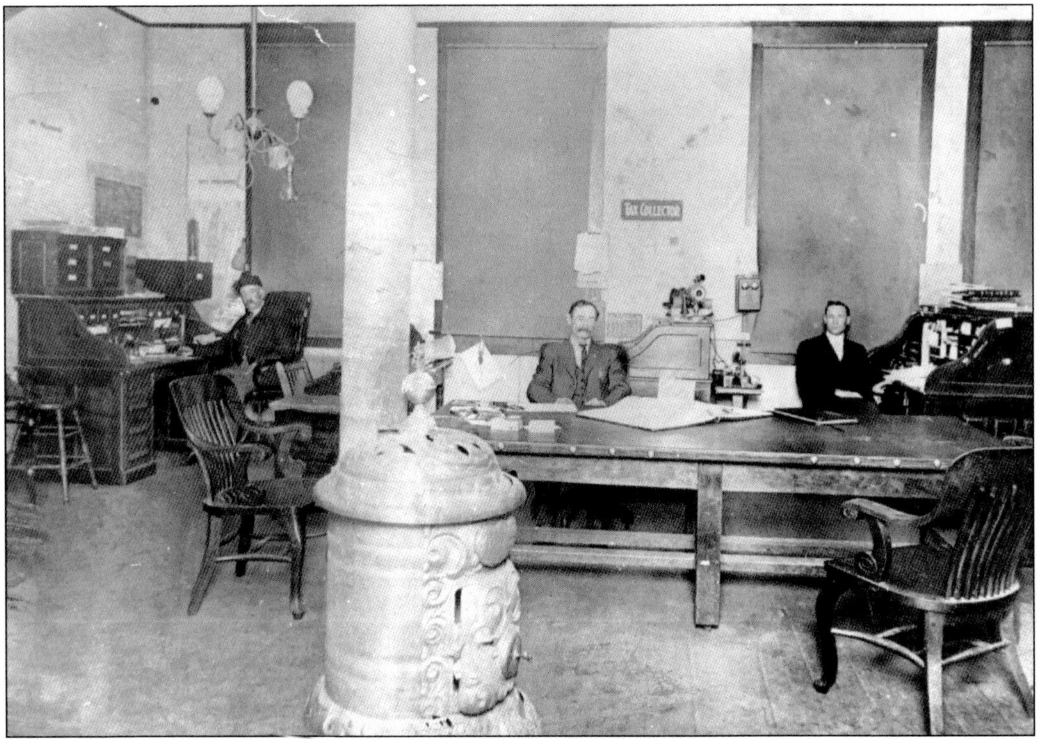

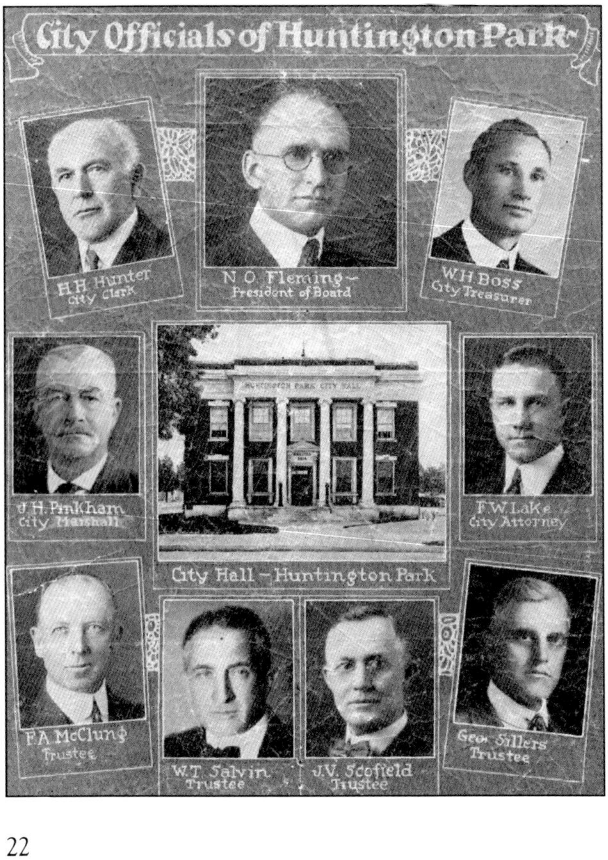

INSIDE CITY HALL. This photograph was taken inside city hall in 1914. J. H. Pinkham (left) was the city marshall, William Ford (center) was the street superintendent, and William Boss (right) was the city treasurer. William Ford was first employed by the city as its second city marshall. Tax collecting then was as important as it is now in supporting the city's services.

EARLY CITY OFFICIALS. By 1922, Huntington Park was a full-fledged city, with over 5,000 residents who required well-organized leadership. This photograph depicts the city government during that time period.

Two

ONE HUNDRED YEARS OF PROGRESS

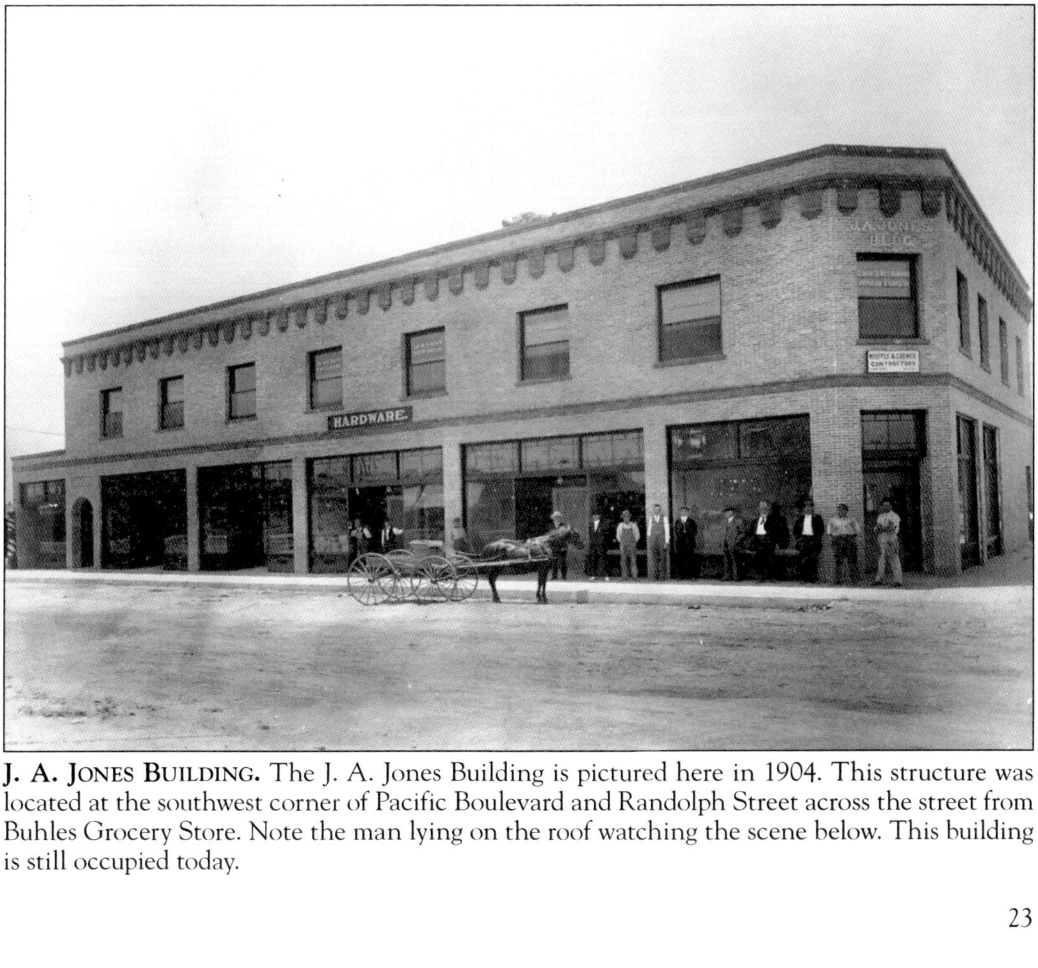

J. A. JONES BUILDING. The J. A. Jones Building is pictured here in 1904. This structure was located at the southwest corner of Pacific Boulevard and Randolph Street across the street from Buhles Grocery Store. Note the man lying on the roof watching the scene below. This building is still occupied today.

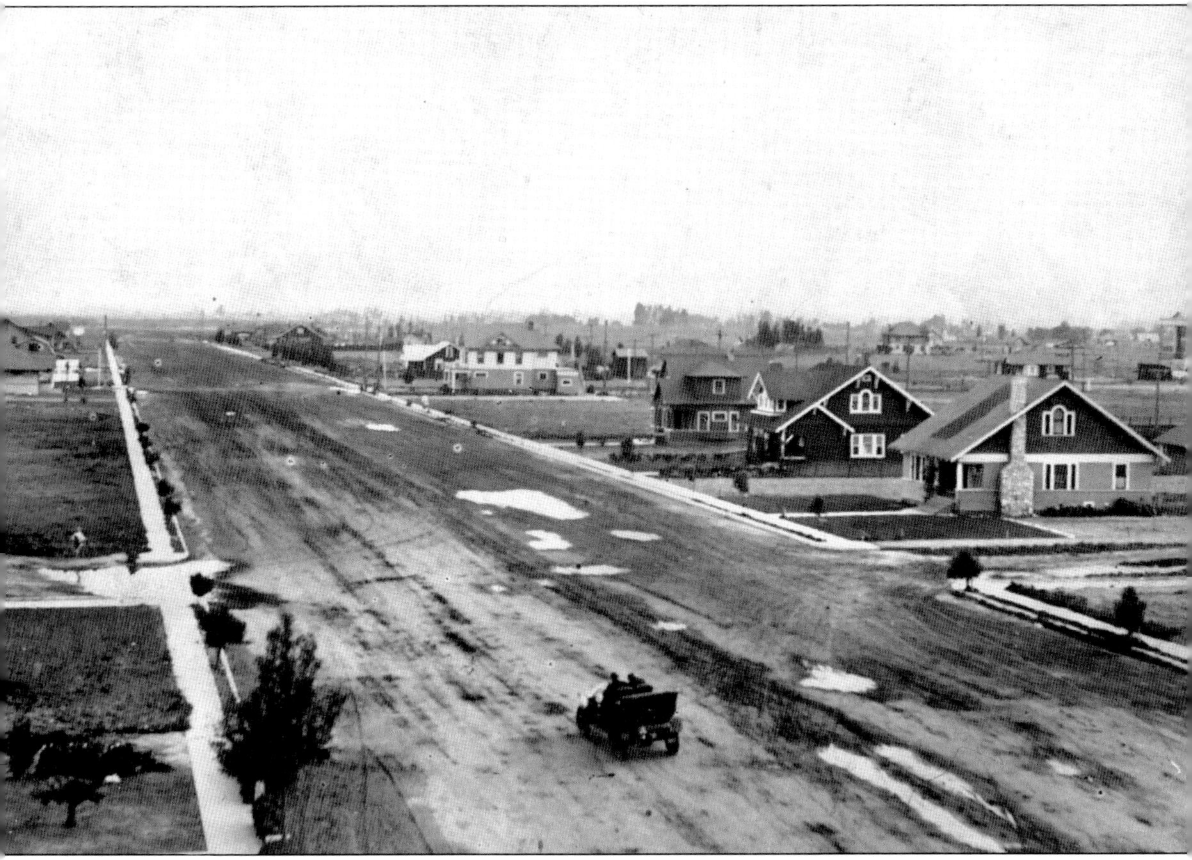

PACIFIC BOULEVARD SOUTH FROM IRVINGTON. This 1909 view of Pacific Boulevard, looking south from Gage Avenue, illustrates the residential nature of the thoroughfare during this time period. Malabar Street School is visible on the right with the George Garlow home a little to the left. Traffic for the few cars on the road was wide open. This condition would soon change. Pacific Boulevard was paved in 1911 and celebrated with a parade and lemonade.

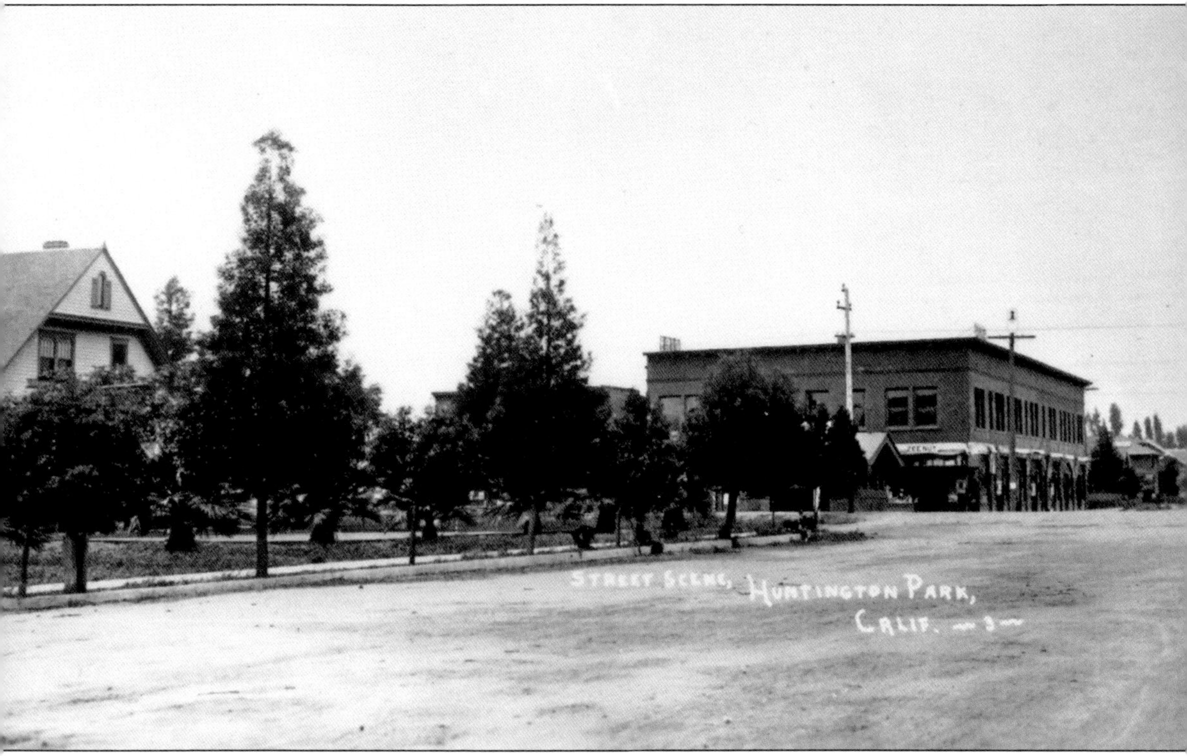

THE WEBER BUILDING. Opened by Mayor Weber, the two-story building on the right was where the first high school classes were held. This building was at the northwest corner of Randolph Street and Pacific Boulevard. A small Pacific Electric waiting room for the Red Cars is visible next to the Weber Building. This structure, condemned at the time, survived the earthquake of 1933.

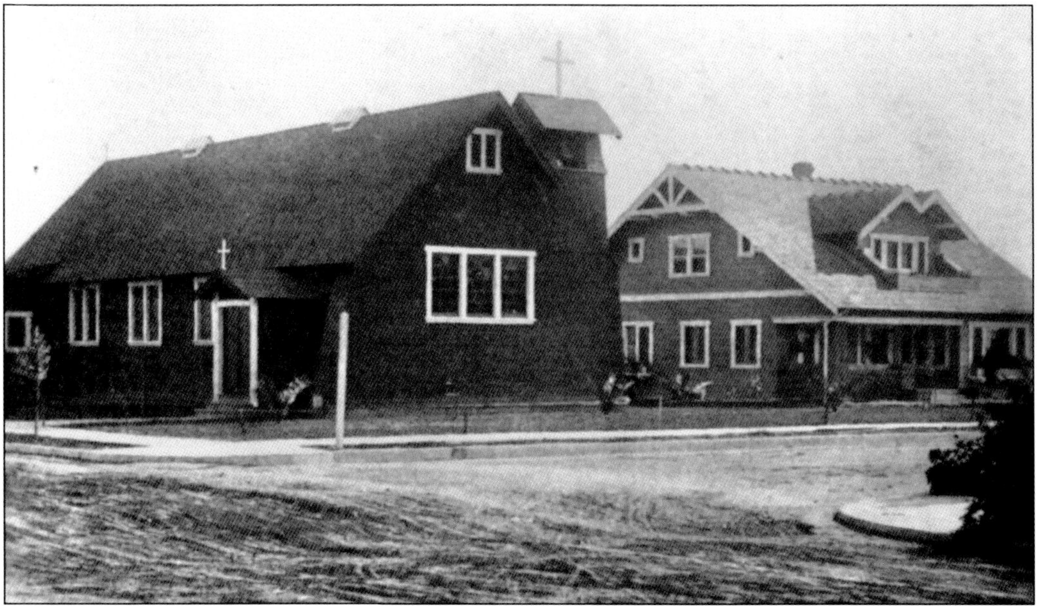

ST. MATHIAS CATHOLIC CHURCH. Pictured above is the original St. Mathias Church and Rectory in 1913. During this time, the church was located at Belgrave Avenue and Seville Avenue. It was later relocated to Florence Avenue and Mission Place. The original location is now occupied by St. Martha's Catholic Church. Pictured below is the confirmation class of St. Mathias Catholic Church on March 30, 1924. This Catholic church has always played an important role in the community, but it is even more so in modern times with the influx of the Hispanic culture.

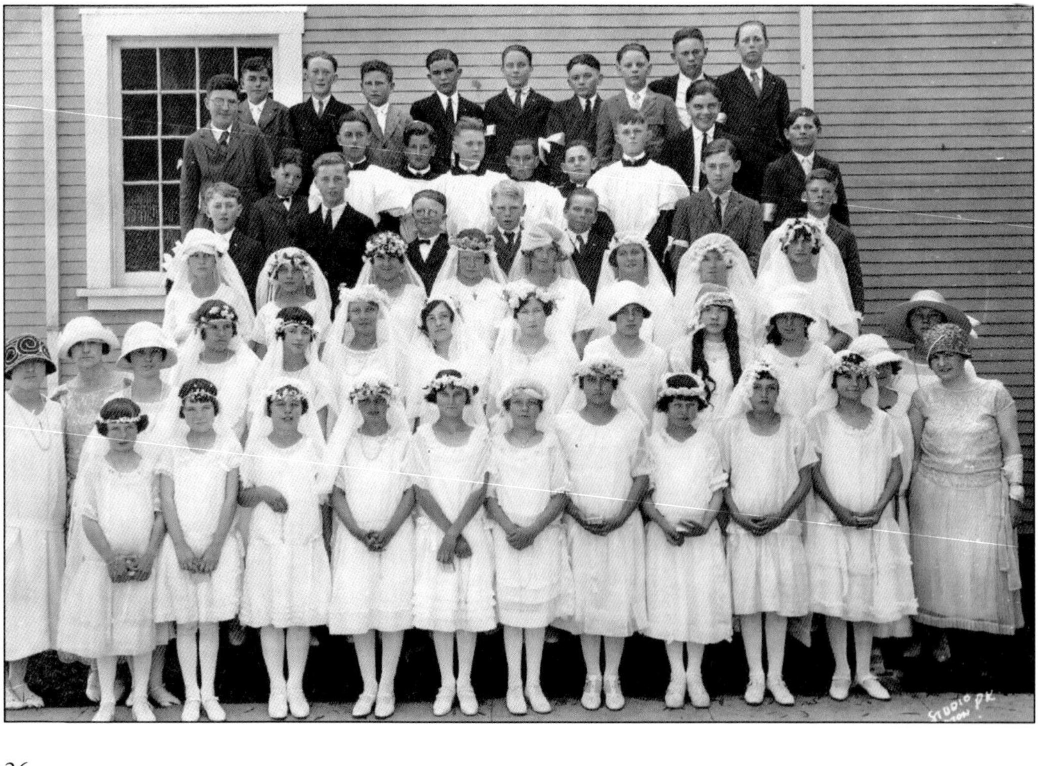

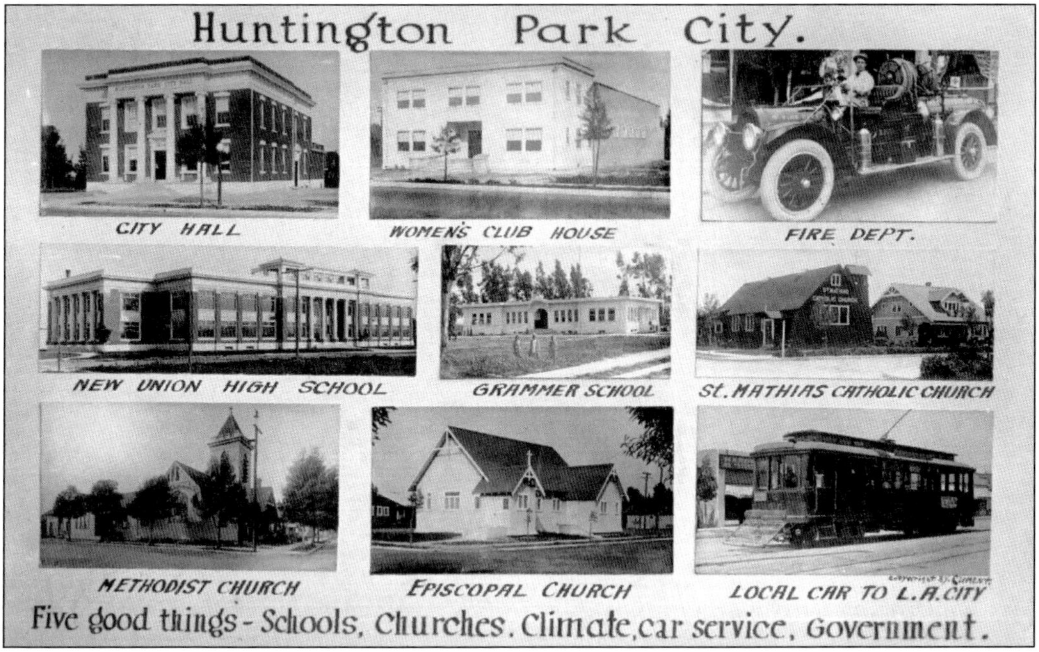

HUNTINGTON PARK POSTCARD. This c. 1920 postcard appears to have been produced to advertise the growing city. It illustrates "five good things" that might appeal to future residents—schools, churches, public safety, public transportation, and a good climate.

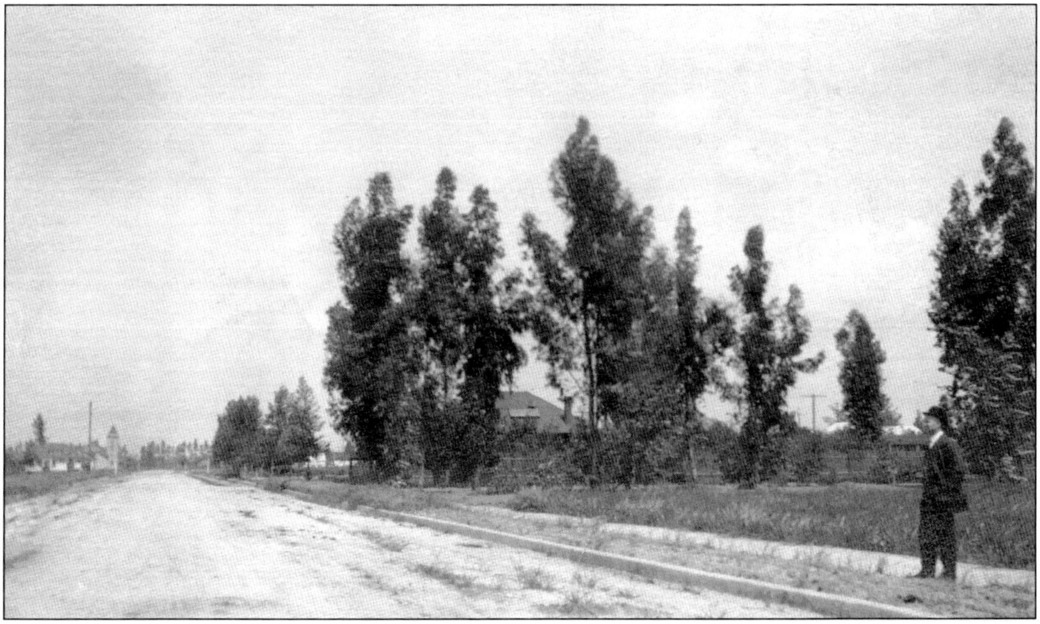

MANY TREES WERE PLANTED. This photograph depicts Rugby Avenue looking north from Randolph Street in 1918. In the background, many eucalyptus trees are visible adjacent to Pacific Boulevard. Many of the original trees were planted by pioneer George Garlow. By 1935, there had been 7,800 trees planted throughout the community by street superintendent (and former town marshall) W. E. Ford. Four hundred forty-four trees were set in parkways along Pacific Boulevard. The Methodist Episcopal Church is visible in the distance.

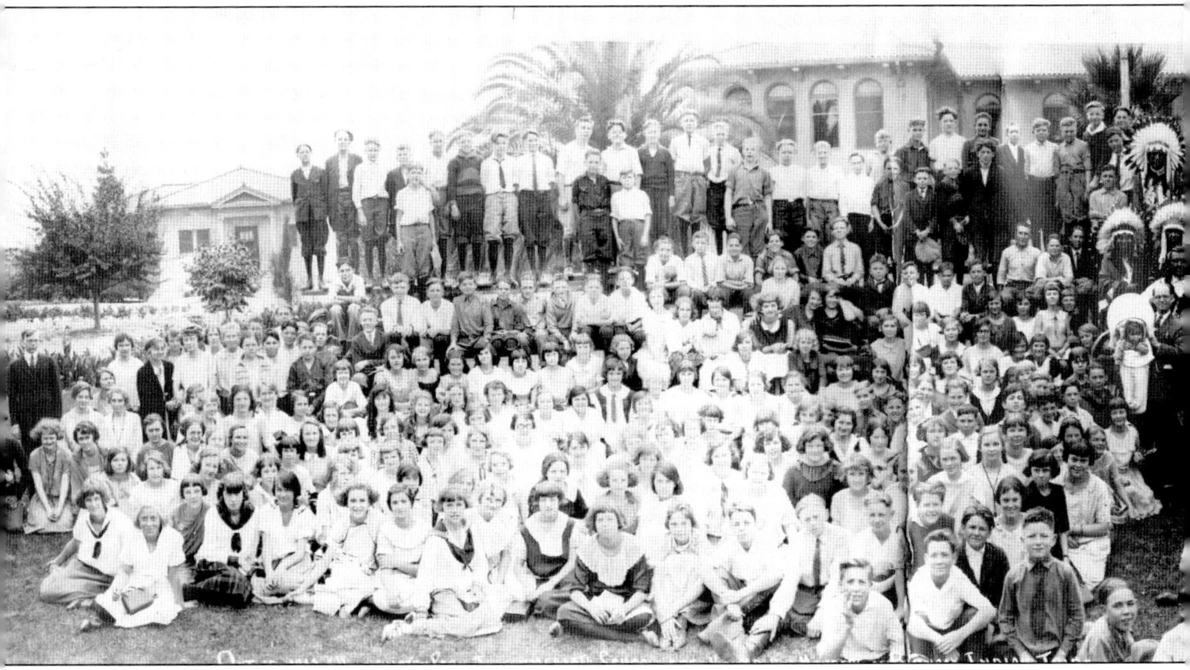

BANNOCK INDIANS VISIT HUNTINGTON PARK. In 1923, the Bannock Indian tribe visited Huntington Park Middle School (also known as Irvington). This school was originally a Jewish orphanage and was located at Gage Avenue and Miles Avenue, where Gage Middle School now

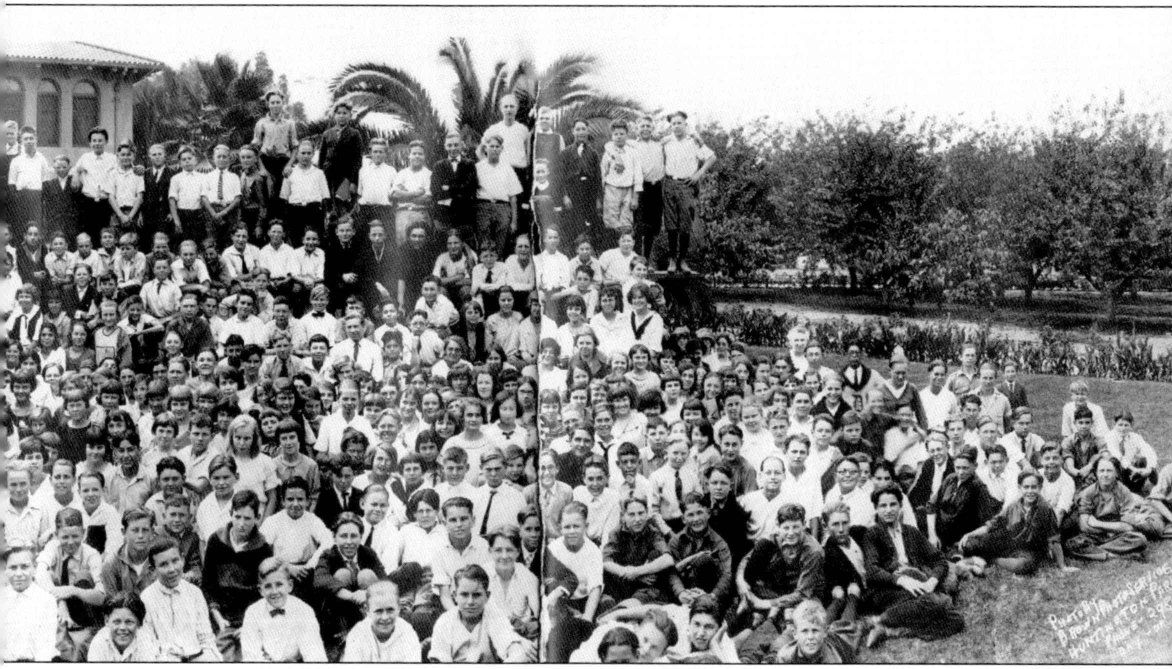

stands. The Bannocks are believed to be a branch of the Shoshones, originally from Oregon and Idaho. Their reservation is in southeastern Idaho at Fort Hall.

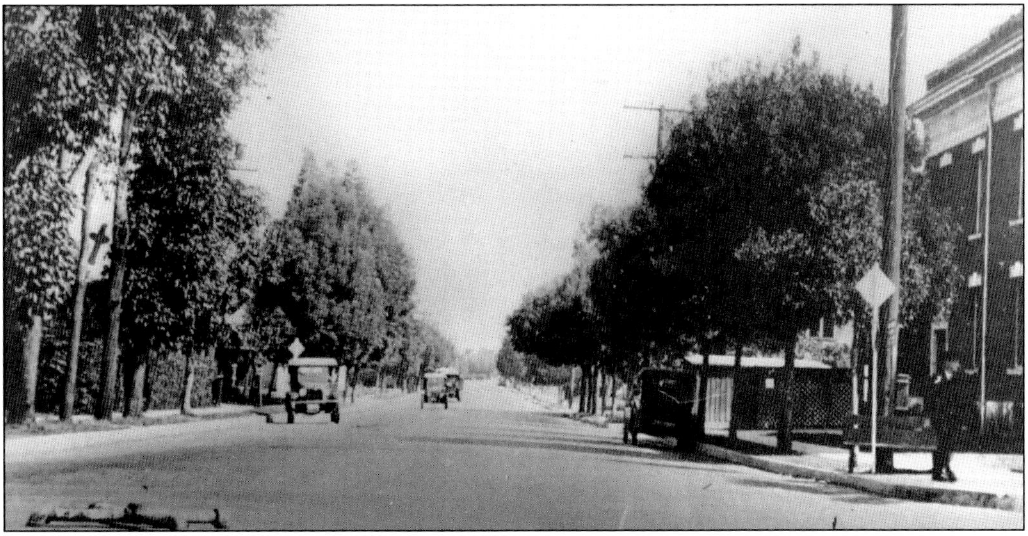

PACIFIC BOULEVARD AND IRVINGTON STREET. This is a 1915 photograph of Irvington Street looking east from Pacific Boulevard; city hall is on the right. Irvington was first called Baker Street, and around 1930, the name of the street changed again to Gage Avenue after former California governor Henry T. Gage (1899–1903) who lived in the area.

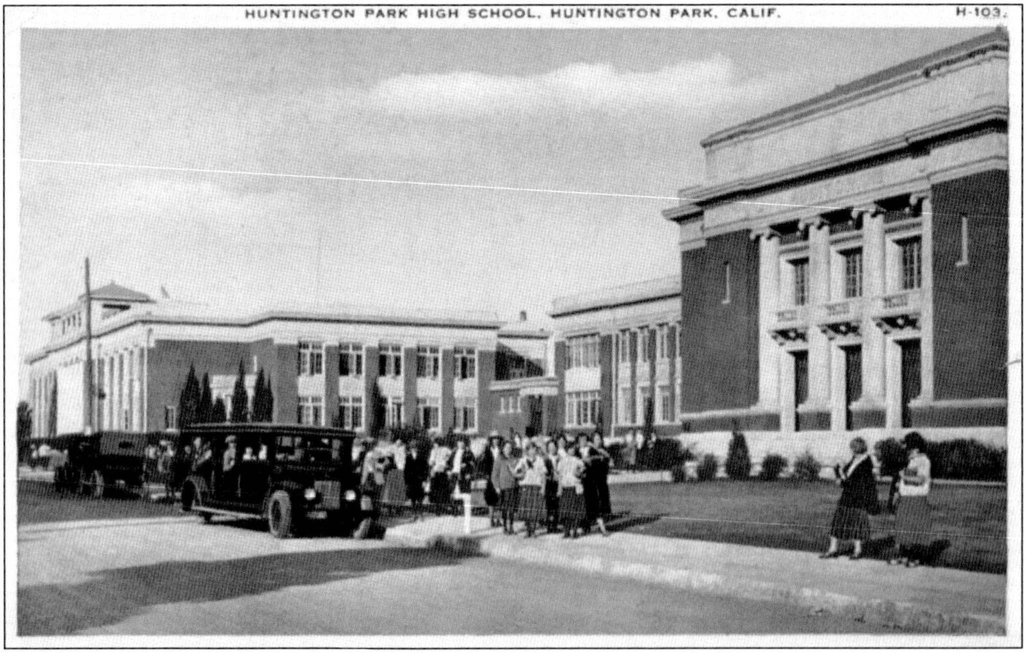

HUNTINGTON PARK HIGH SCHOOL. This postcard depicts the beautiful Huntington Park High School in the 1920s. This high school was destroyed by fire following the 6.2 earthquake on March 10, 1933. This school became part of the Los Angeles Unified School District, along with the other Huntington Park schools, in 1932.

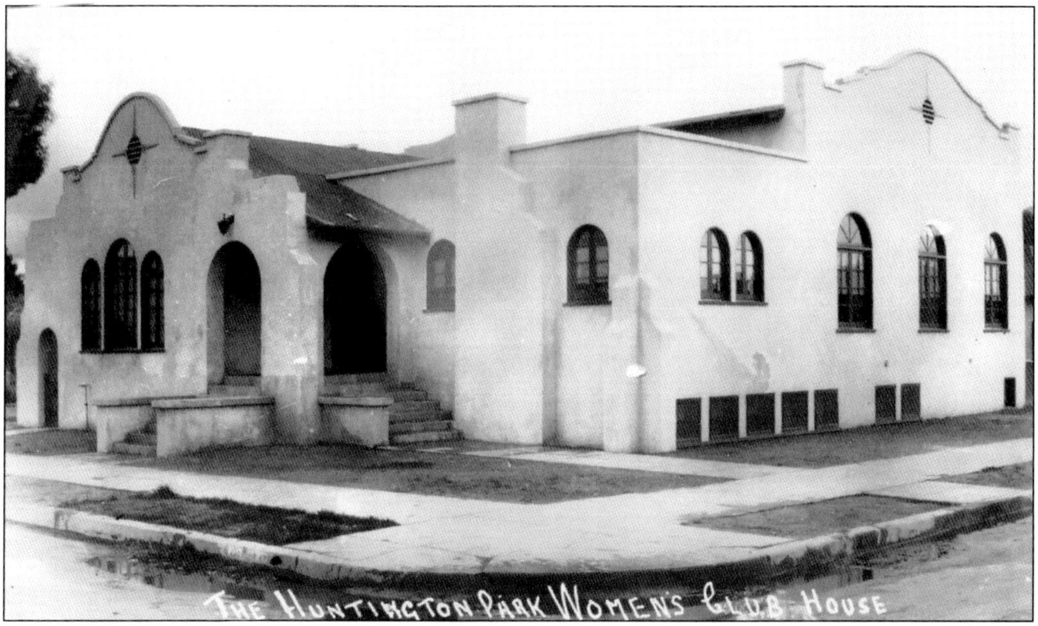

THE EBELL CLUB. This was the pioneer of women's clubs in Huntington Park. Incorporated in 1906, it was originally known as the Woman's Improvement Club. It was founded by May Moncreiff. Its second clubhouse, pictured here, opened in 1923 at Malabar Street and Clarendon Avenue, where it stands today. This club was very active with the Red Cross during World War I. The Woman's Improvement Club merged with the Women's Club in the late 1920s.

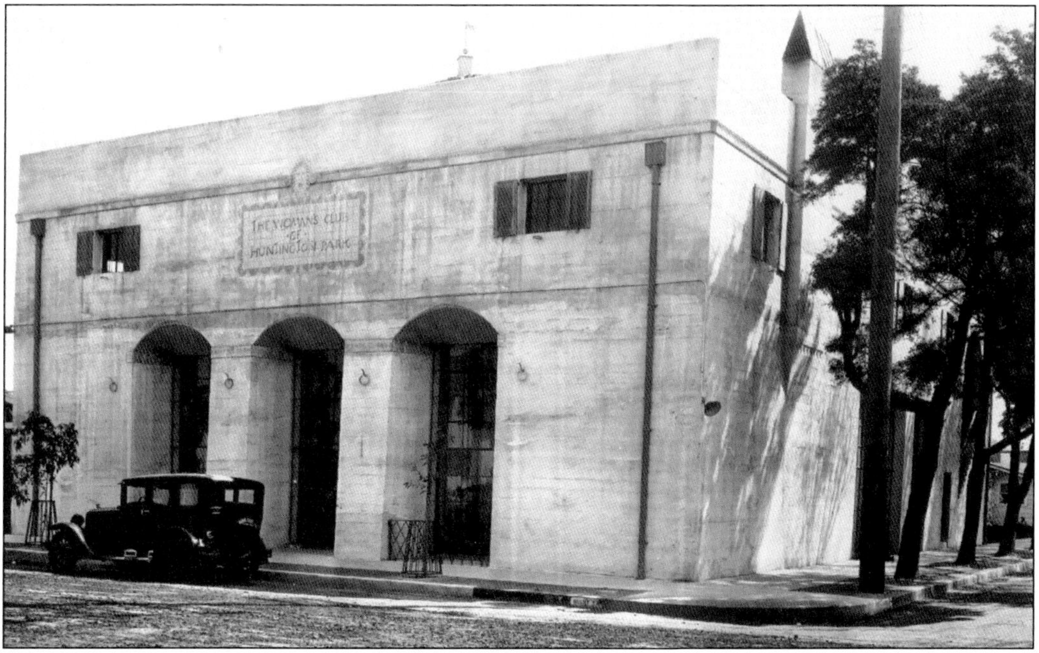

THE WOMAN'S CLUB OF HUNTINGTON PARK. The Woman's Club was founded in 1907 and was originally organized as a small reading club "to promote advancement in general culture." In 1911, it joined the California Federation of Woman's Clubs and continued operation until the 1990s. The building, pictured here, still stands today as a church.

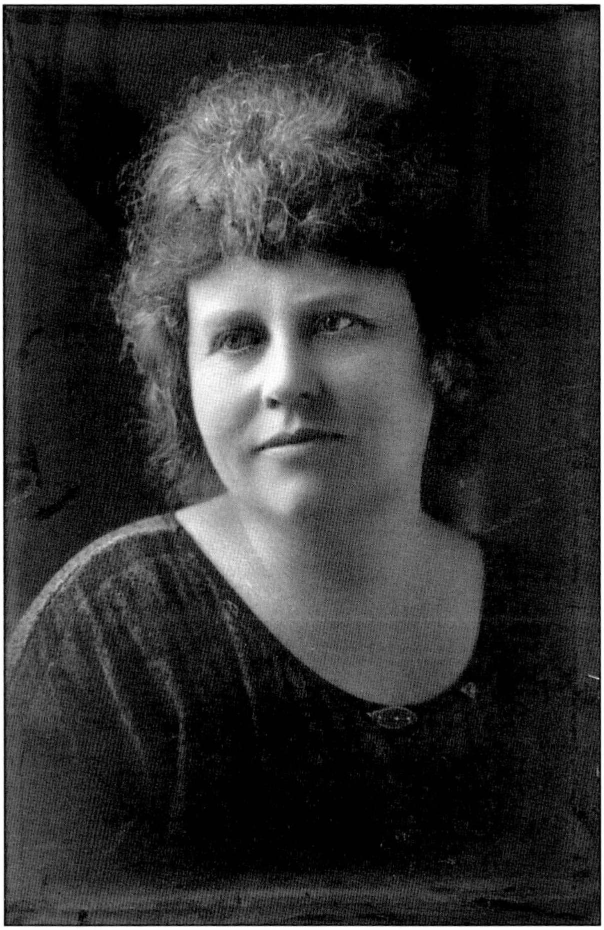

ANNA GECK. Anna Geck (left) was one of the most influential women in the history of Huntington Park. She moved to Huntington Park with her husband and two children in 1903. With a great interest in public affairs, Geck was a charter member of the Woman's Improvement Club, the treasurer of the first city PTA and a school trustee from 1911 to 1925, and was a member of the Students Art League. She became the city historian in 1935 and was an associate editor of the city's history book. Much of the information found in this book was available as a result of her work. Pictured (below) is the 1915 award-winning Huntington Park Parade float that Geck was closely involved with. The boy on the float is Archie Jones, and the girl is Reba Van Loon (Leonard.)

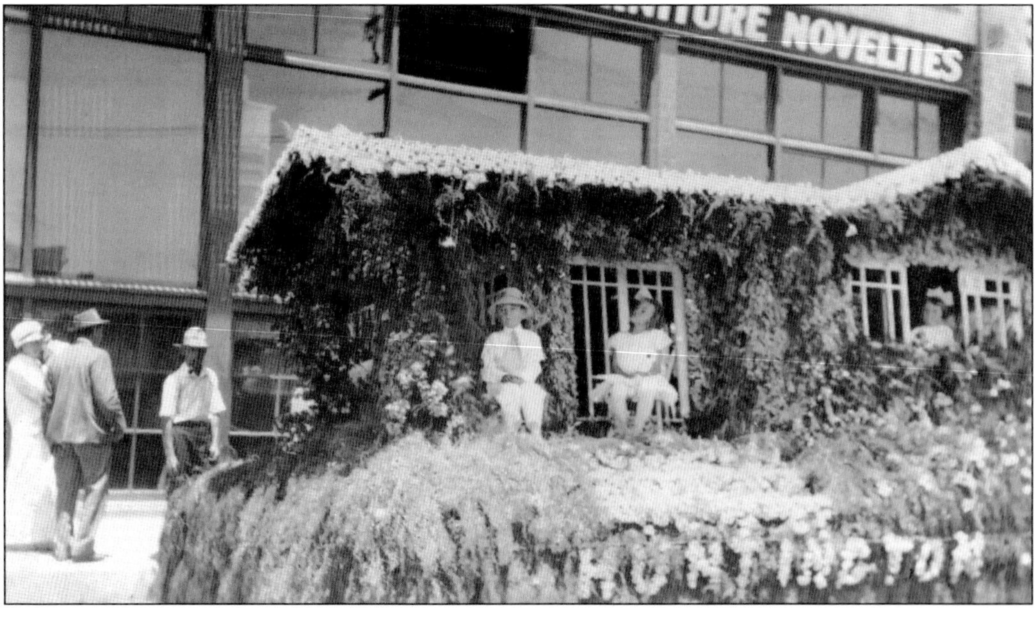

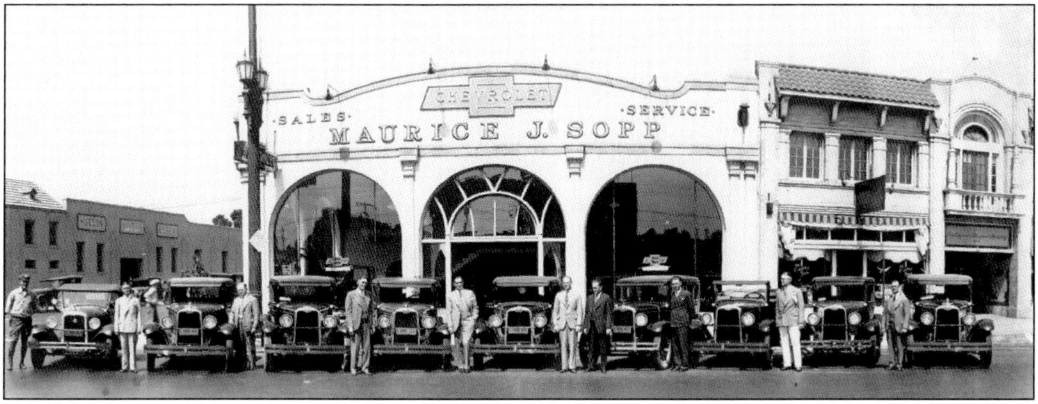

SOPP CHEVROLET. Maurice Sopp, pictured at below center in the 1950s, opened a Chevrolet car dealership. The above photograph depicts the Sopp sales team in 1928, when they were located at the northwest corner of Pacific Boulevard and Belgrave Avenue. In 1929, the business moved to 5801 Pacific Boulevard and a much larger facility. Eventually, Randy Sopp, Maurice's grandson, took over the business and leads it today. In 1988, the structure housing the dealership burned down and was relocated to the city of Bell. Ken Sopp, Randy's son, operates a truck dealership at the same Pacific Boulevard location. Randy is very active in community projects associated with the YMCA and the Kiwanis.

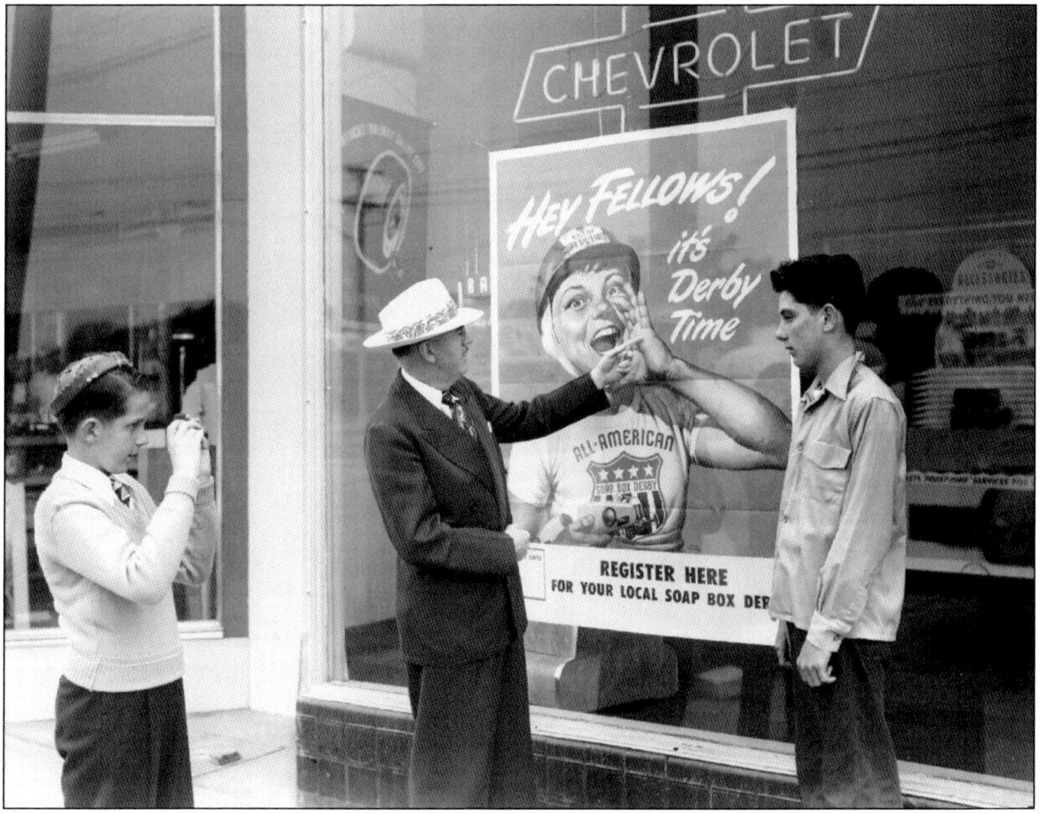

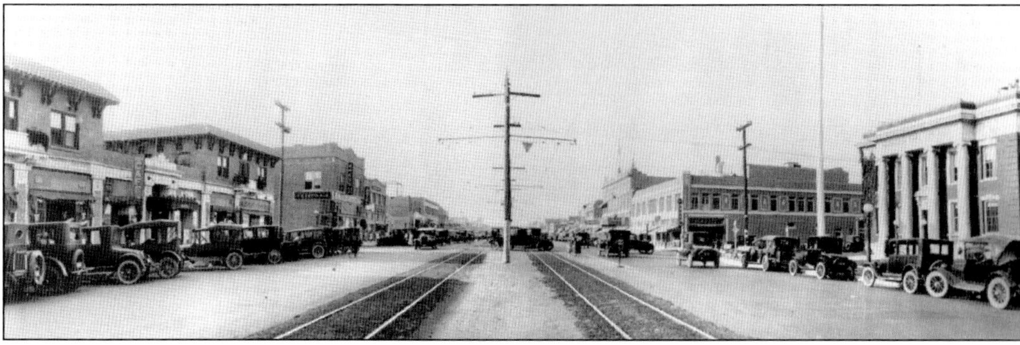

HUNTINGTON PARK, 1929. In the 1920s, major changes took place within rapidly developing Huntington Park. The city's population grew from 4,513 in 1920 to approximately 30,000 in 1935. The city slogan of "The City of Beautiful Homes" changed to "The City of Perfect Balance," illustrating a change in emphasis. A group referred to as the Reform Slate replaced the long-entrenched city council. Finally, the Great Depression began October 29, 1929. These two photographs, looking north on Pacific Boulevard towards city hall (above) and looking northwest from Clarendon Avenue (below), were taken on November 14, 1929, just two weeks after the stock market crash.

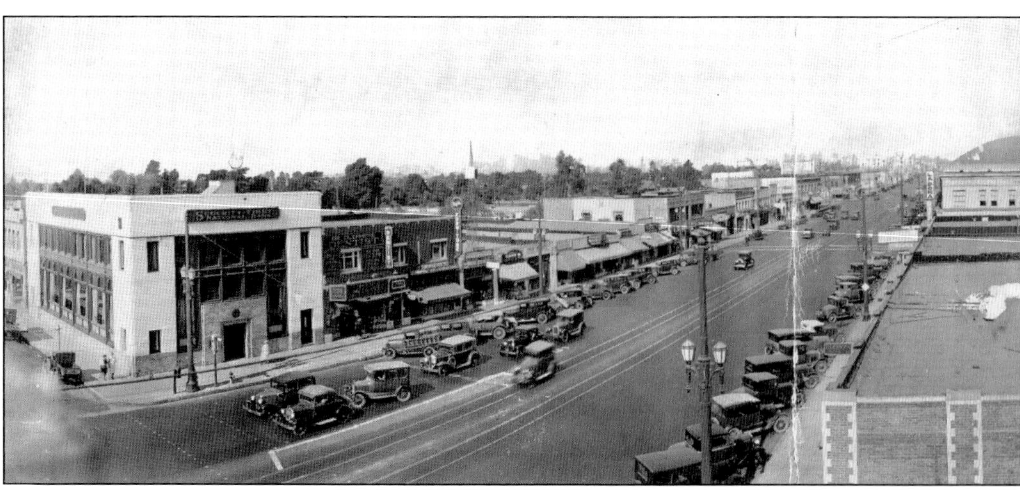

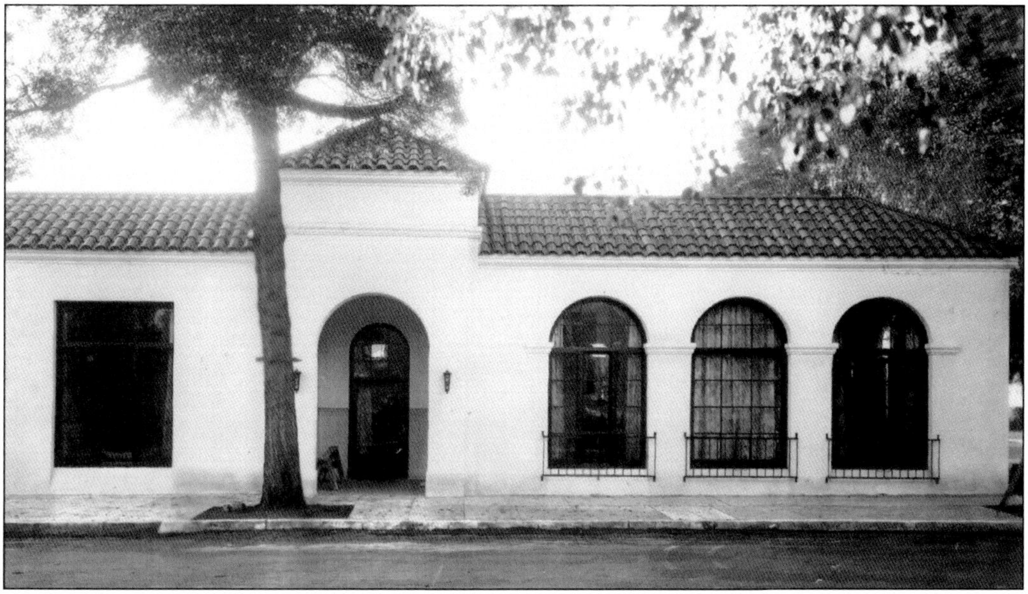

LIBRARIES IN HUNTINGTON PARK. The first library in Huntington Park, located above the hardware store at Pacific Boulevard and Park Place, was vacated by the city when city hall was moved in 1914. This library was established by Mrs. C. L. Byam, who was also the librarian. Pictured here in the 1930s is the Huntington Park Library located on Zoe at Rugby Avenue. The library then moved to the county health building next to the police station on Miles Avenue and then to its own building next door, where it stands today.

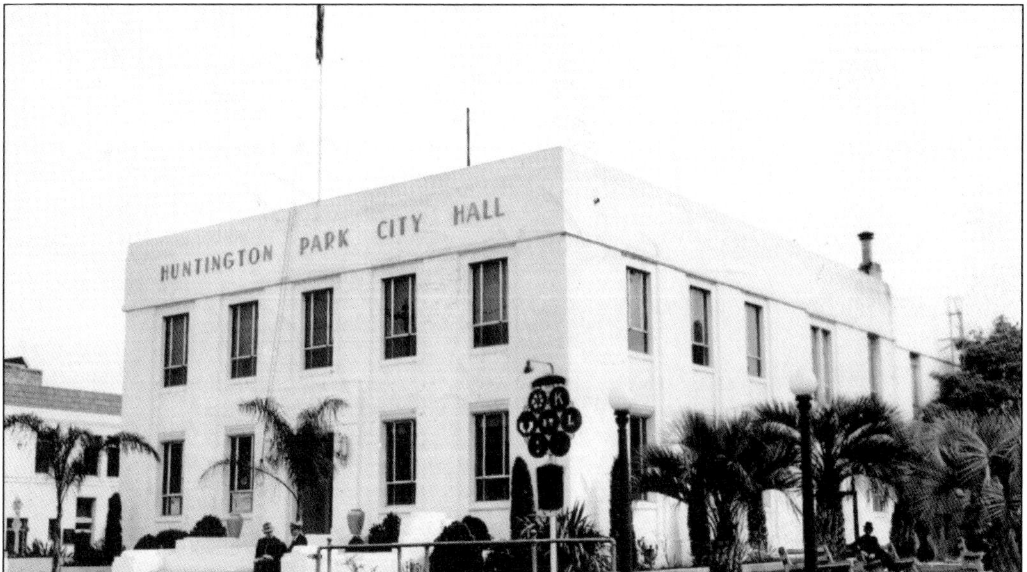

CITY HALL, REBUILT. As a result of the earthquake in 1933, the second floor of city hall was so badly damaged it had to be demolished. In 1934, it was rebuilt and given a new art deco exterior design. It remained in use until 1947, when city hall was moved to Miles Avenue.

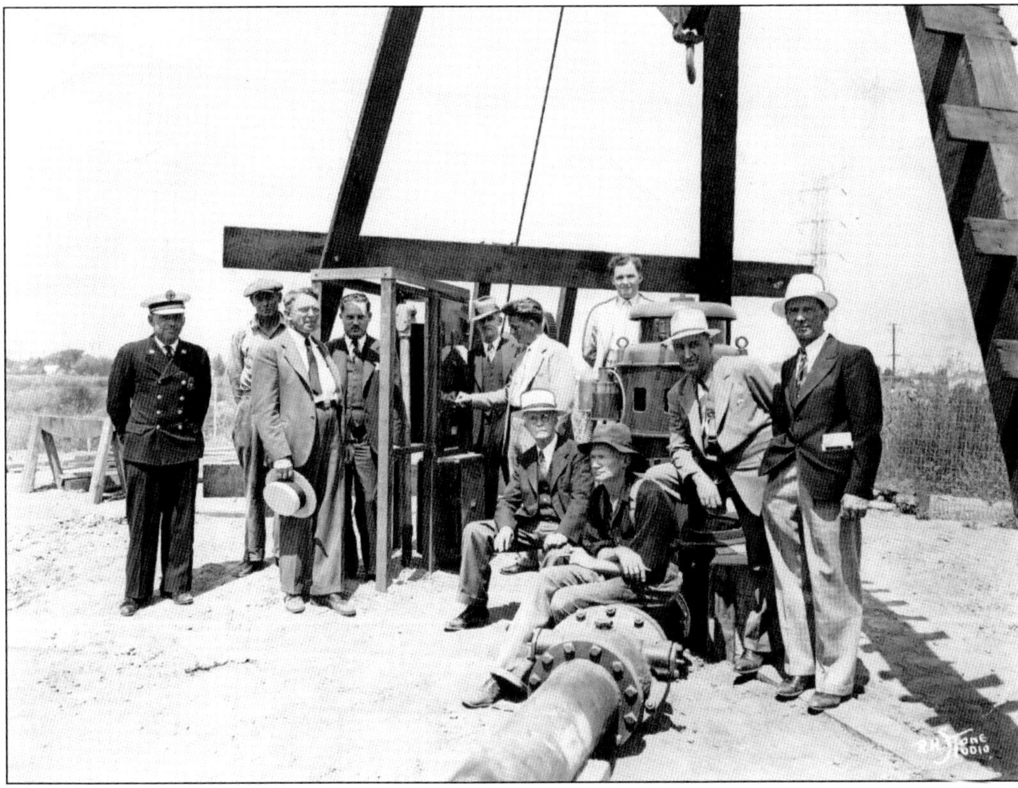

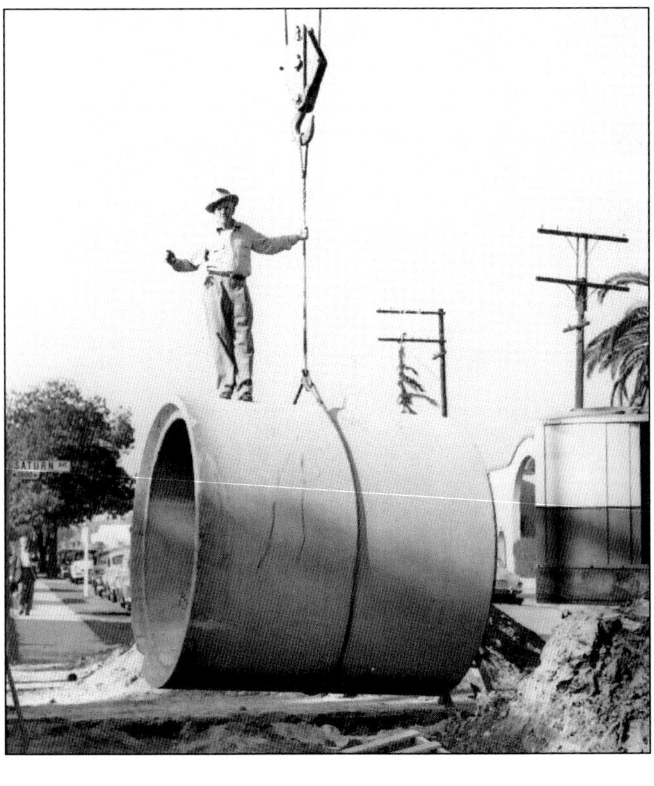

PUBLIC IMPROVEMENTS. As Huntington Park grew, so did its infrastructure. Streets had to be cleaned, buildings had to be inspected, water had to be pumped, and sewers had to be maintained to service the city's booming population. These photographs, taken in the 1930s, illustrate such projects. Above, a new pump is installed at one of the city's wells where fire chief and water foreman Arthur Weis is standing at left. In the image below, city engineer A. E. Robinson is riding a sewer pipe during installation on Saturn Avenue.

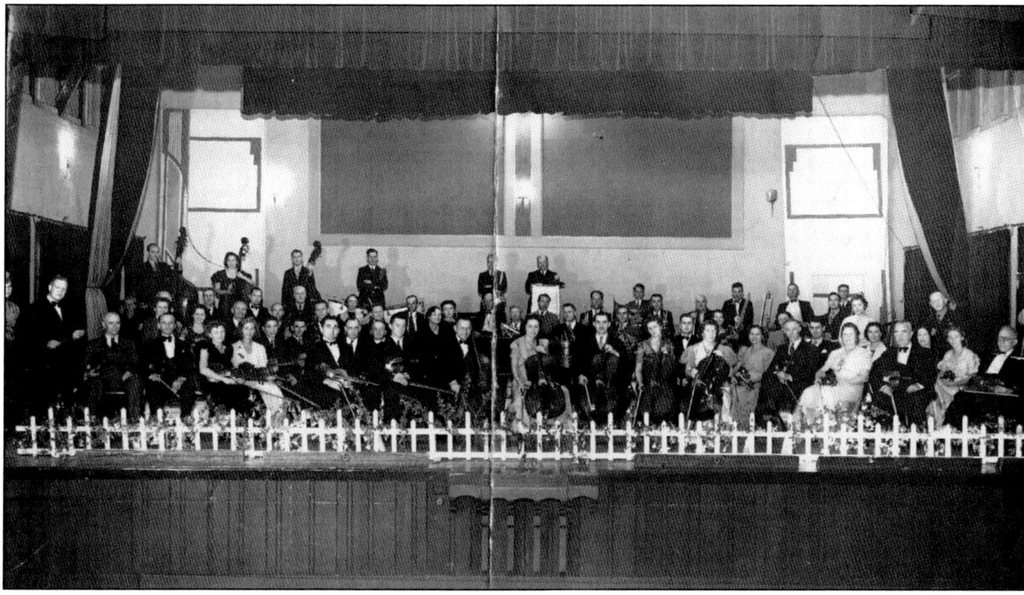

THE HUNTINGTON PARK SYMPHONY ORCHESTRA. Formed in 1937 by its director, Glen Cadwell, the orchestra had about 60 pieces. The musicians were volunteers, and they presented hundreds of free concerts. Cadwell came to Huntington Park in 1907 as a professional musician, playing with the Los Angeles Symphony Orchestra.

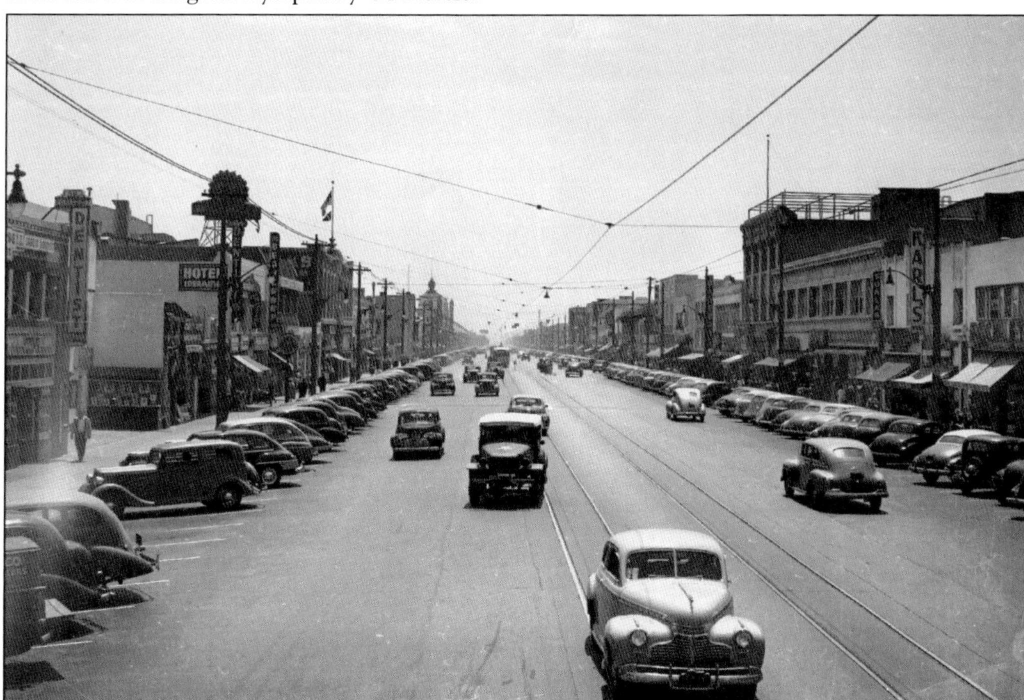

PACIFIC BOULEVARD, 1939. This photograph is a view of Pacific Boulevard looking south from Clarendon Avenue in 1939. The wires hanging across the street powered the Yellow Cars. The tall building on the right was the Rising Light Masonic Lodge. The building at left with the flag was the Elks Lodge. Both organizations were very active in the community for most of the city's history.

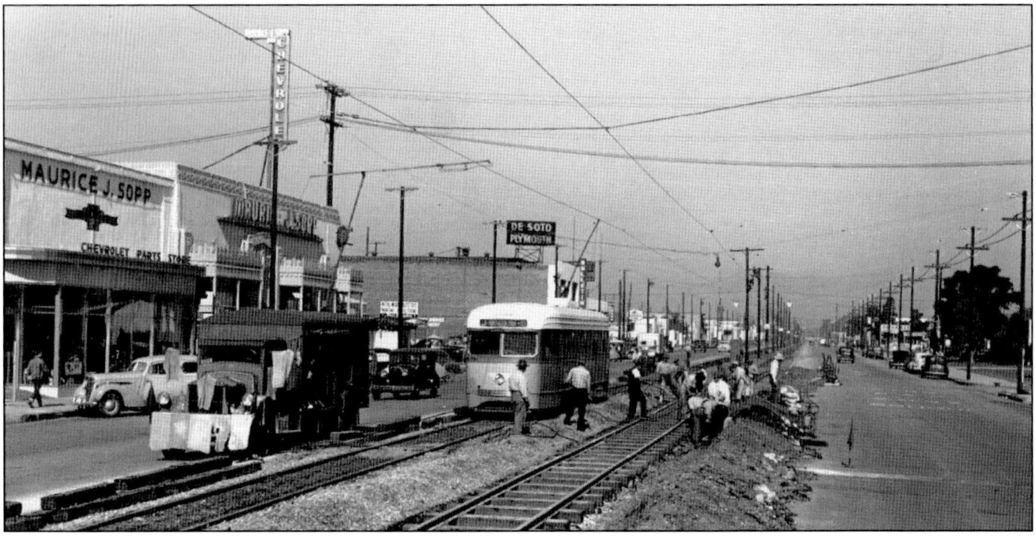

PACIFIC BOULEVARD NORTH OF SLAUSON. This photograph depicts Pacific Boulevard north of Slauson Avenue in 1948 undergoing rail-line improvements. By this time, Sopp Chevrolet had moved to this location at Fifty-eighth Street and Pacific. Pacific School is on the right and a Yellow Car is approaching. The north end of Pacific was never developed to the degree south of Slauson had, and much of the area is still industrial.

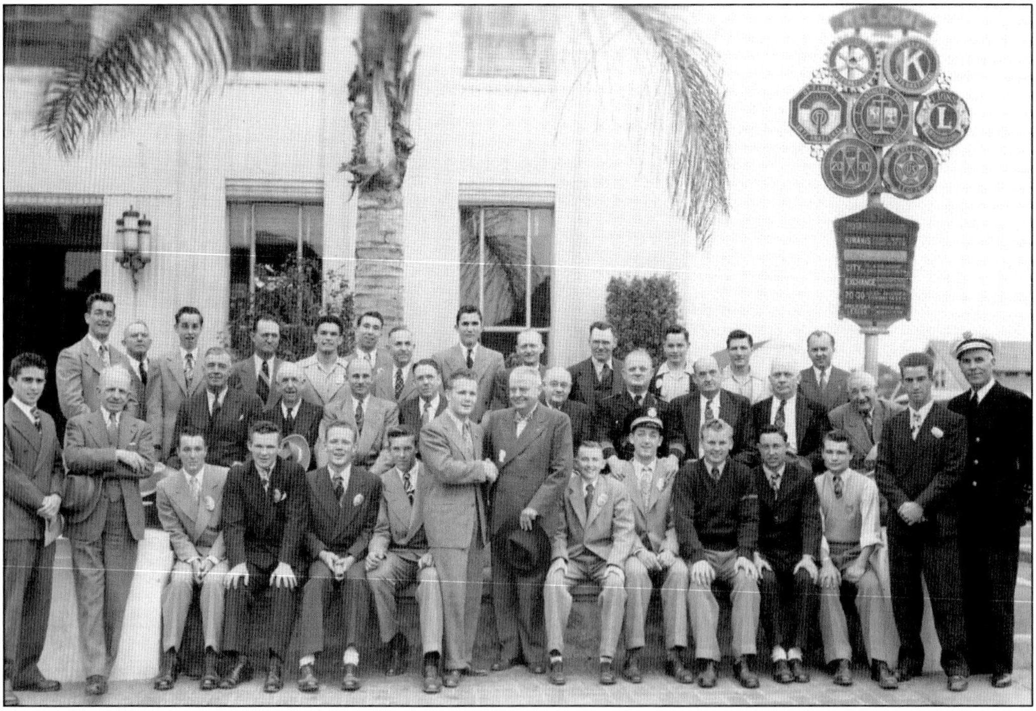

BOYS DAY IN GOVERNMENT. This photograph depicts Boys Day in Government in the early 1940s. Mayor Hollis Peavy is standing in the middle of the picture shaking hands with his assistant for the day. This tradition later added Girls Day and continues today as Student Government Day. During these events, students get a taste of local government by spending the day with different local departments.

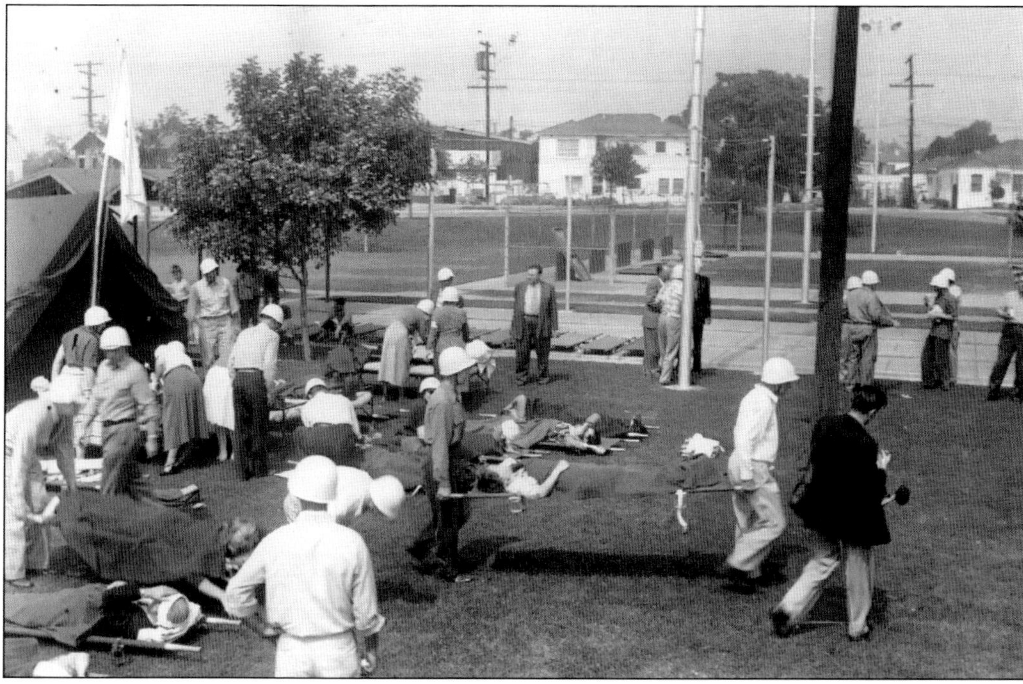

World War II Hits Huntington Park. This air-raid drill (above) was held in the city park during World War II, complete with role players. The participants are wearing the white civil defense helmets, and the Red Cross was always on hand. The V for Victory War Bond Rally (below) was held in City Hall Park on June 18, 1945, just two months before the end of the war. The agenda included entertainment, as seen, and speakers from the military.

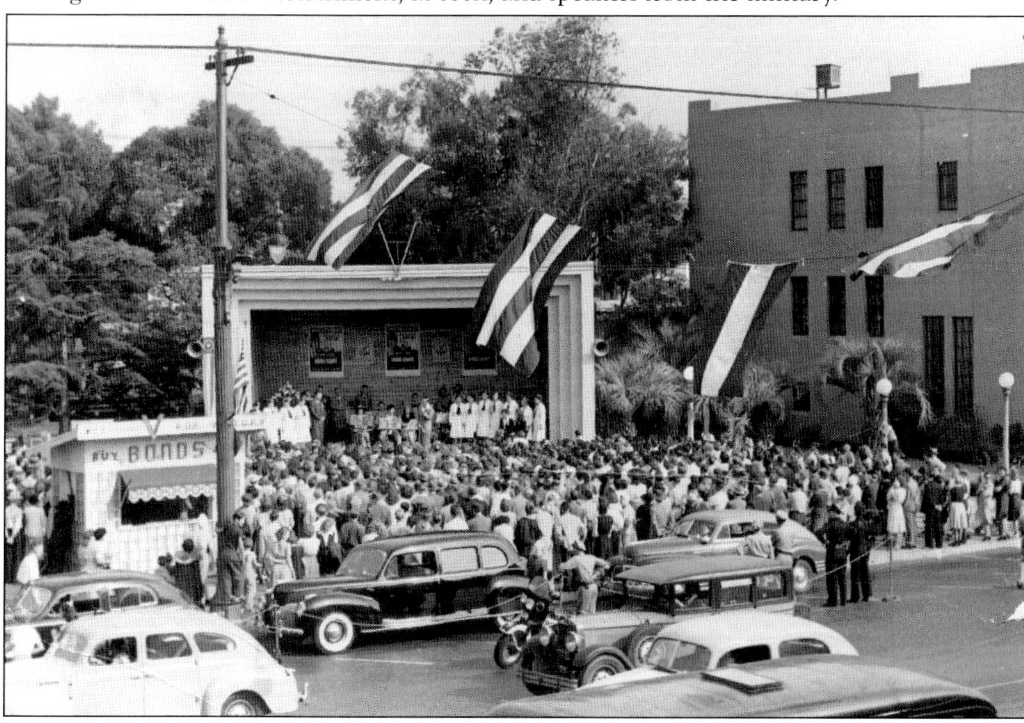

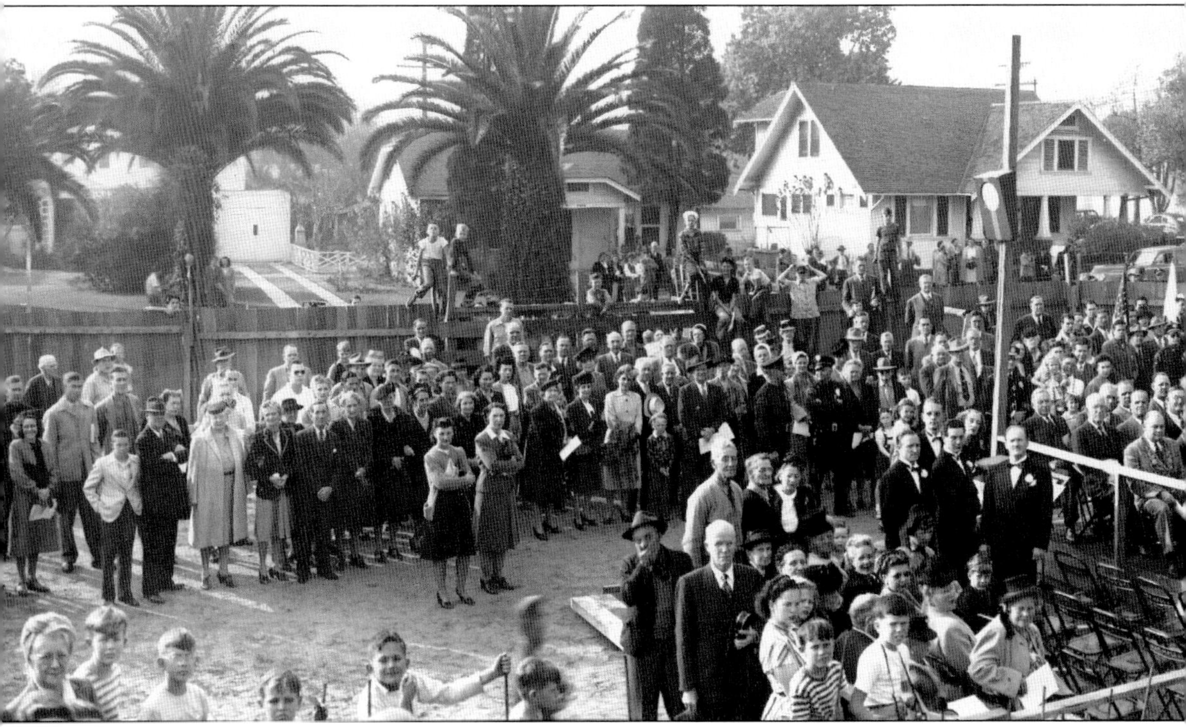

The Laying of the Cornerstone. The sale of the city hall property was approved by special election on November 7, 1944. The James I. Barnes Construction Company was awarded the contract for the new city hall on Miles Avenue at Zoe Avenue. This is a ceremony for the laying

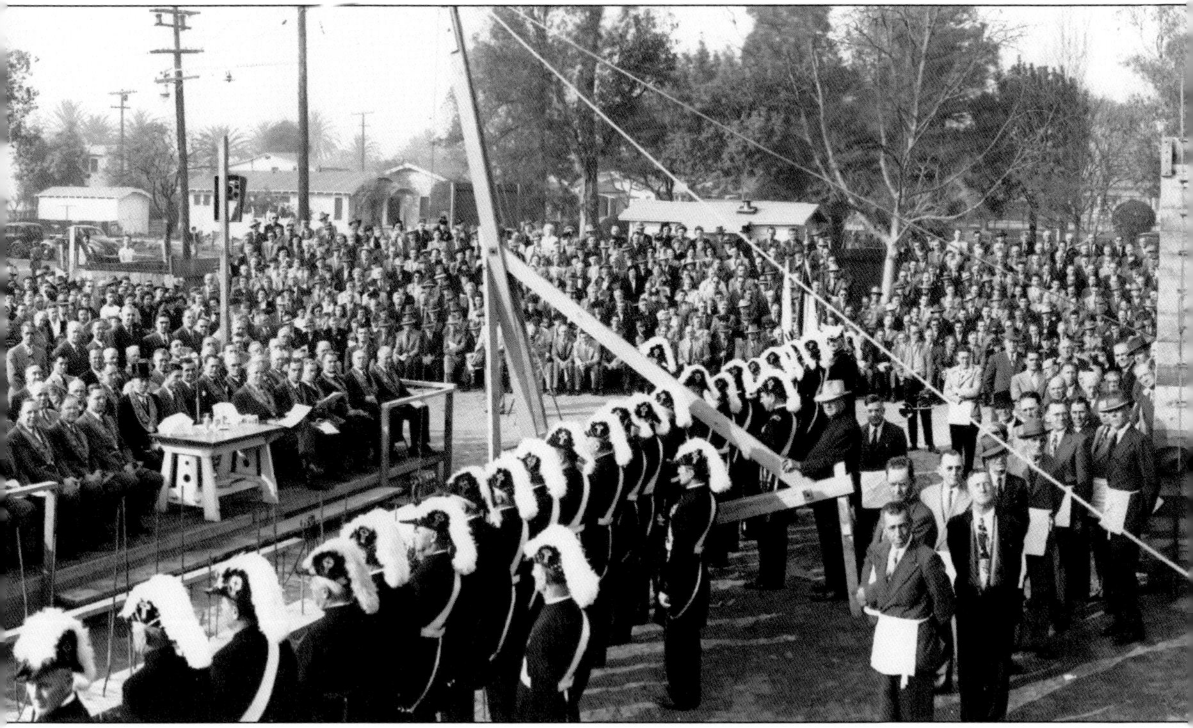

of the cornerstone, or the city hall dedication, conducted by the California Grand Lodge of Masons on November 1. Rising Light Masonic Lodge No. 397 was founded in Huntington Park in 1908 on Pacific Boulevard.

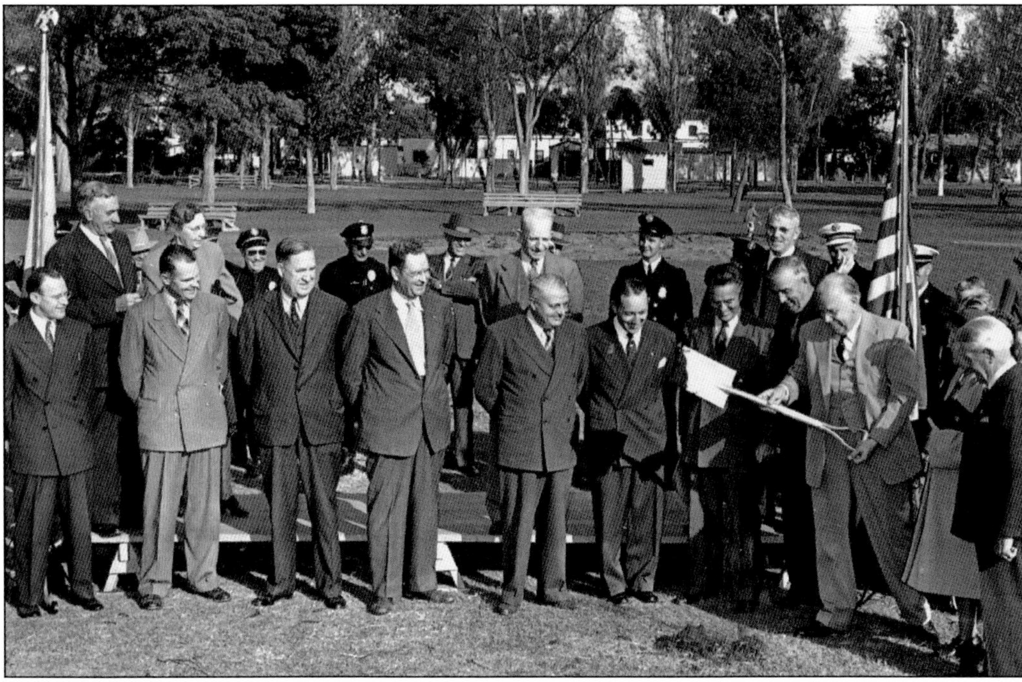

GROUNDBREAKING FOR CITY HALL. On October 21, 1946, Huntington Park city officials gathered in Miles Avenue Park at the 6500 block of Miles Avenue to break ground for a new city hall. Mayor Hollis Peavy is at center, and city historian Anna Geck, who was also among those invited to participate, is at right.

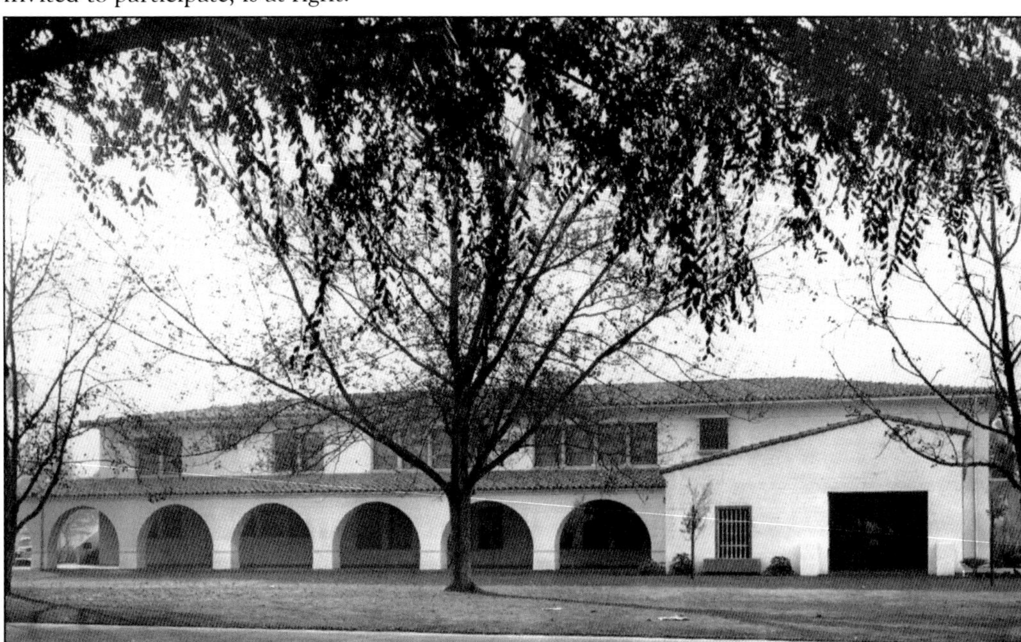

CURRENT CITY HALL. This c. 1947 photograph shows city hall shortly after completion. Note that construction on the walkway leading to the future police department had not yet begun. Miles Avenue Park, though much smaller, remains.

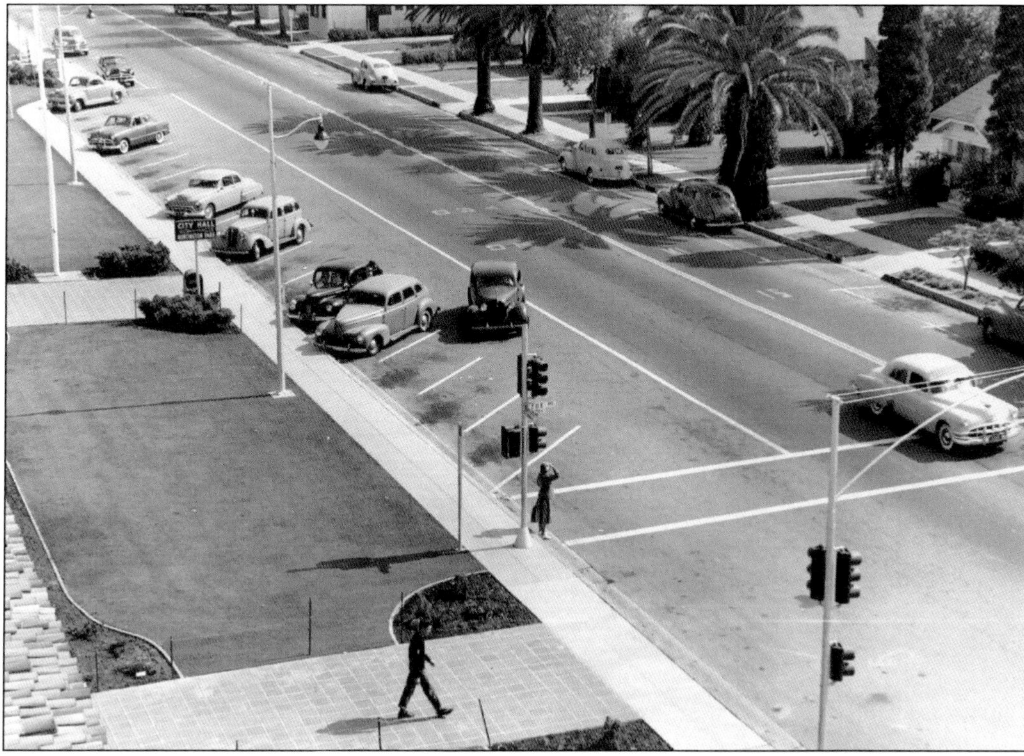

THE CLOCK TOWER. This 1950 photograph is of Miles Avenue looking south from the police station clock tower. Chief of police Randy Narramore added chimes to the clock tower in 2005.

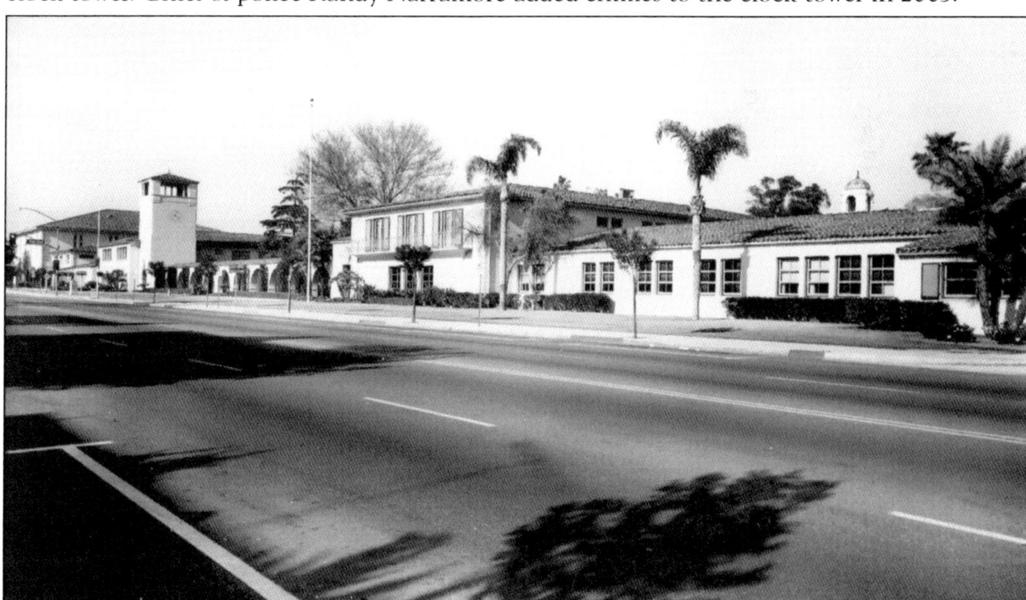

THE COMPLETED CITY HALL COMPLEX. This photograph shows the completed civic center complex. In the background, on the right, the dome of the beautiful Southeast Municipal Courthouse Tower is visible. The police station, under the clock, was built in 1950. The county health center and public library are at the far left.

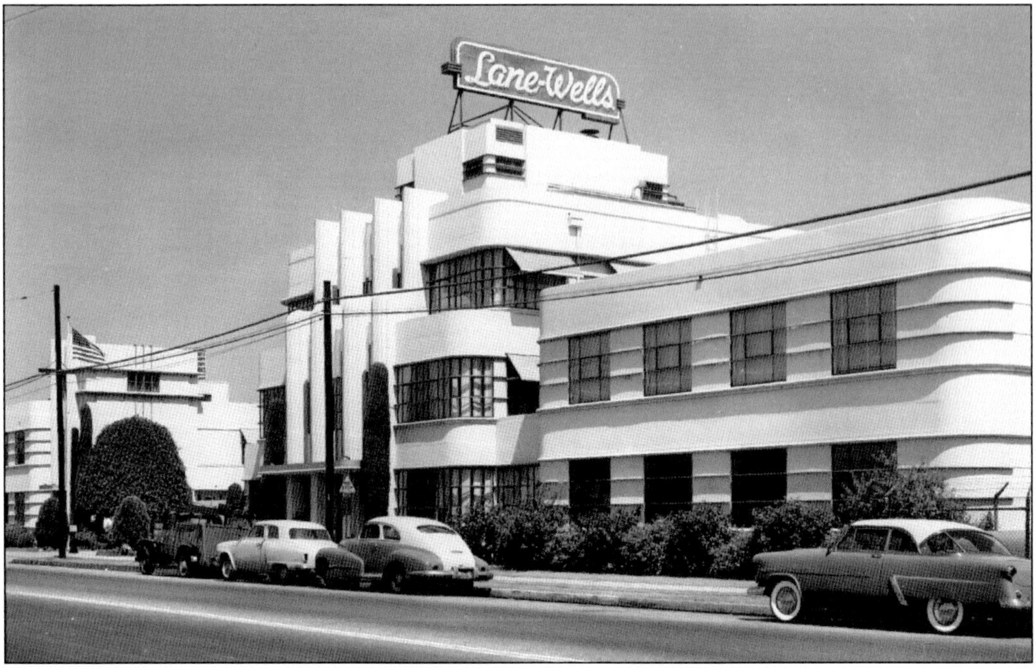

HUNTINGTON PARK INDUSTRY. Industry was, and is, as much a part of the city's development as its residential or retail sales. As the Depression ended and the country entered World War II, Huntington Park industry rebounded. Defense contracts provided jobs that resulted in a migration of new workers and subsequently more shoppers. Lane Wells (above), located on Soto Street north of Slauson Avenue, was built between 1935 and 1940 in Streamline Modern design. This building has been seen in several movies, including *The Two Jakes*. Columbia Steel (below), located on Slauson Avenue near Alameda Street, was a supplier of World War II steel.

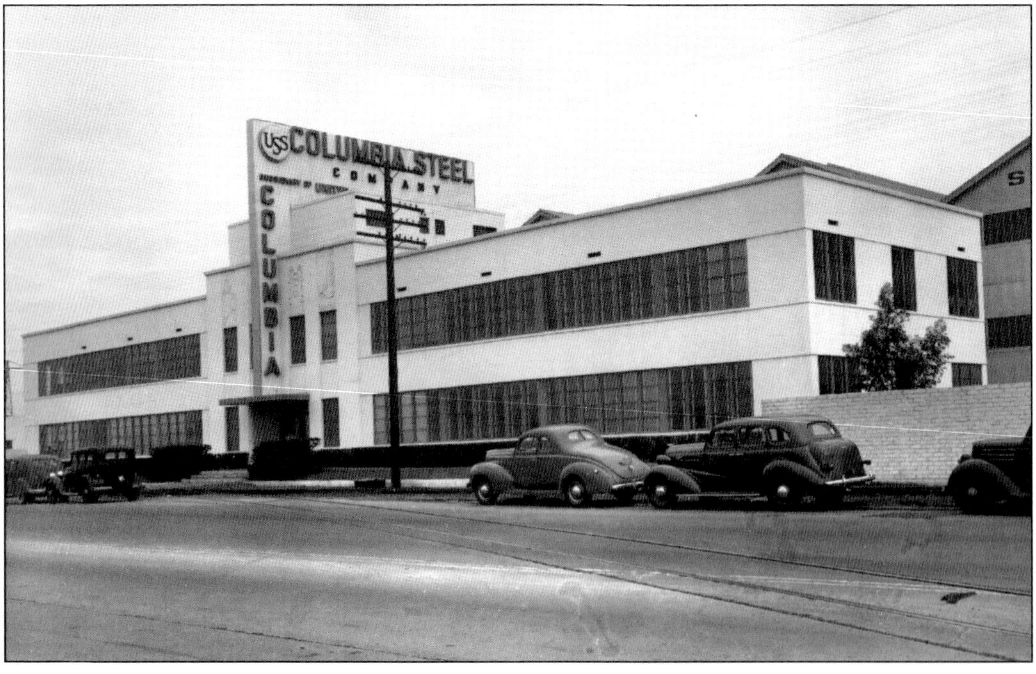

SHOP IN HUNTINGTON PARK. This banner, affixed to the two city water tanks on Slauson and Florence Avenues, is a longtime city icon. Sponsored by the chamber of commerce, "We Girls Shop in Huntington Park" declares the city's emphasis on retail sales. The signs remain today, although they are worded a little differently and now state, "Shop in Huntington Park."

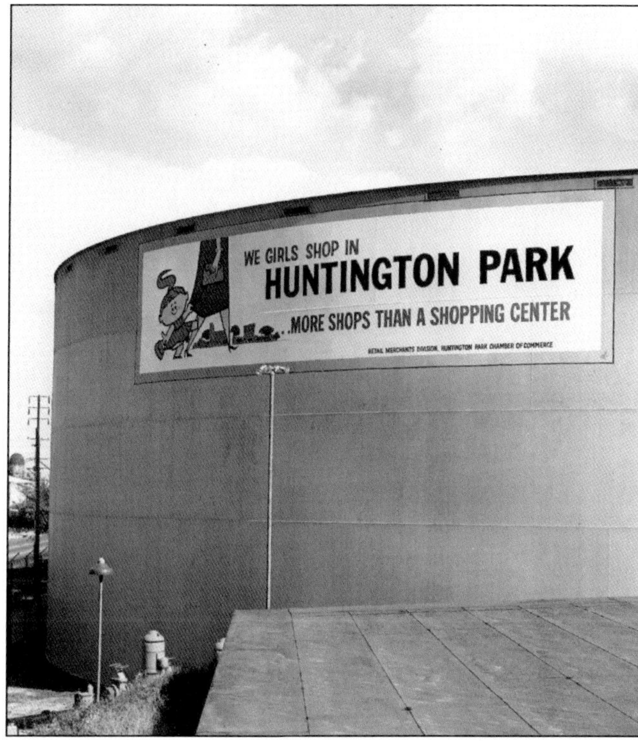

OFF-STREET PARKING. As the popularity of Huntington Park shopping grew, so did the need for parking for the thousands of shoppers. The city purchased three lots with general funds. Nine more lots were purchased with parking meter revenues. These meters were a major political issue in the mid-1930s and were eventually removed from the lots.

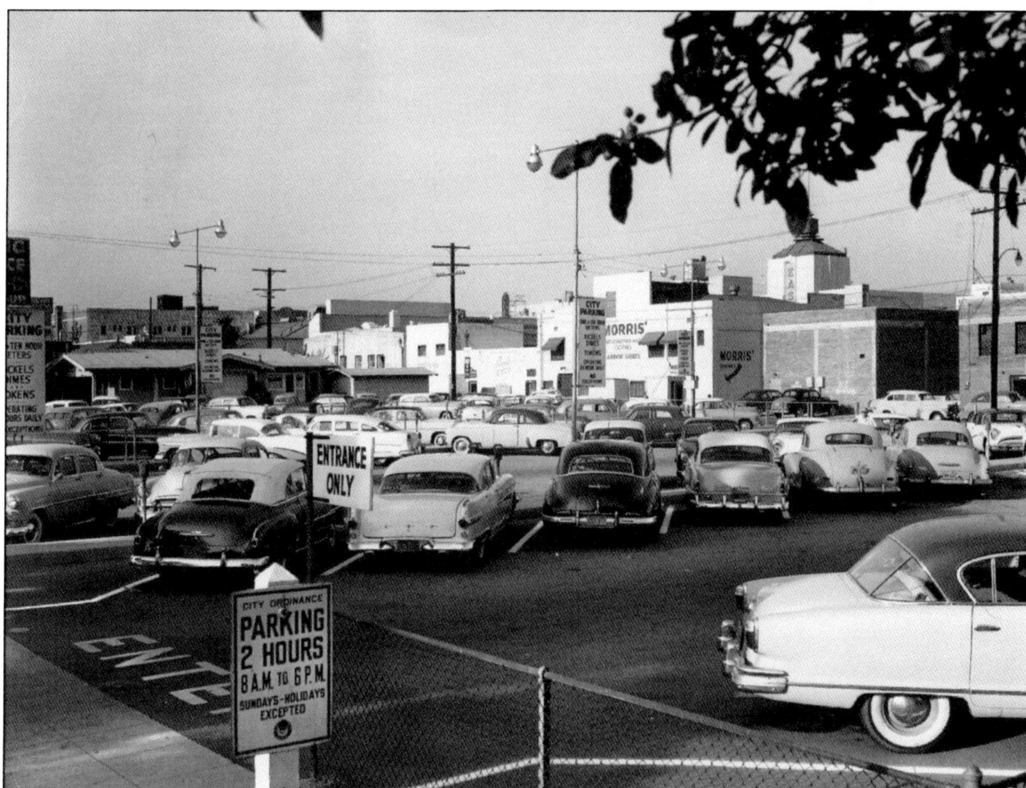

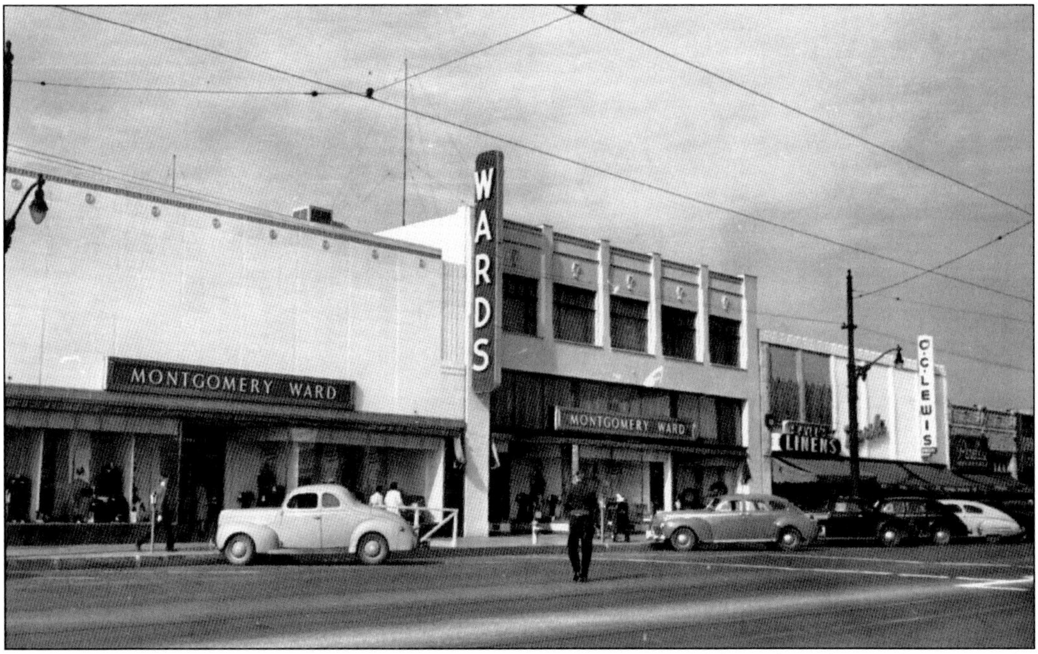

MONTGOMERY WARD. Montgomery Ward was one of what would be referred to today as Pacific Boulevard's anchor stores. This photograph was taken in the 1940s. The business used two buildings located on the west side of Pacific Boulevard between Saturn and Zoe Avenues. J. C. Penney is also one of those stores and still operates there.

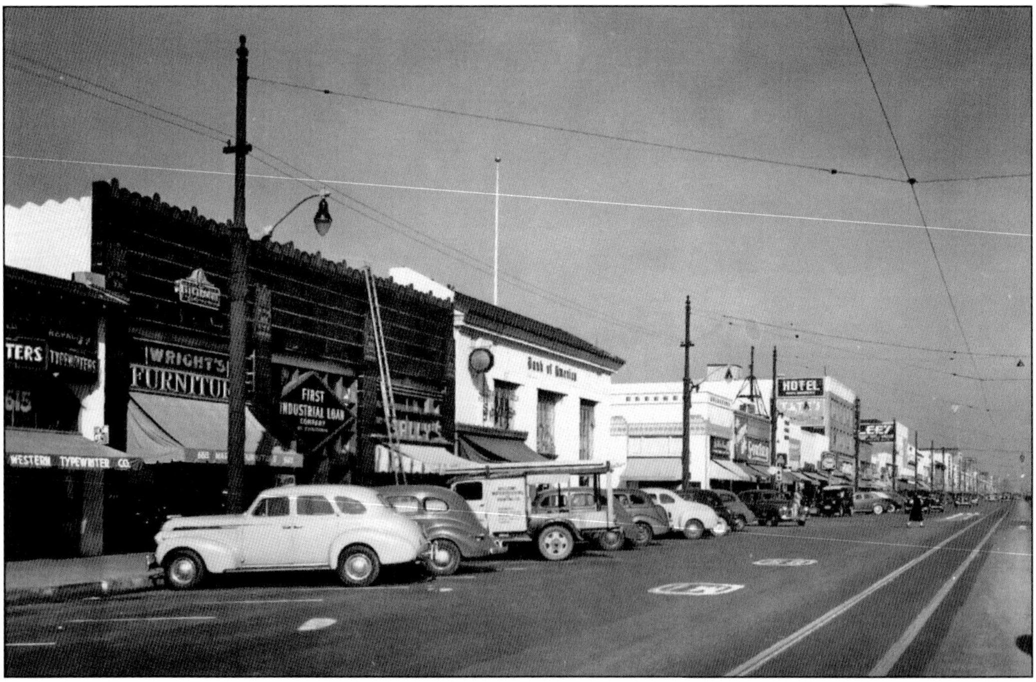

BANK OF AMERICA. This Bank of America branch, taken during the 1940s at Pacific Boulevard looking north towards Zoe Avenue, is still operating today. The black truck on the right side is delivering ice. The banking industry has always played an important role in community development.

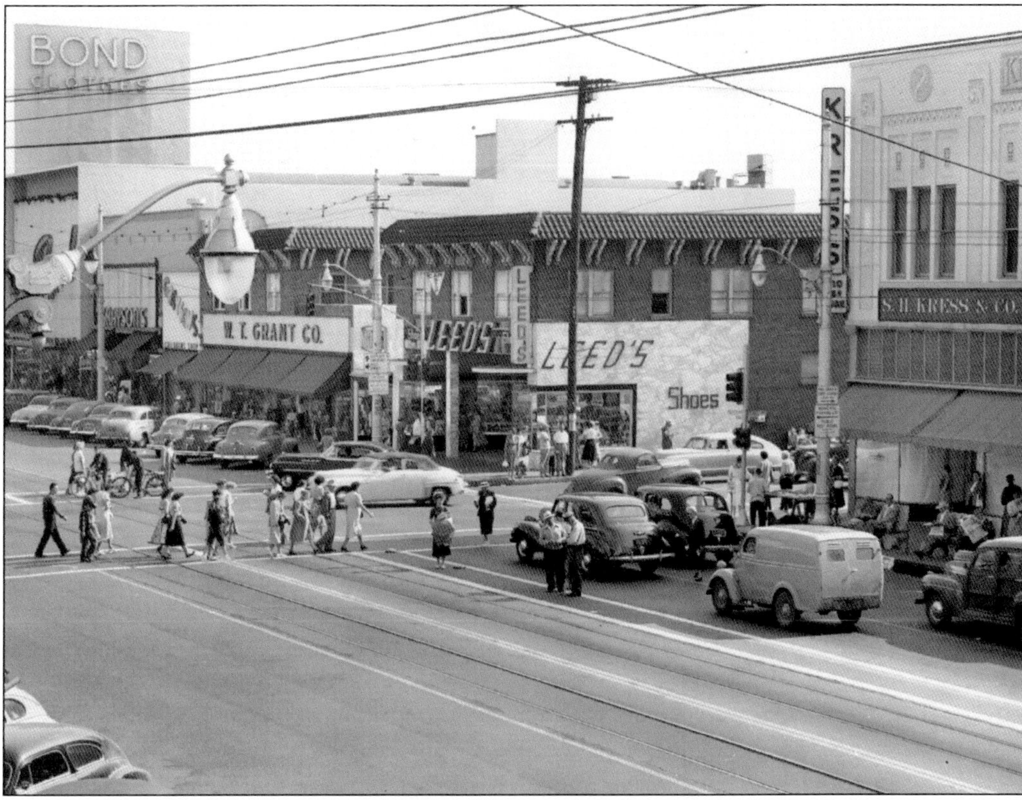

PACIFIC BOULEVARD AND GAGE AVENUE. This 1950 photograph depicts the west side of Pacific Boulevard at Gage Avenue. The man with a cap in the center of the photograph is a "traffic loader" directing people on and off the Yellow Cars and buses.

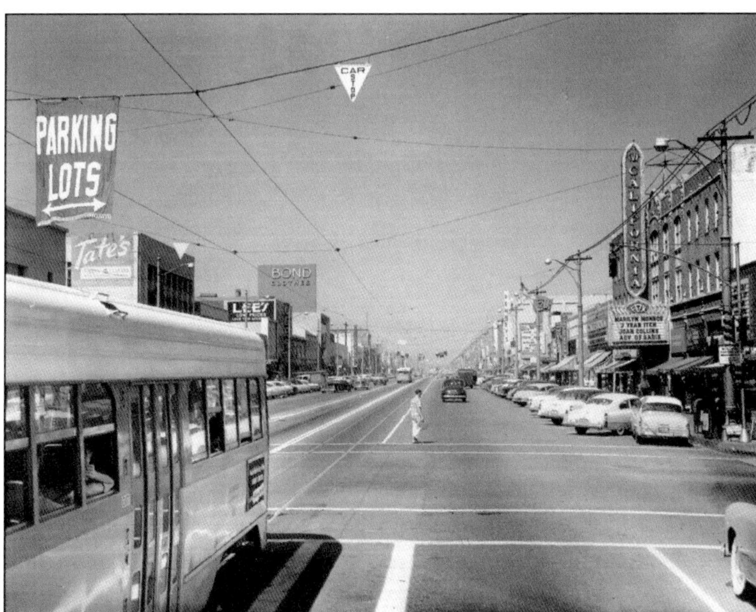

PACIFIC BOULEVARD, 1955. This 1955 photograph is of Pacific Boulevard looking north from Zoe Avenue. *Seven Year Itch*, starring Marilyn Monroe, is playing at the California Theater, and Richard Witmark is starring in *Hell and High Water* at the Park Theater. The Park is advertising "50 Cents—All Seats."

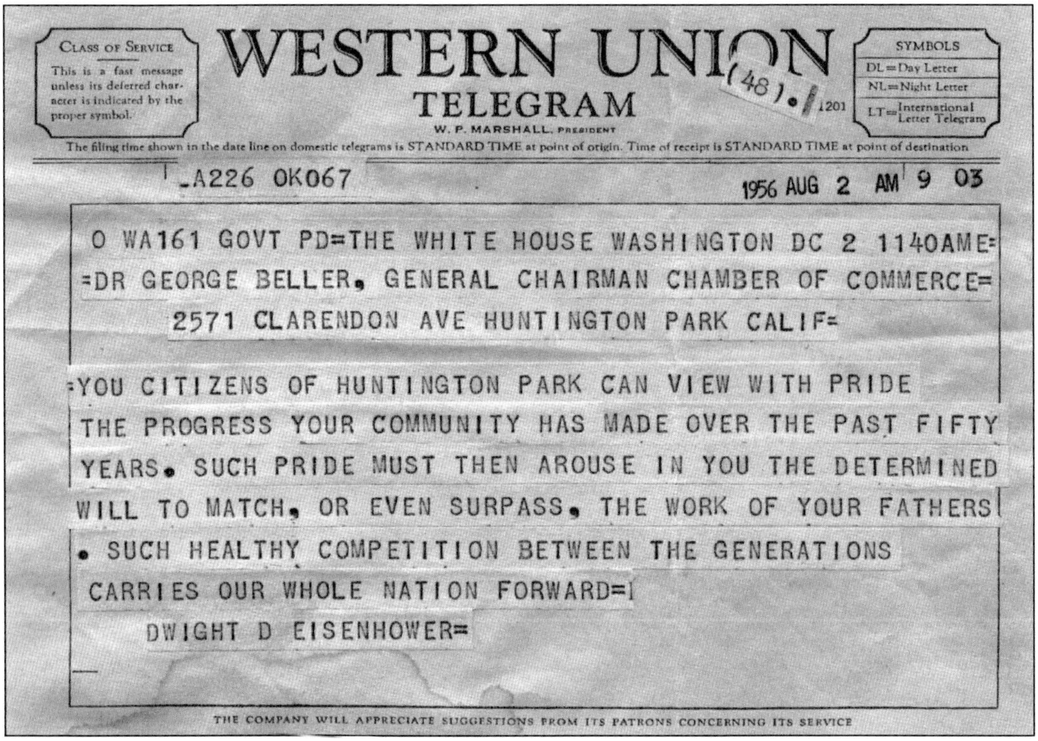

CLASS OF SERVICE
This is a fast message unless its deferred character is indicated by the proper symbol.

WESTERN UNION
TELEGRAM
W. P. MARSHALL, PRESIDENT

(48). 1201

SYMBOLS
DL=Day Letter
NL=Night Letter
LT=International Letter Telegram

The filing time shown in the date line on domestic telegrams is STANDARD TIME at point of origin. Time of receipt is STANDARD TIME at point of destination

.A226 OK067 1956 AUG 2 AM 9 03

O WA161 GOVT PD=THE WHITE HOUSE WASHINGTON DC 2 1140AME=
=DR GEORGE BELLER, GENERAL CHAIRMAN CHAMBER OF COMMERCE=
2571 CLARENDON AVE HUNTINGTON PARK CALIF=

=YOU CITIZENS OF HUNTINGTON PARK CAN VIEW WITH PRIDE THE PROGRESS YOUR COMMUNITY HAS MADE OVER THE PAST FIFTY YEARS. SUCH PRIDE MUST THEN AROUSE IN YOU THE DETERMINED WILL TO MATCH, OR EVEN SURPASS, THE WORK OF YOUR FATHERS . SUCH HEALTHY COMPETITION BETWEEN THE GENERATIONS CARRIES OUR WHOLE NATION FORWARD=

DWIGHT D EISENHOWER=

THE COMPANY WILL APPRECIATE SUGGESTIONS FROM ITS PATRONS CONCERNING ITS SERVICE

FIFTIETH ANNIVERSARY. In 1955, Huntington Park celebrated its 50th birthday. In recognition of the event, Pres. Dwight D. Eisenhower sent this telegram to the Huntington Park Chamber of Commerce. The official anniversary celebration took place September 15–23, 1956. The *Daily Signal* published a special Golden Years edition on September 17, 1956. Much of the information from that edition is reflected in this publication.

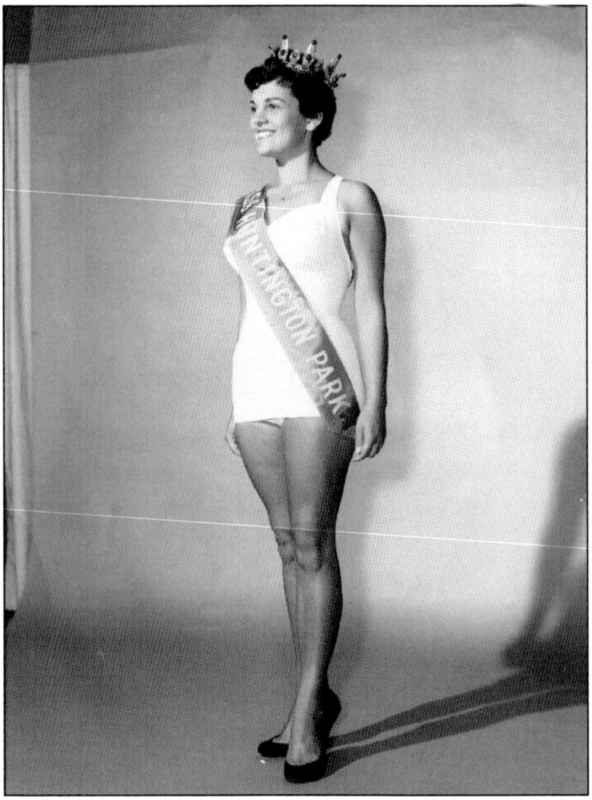

MISS HUNTINGTON PARK. Pictured in 1956 is Glenda McMinn, who was selected as Miss Huntington Park and queen for the city's 50th anniversary celebration during an event held at Warner's Theater hosted by actor Richard Boone. Glenda McMinn and the four other girls of her court participated in several anniversary events.

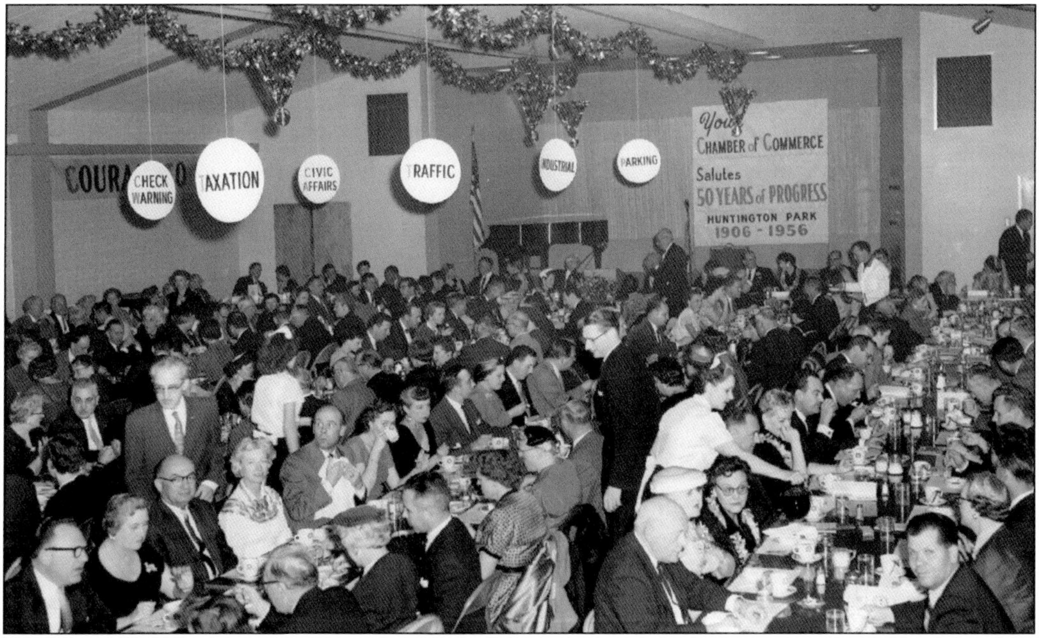

THE CHAMBER OF COMMERCE. Among the 50th anniversary events was this chamber of commerce–sponsored dinner. The chamber played a key role in the development of Huntington Park. Its roots are in the improvement foundation, established in 1904, and approximately one year later it expanded into the board of trade. In 1915, the existing chamber of commerce was founded, and it was incorporated on June 30, 1921. The role of the chamber is to promote the growth and economic health of the business community.

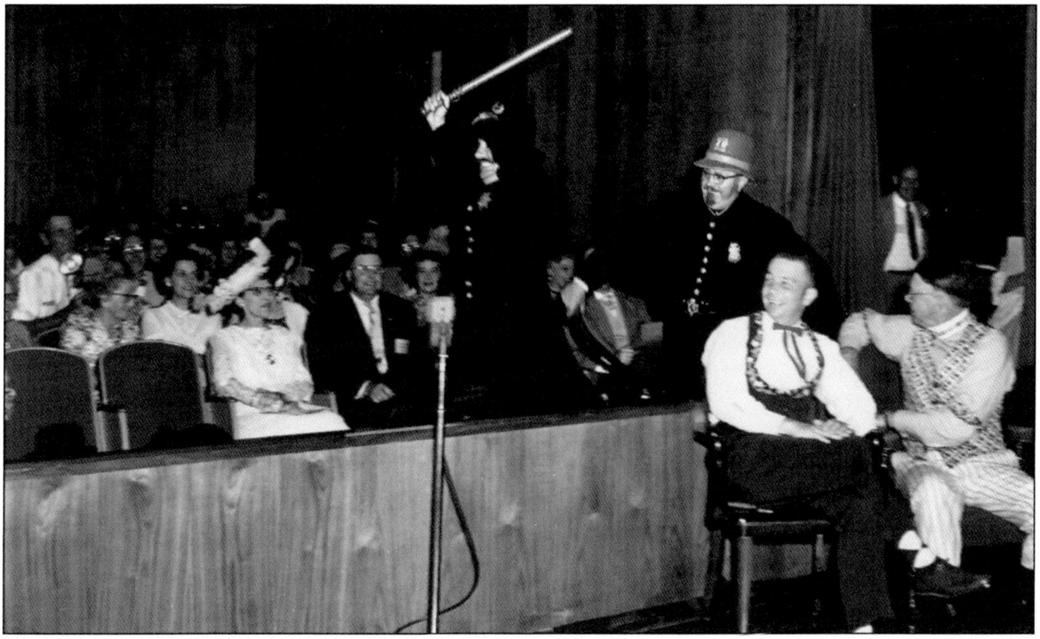

THE KEYSTONE COPS AT COUNCIL. During one of the many 50th anniversary events, these Keystone Cops make an appearance at a city council meeting. Note that many of the attendees are dressed in period attire.

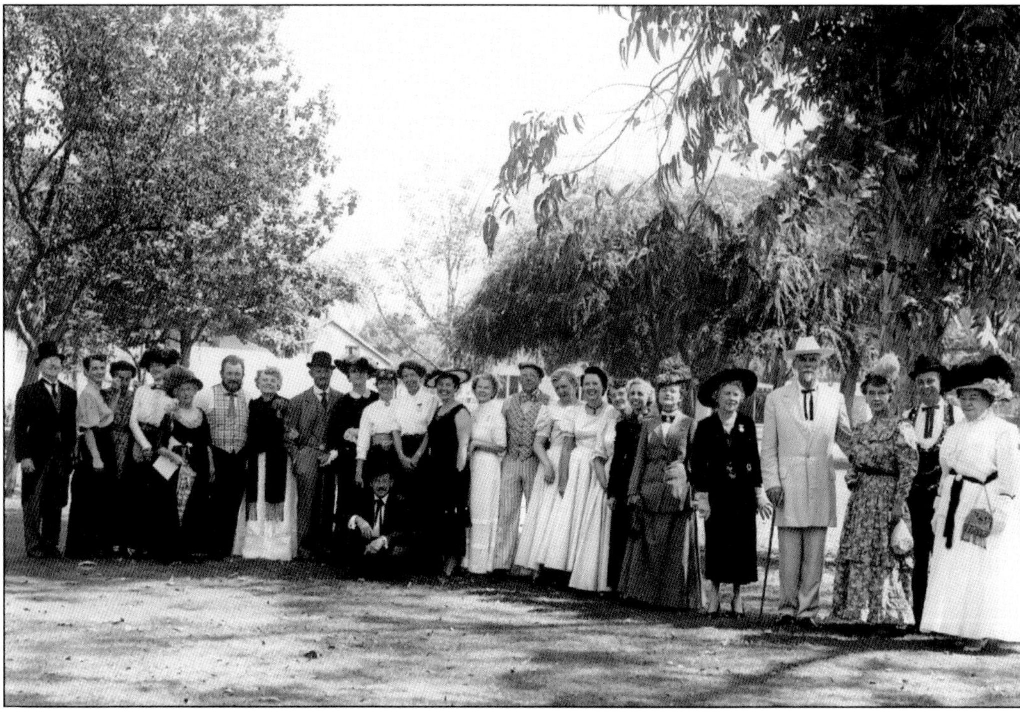

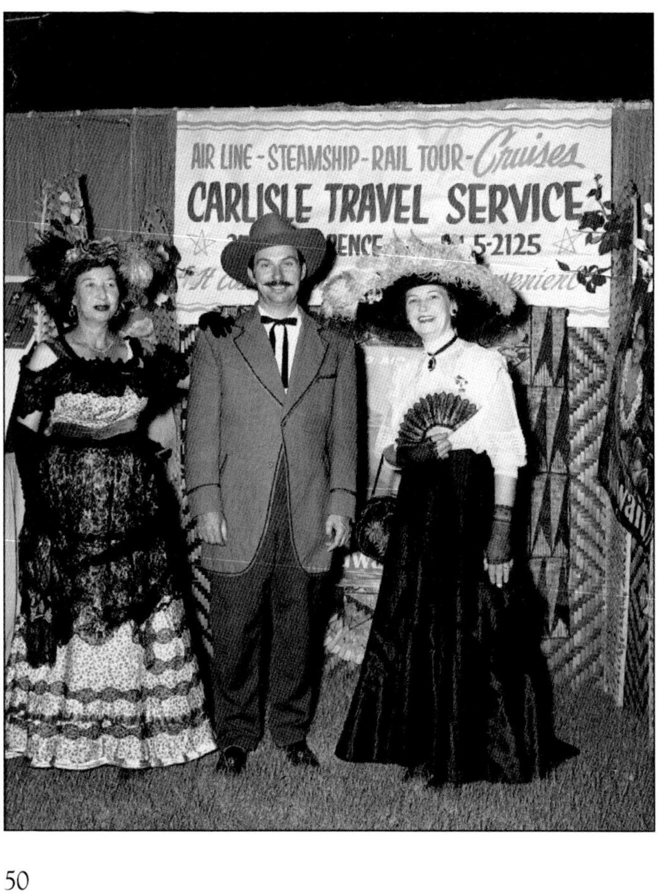

FIFTIETH ANNIVERSARY EVENTS. Among the 50th anniversary celebration events was a period dress-up day for city hall employees (above). This photograph was taken in Miles Avenue Park next to city hall. Golden anniversary events included a parade, an ice cream social, a square dance, concerts, a costume contest, and a banquet as the climax of the event was held at the Elks Lodge. The anniversary chairman was George Beller (left), who was also in costume.

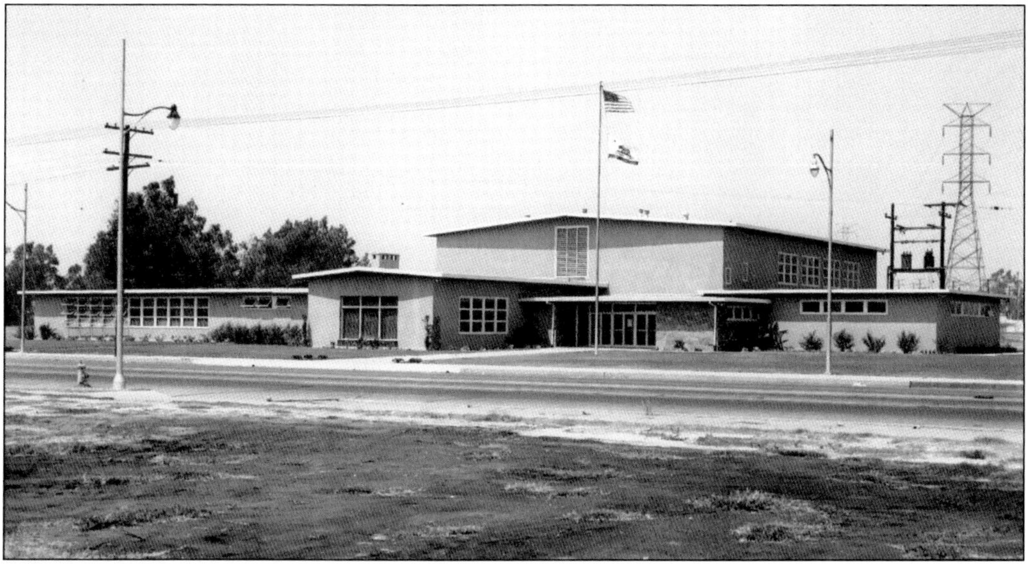

PARKS AND RECREATION. This photograph of Huntington Park's current parks and recreation building was taken in the 1950s shortly after its construction. The building, located at Florence and Bissell Avenues, contains an indoor basketball court, a gymnasium, and classrooms where it hosts many programs, including music, dance, and self-defense classes.

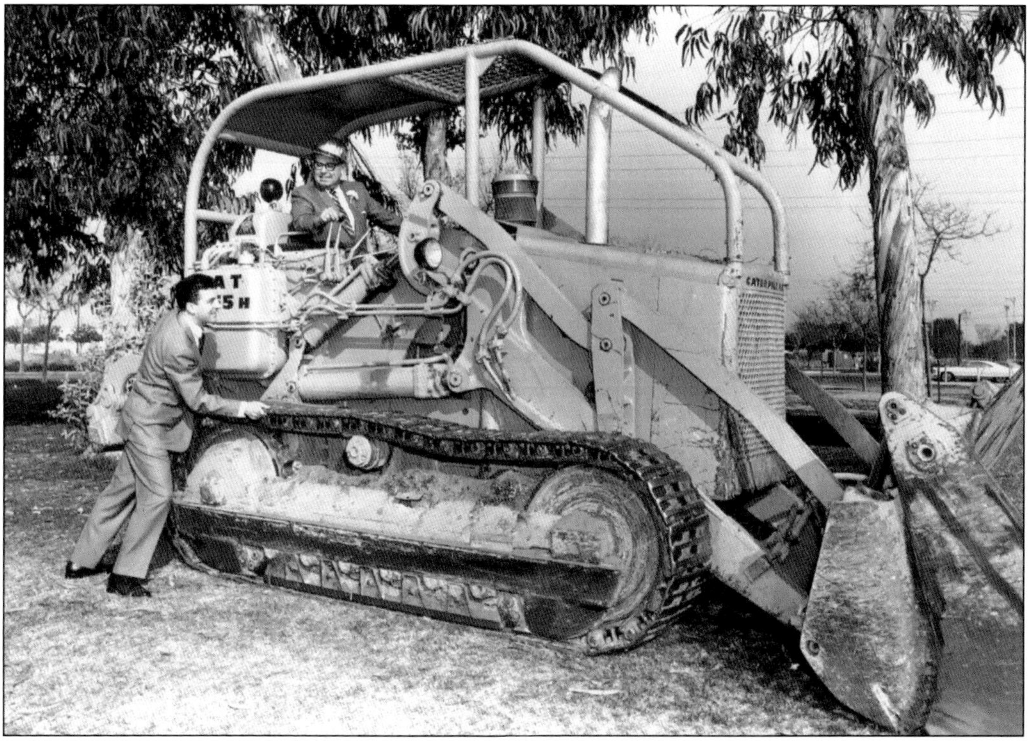

THE NEW MUNICIPAL PARK. Mayor Kermit Bill drives the bulldozer with parks and playgrounds supervisor Mike Maramonte giving him a push in this 1968 photograph during groundbreaking ceremonies at Municipal Park. Now known as Salt Lake Park, the large eucalyptus trees were removed as part of the park's redevelopment.

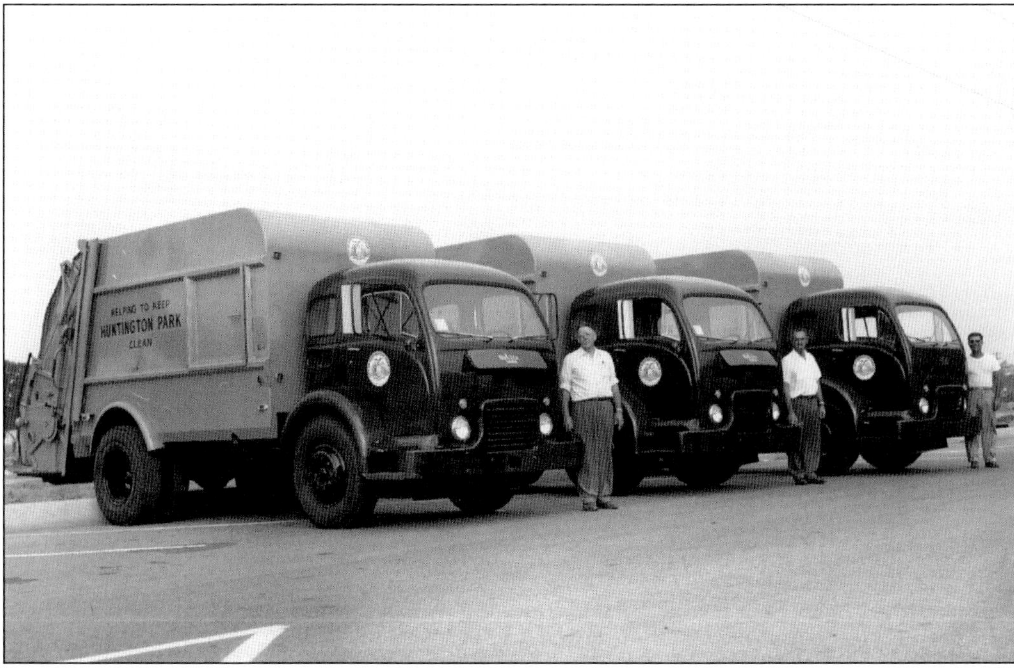

NEW TRASH TRUCKS. As pictured in the 1940s (above), then again in the 1970s (below), the city purchased modern trash trucks in an effort to keep up with the growing quantities of rubbish generated by a growing modern city. Once under the control of the street superintendent, trash collection is now contracted out to a private company.

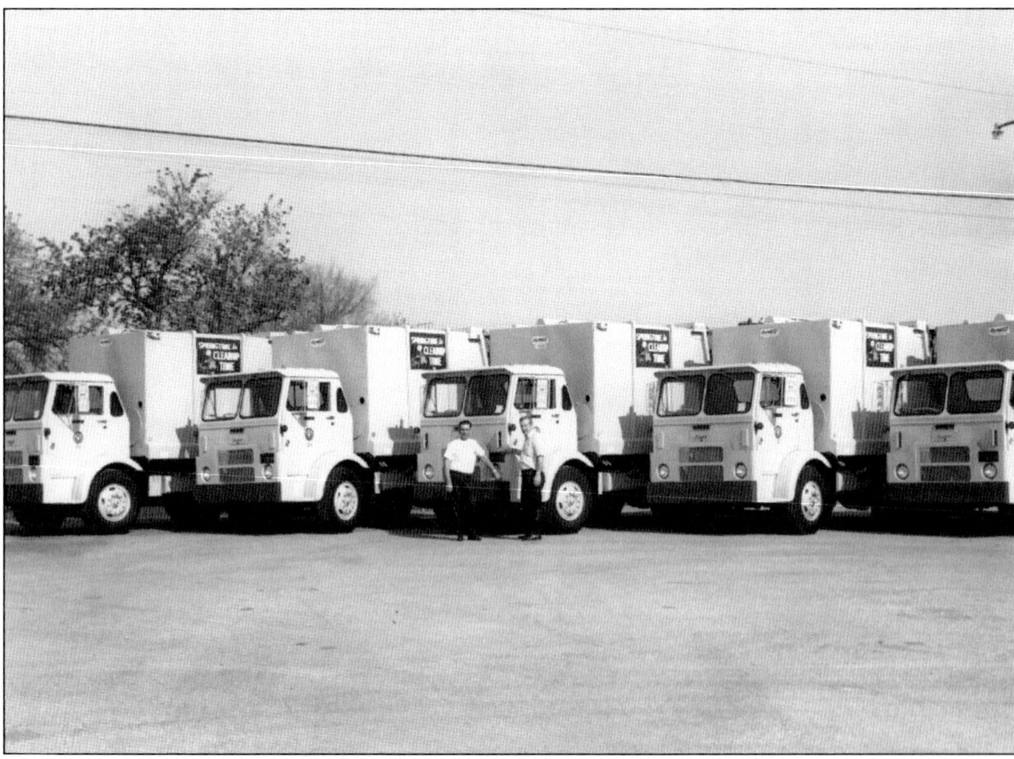

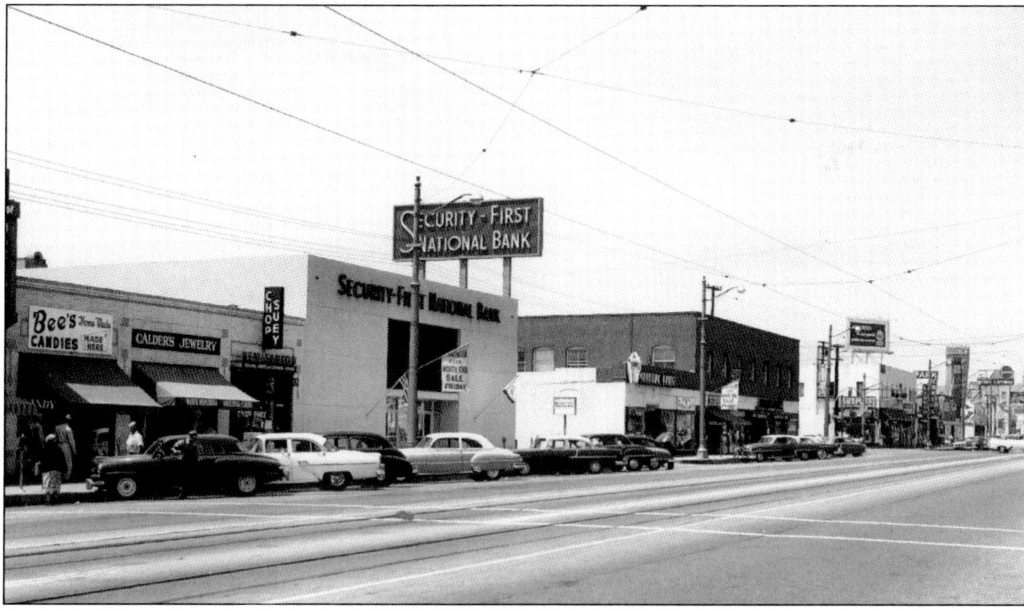

PACIFIC BOULEVARD AND RANDOLPH STREET, 1950S. In the 1950s, Pacific Boulevard remained the hub of southeast Los Angeles retail shopping, serving a market area of over 350,000 people. Pacific Boulevard hosted 38 shoe stores and 26 jewelry stores. This photograph was taken looking northwest from Park Place towards Pacific Boulevard and Randolph Street. The dark building on the right is the J. A. Jones Building, constructed 50 years earlier (see page 24).

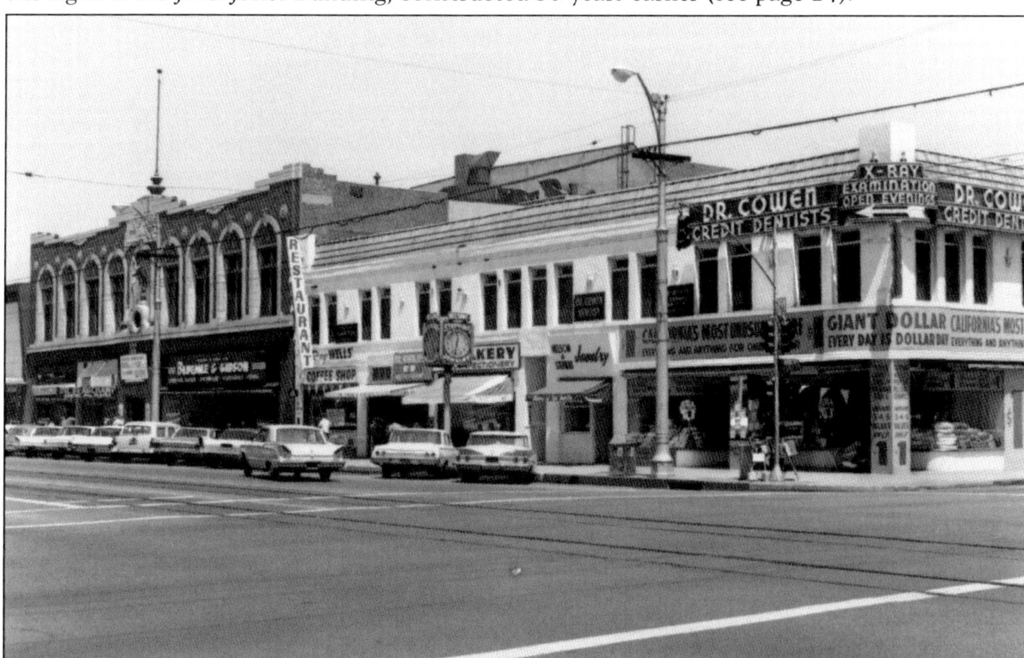

PACIFIC BOULEVARD AND GAGE AVENUE, 1960S. This *c.* 1960 photograph is of the Pacific Boulevard and Zoe Avenue intersection looking northeast, and the buildings are showing their age. In 1963, the Yellow Car line was replaces by buses. Vacancy of storefronts rose to 20 percent. Additionally, this was the beginning of the age of the regional shopping center or shopping mall.

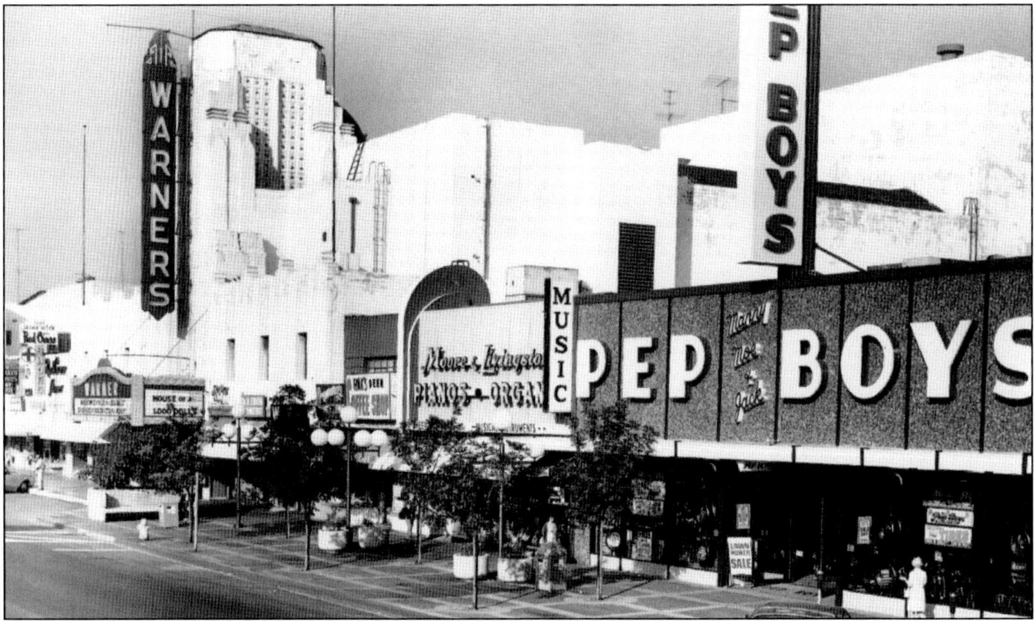

REDEVELOPMENT IN THE 1970S. These photographs were taken on Pacific Boulevard during the redevelopment era of the 1970s. The decline of business on Pacific significantly reduced tax revenues compounded by the Proposition 13 Jarvis Tax Revolt. A broad redevelopment plan was enacted by the city council, making the rejuvenation of the central business district a priority. At this same time, older housing in the city was demolished and replaced with new homes and condominiums. As time passed, Pacific Boulevard rebounded and today has few, if any, vacancies.

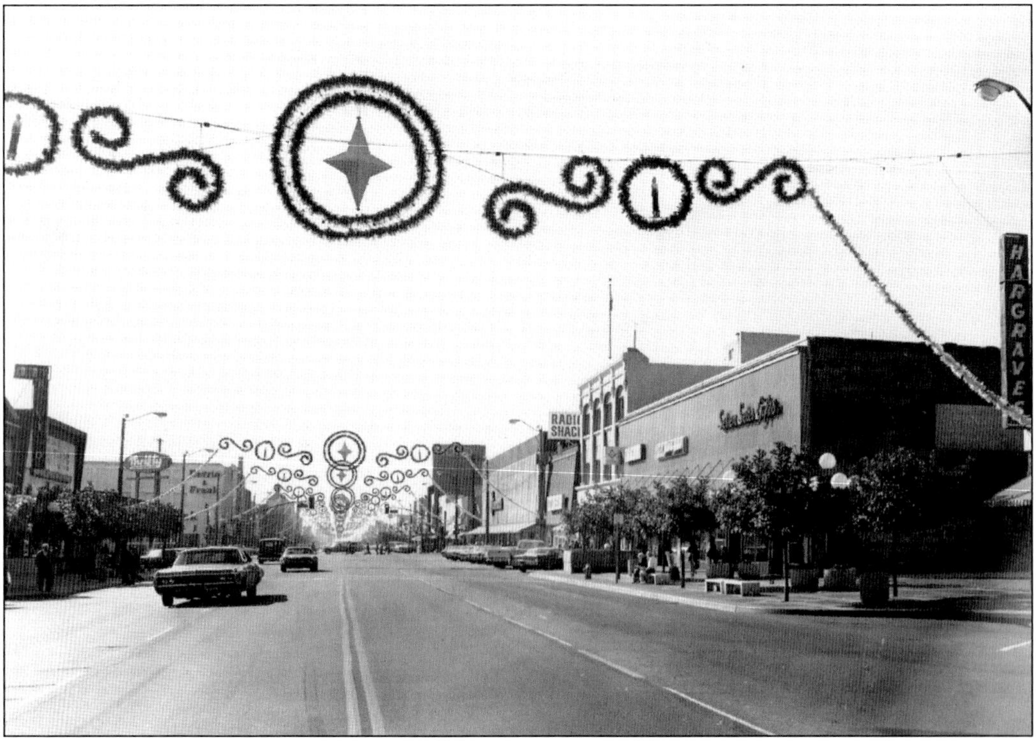

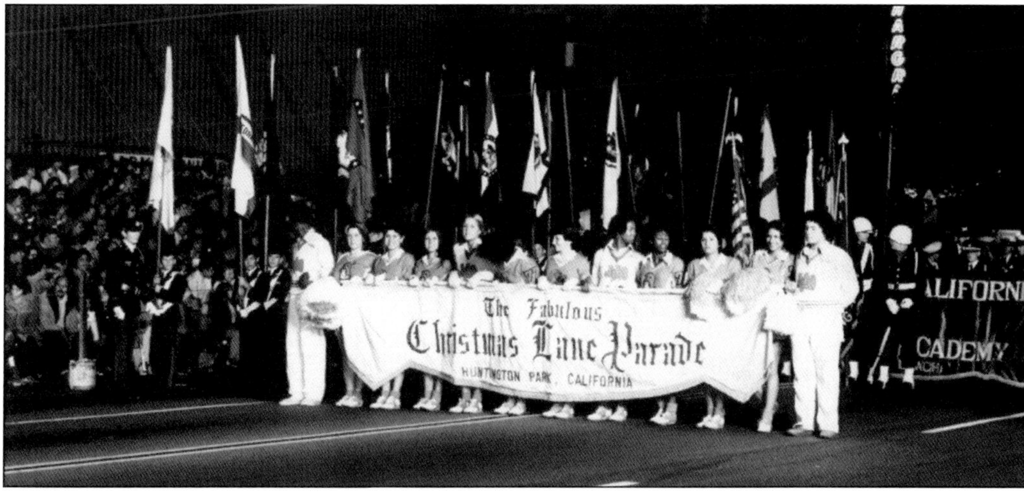

THE FABULOUS HUNTINGTON PARK CHRISTMAS PARADE. Huntington Park's Christmas parade was first held in 1946. It has been sponsored by the chamber of commerce, the junior chamber of commerce, or both since its inception. Arguably the most popular Christmas parade in the Los Angeles area throughout the 1950s, it had many famous personalities serve as grand marshall. The first was singer and actor Pat Boone; others have included Danny Thomas, Ernest Borgnine, and Jane Mansfield. In 1952, it was the first live televised event in the Los Angeles area to be simulcasted on radio and television in both Spanish and English. Although the parade is shorter in length, the tradition continues today.

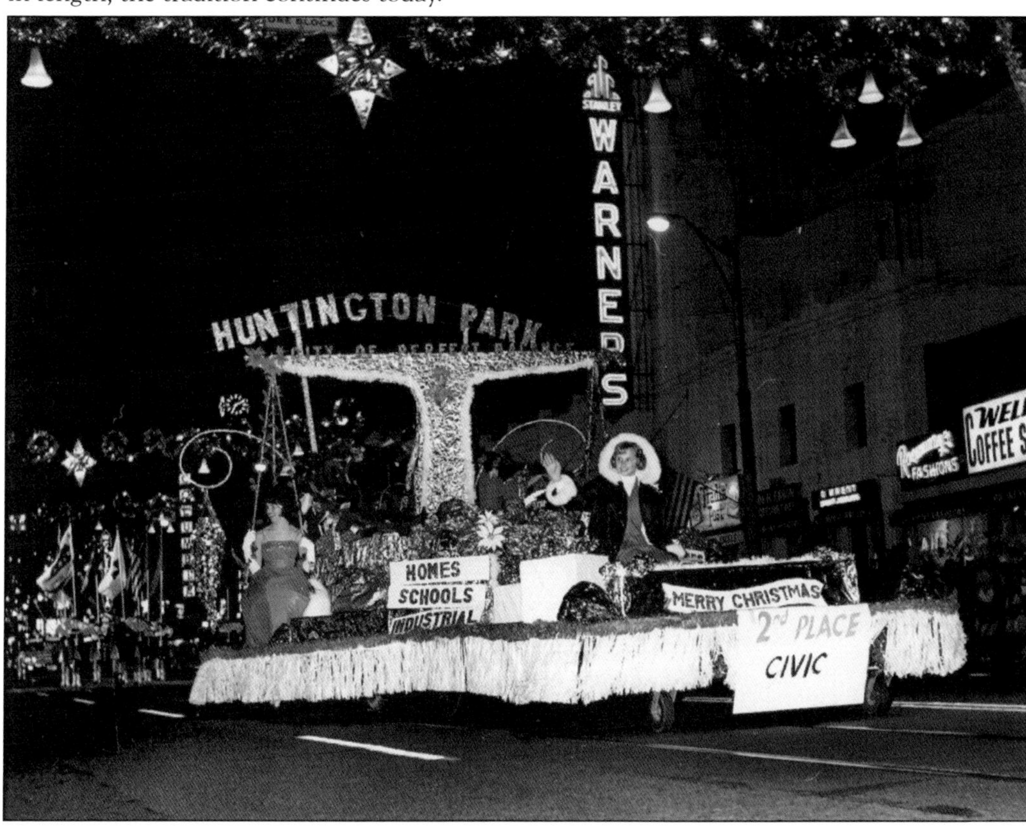

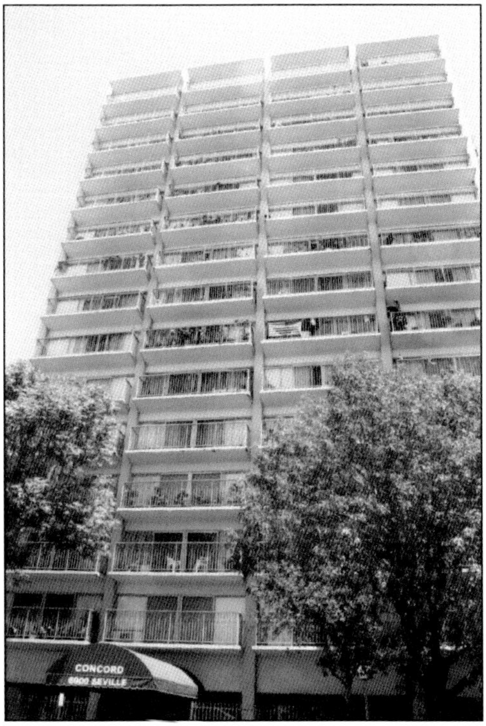

THE CONCORD. The Concord Apartments, seen as it appears today, was built in 1973 during the redevelopment years. At 15 stories, it is the tallest building in Huntington Park and probably the entire southeast area. It is occupied by senior citizens, who are offered many activities and a secure environment.

DIAL-A-RIDE. Also initiated during the redevelopment of the 1970s was the city's Dial-a-Ride program. It was primarily intended for senior citizens and the disabled and provided rides to local shopping outlets, doctor's appointments, and other places at a very low cost. Fiesta Taxi holds the city's current Dial-a-Ride contract. Pictured in 1972 are, from left to right, Huntington Park mayor Herb Hennes, unidentified, Sam Oliveto from Dial-a-Ride, City of Bell council member Jay Price, and city manager Harold Campbell.

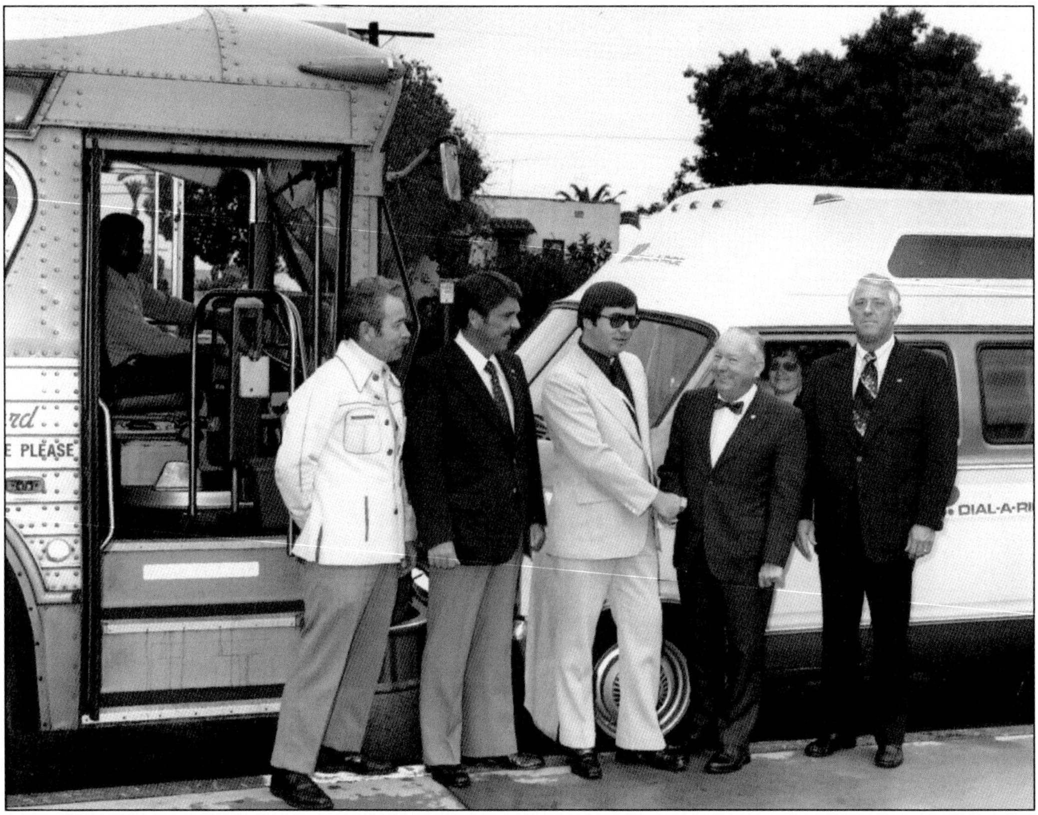

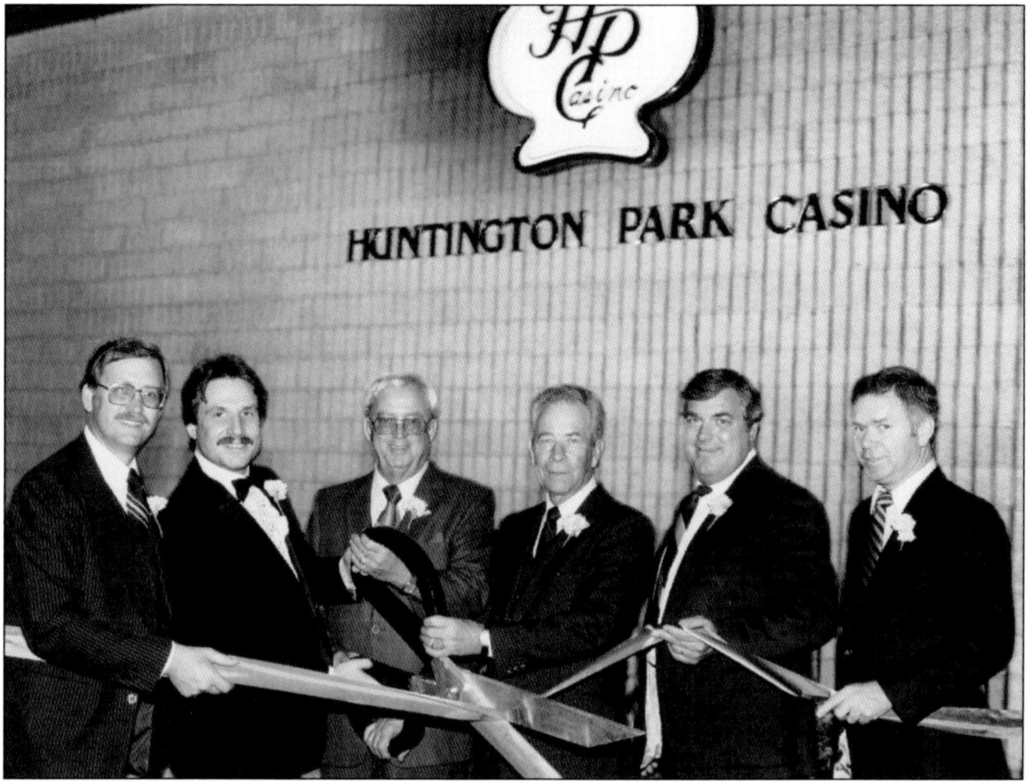

THE HUNTINGTON PARK CASINO. On March 23, 1984, a ribbon-cutting ceremony took place celebrating the grand opening of the Huntington Park Casino at Sixty-seventh and Alameda Streets. Pictured above from left to right are councilman Tom Jackson, casino president Curt Fresch, Mayor Jack Parks, councilman Herb Hennes, mayor pro-tem Bill Cunningham, and councilman Jim Roberts. The casino was part of the city's west side industrial redevelopment program, seen below. The 40,000-square-foot building was expected to generate $1 million per year, but it fell far short of that. It is now Leonardo's Restaurant and Nightclub.

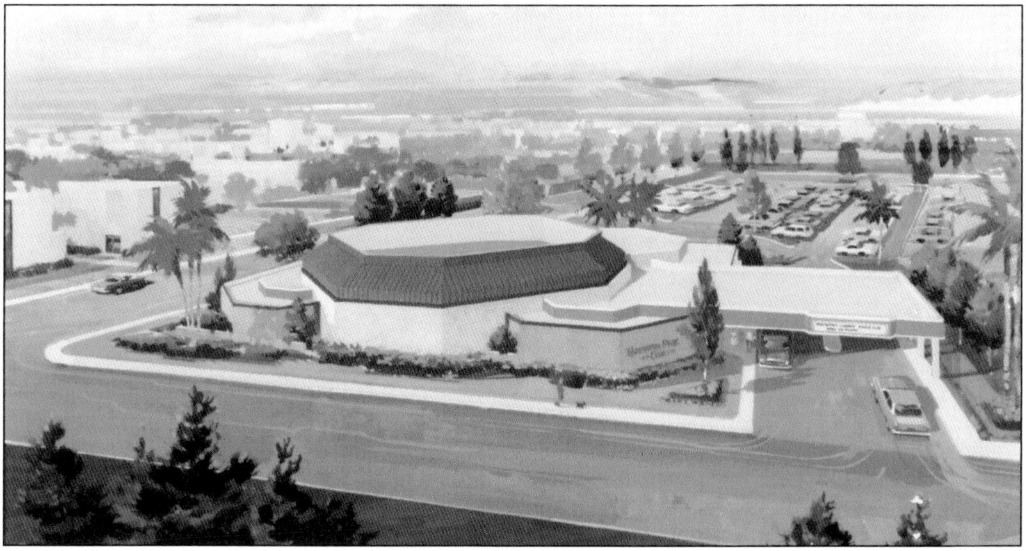

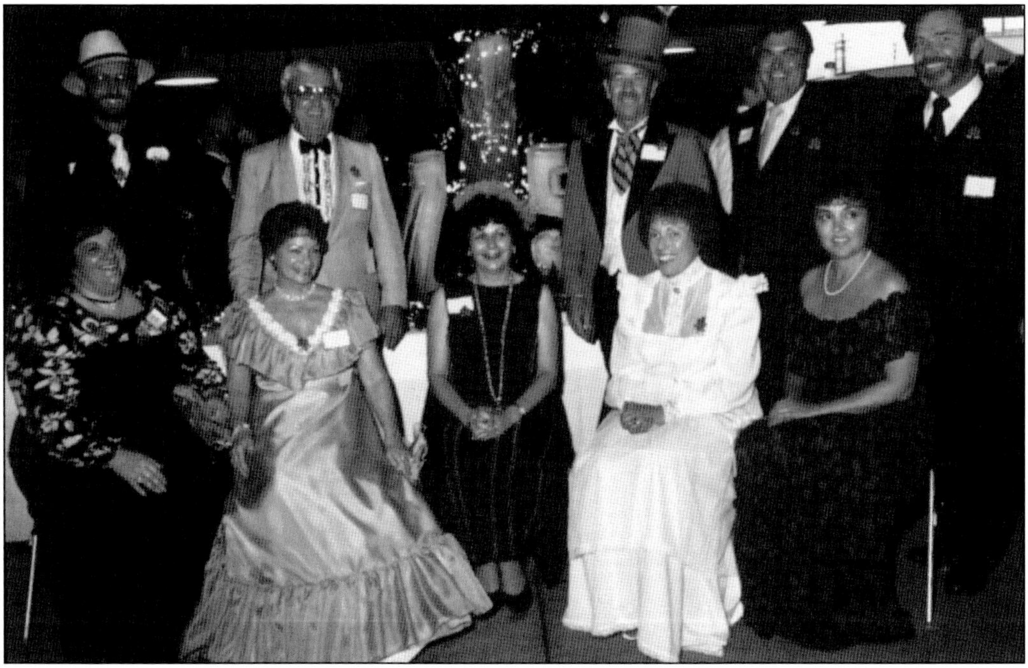

THE 75TH ANNIVERSARY. In 1981, the City of Huntington Park celebrated its 75th anniversary. This photograph was taken at the celebratory dinner on August 29, 1981, at the Elks Lodge. Pictured with their wives are, from left to right, mayor pro-tem Thomas E. Jackson, councilman Jack W. Parks, Mayor Herbert A. Hennes, councilman William Cunningham, and councilman Jim Roberts.

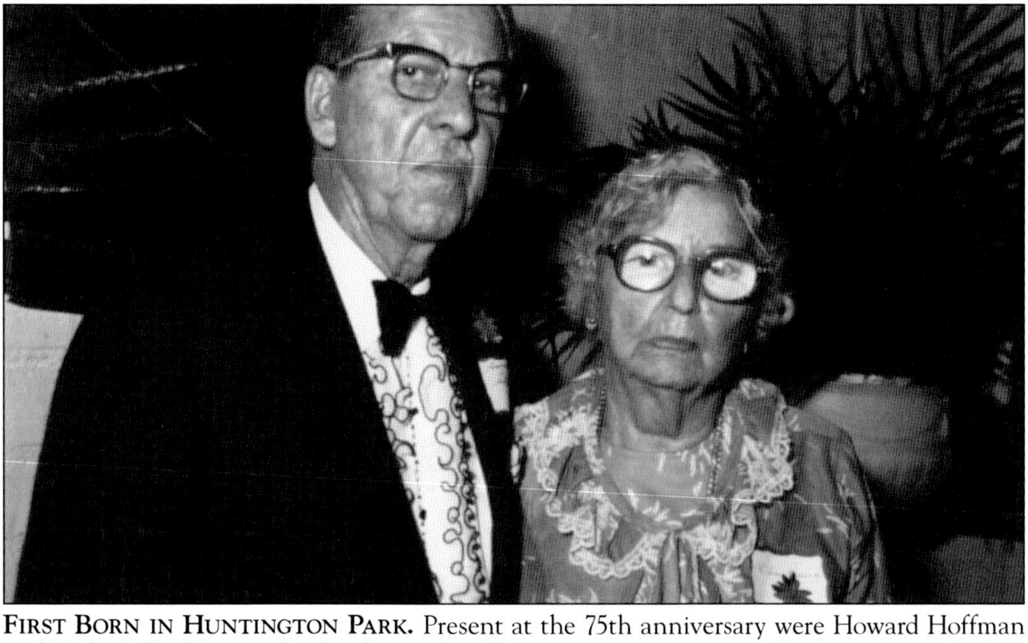

FIRST BORN IN HUNTINGTON PARK. Present at the 75th anniversary were Howard Hoffman and Viola Gifford Bruce, the first boy and girl born in Huntington Park; both in 1905. The first twins in the city were born a short time later to a family named Harrah. The twins were cared for, according to a 1956 *Daily Signal* article, by Evelena Caywood, who purchased the first Daily Signal Building and moved to Middleton, where she lived until 1919.

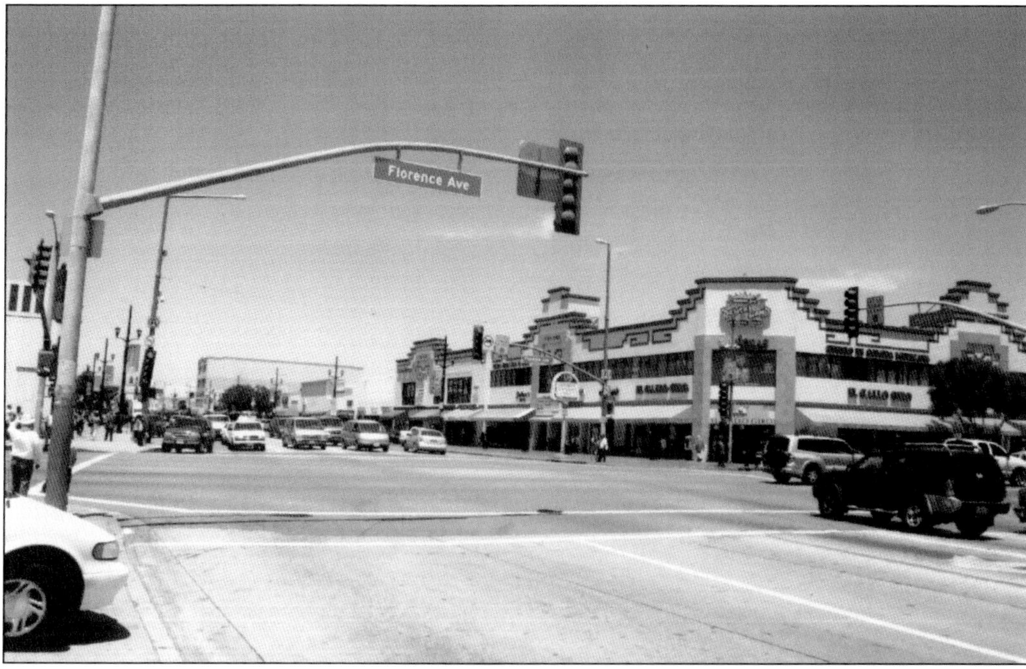

PACIFIC BOULEVARD AND FLORENCE AVENUE. Bordering the unincorporated area of Walnut Park, the intersection of Pacific Boulevard and Florence Avenue is among the best known locations in the city. A major intersection for area traffic, it is also become a gathering place for exuberant soccer fans following world cup victories by the national team from Mexico. Pictured as it appears now, the colorful restaurant Gallo Giro is on the northeast corner.

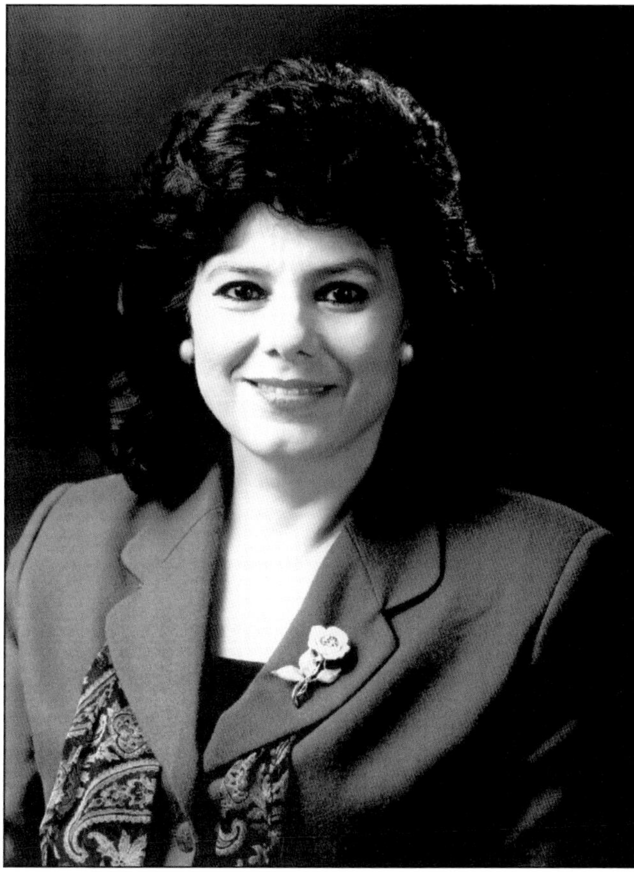

THE FIRST WOMAN MAYOR. Jessica Maes grew up in Huntington Park and attended Huntington Park High School. In 1997, she became the first woman mayor in the city's history, serving two one-year terms in the office. She has been active in the community for 35 years and with her husband is the owner/publisher of *El Adviso* magazine, a Spanish-language publication.

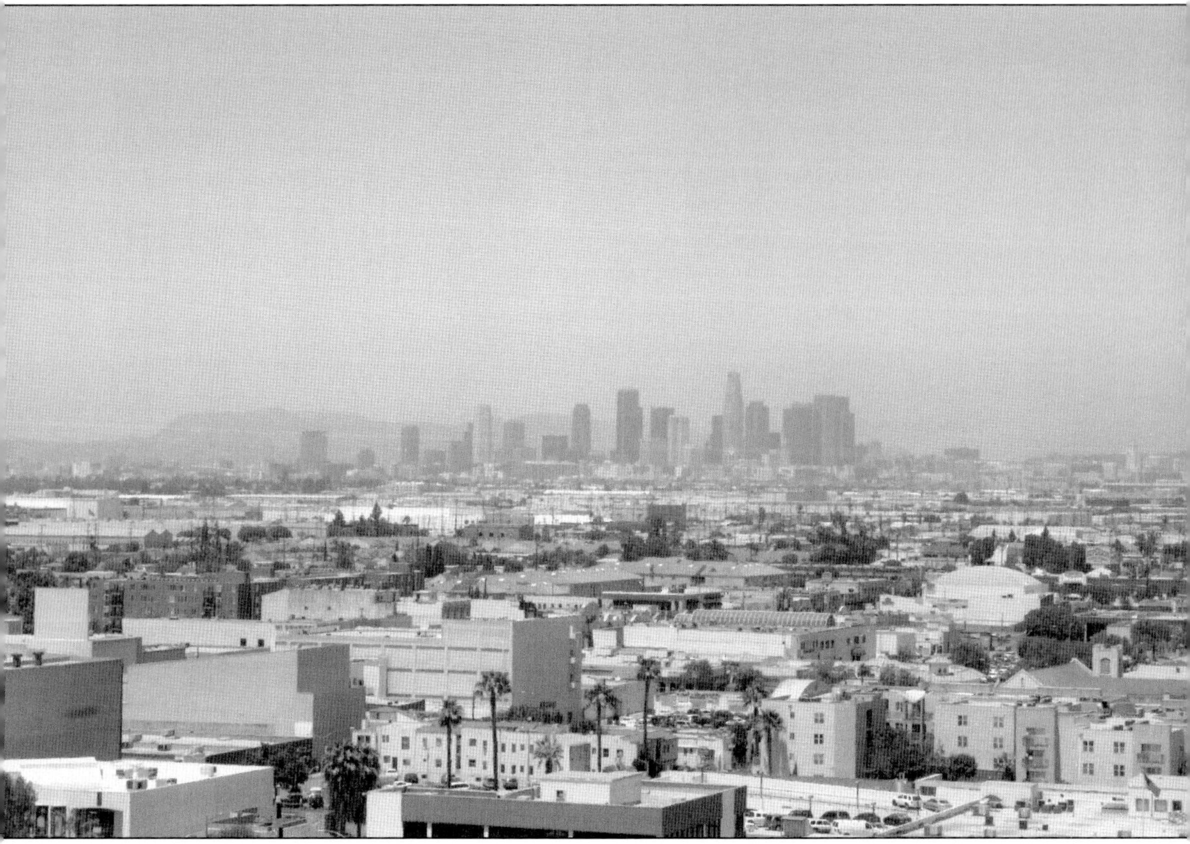

PACIFIC BOULEVARD, 2007. This photograph, taken from the roof of the city's tallest building, the Concord Apartments at 6901 Seville Avenue, looks north at Huntington Park's again booming central business district. Business owners, organized by the chamber of commerce, formed the Business Improvement District (BID) with a mission of returning Pacific Boulevard to retail prominence. In the distance, the skyscrappers of downtown Los Angeles tower above the city.

Three

EARTHQUAKE

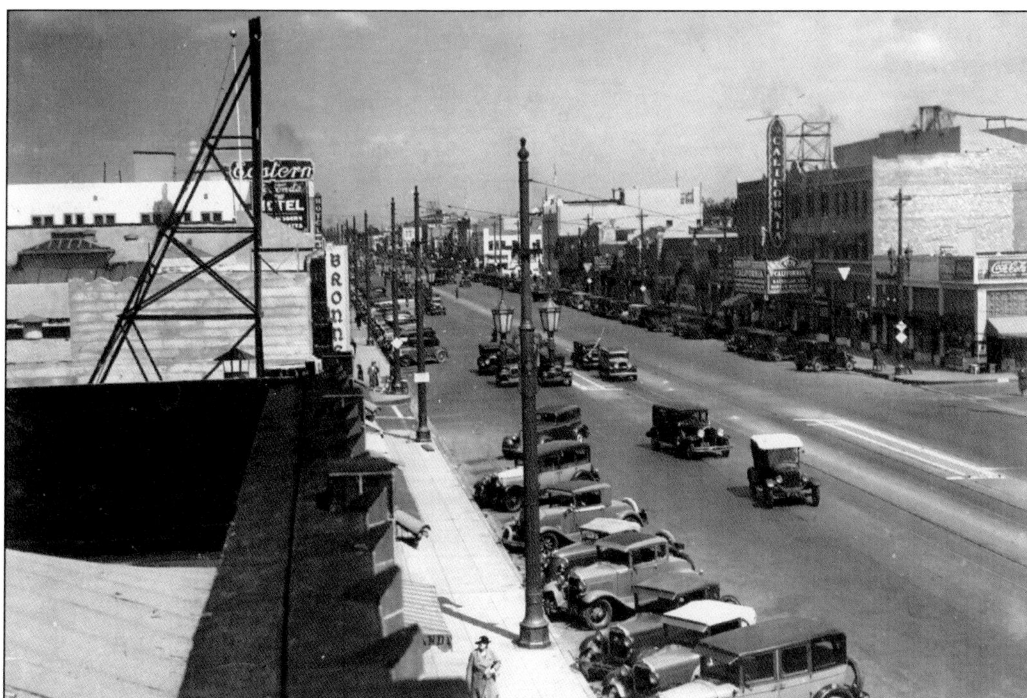

BEFORE THE EARTHQUAKE. Pictured is Pacific Boulevard looking north from Zoe Avenue in 1933 shortly before the earthquake. The California Theatre, which still stands today, is on the right. Although it was the middle of the Depression, Pacific Boulevard was still a successful business district, as can be seen. On March 10, 1933, at 5:54 p.m., an earthquake measuring 6.3 on the Richter scale struck.

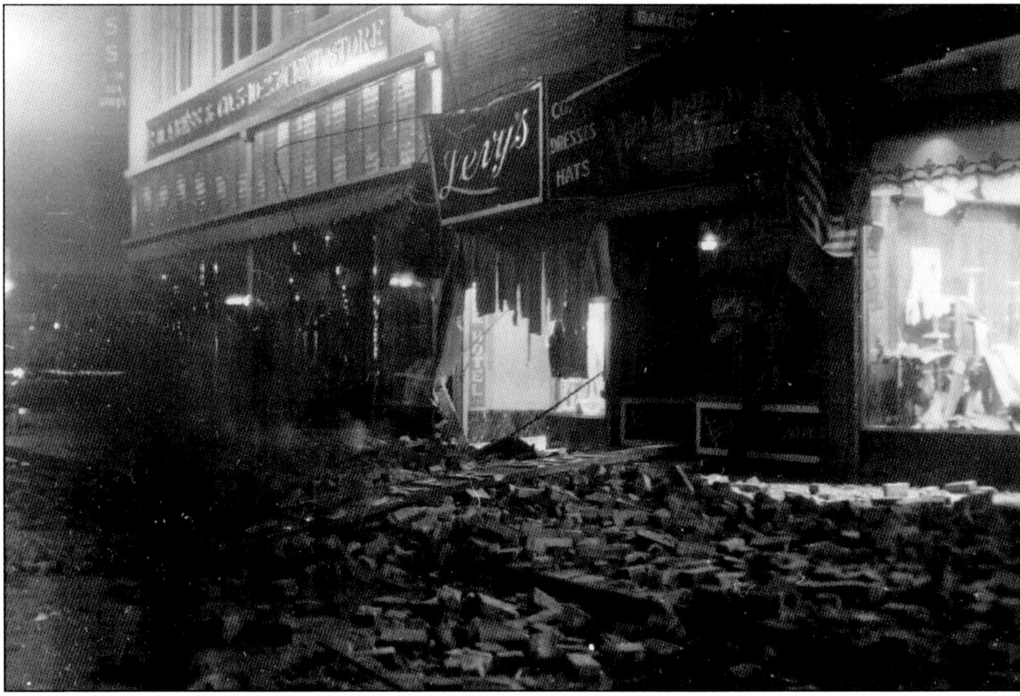

THE LONG BEACH EARTHQUAKE. Called the Long Beach earthquake as a result of the severe damage and many deaths in that city, the quake also killed 12 people in Huntington Park. Pictured is Pacific Boulevard at Gage Avenue on the night of the tremor.

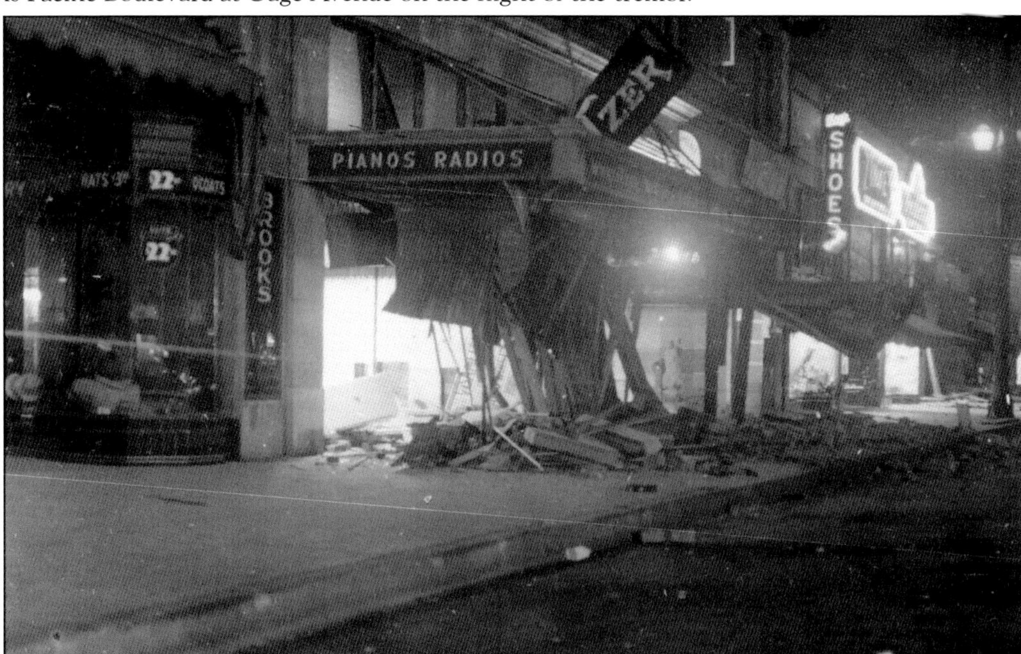

A NIGHT OF TERROR. Pictured is what was left of the Wurlitzer Company Music Store at 6527 Pacific Boulevard on the night of the earthquake. Many severe aftershocks followed, which continued to wreak havoc throughout the night and following days.

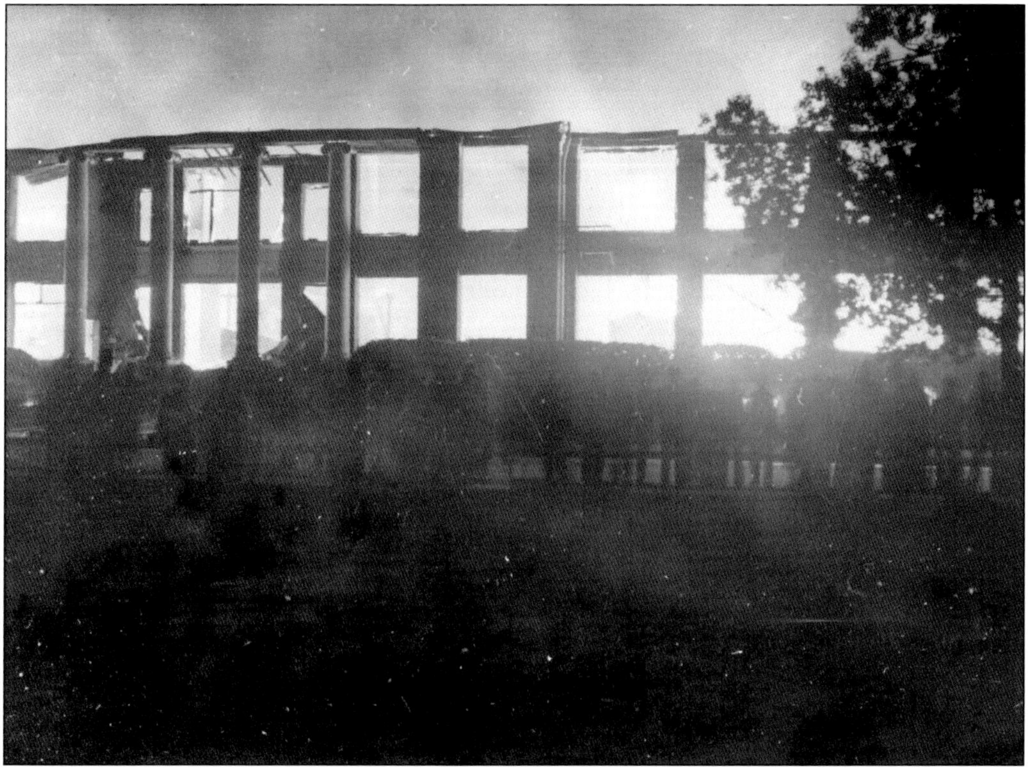

A Night of Fire. On the night of the earthquake, as a result of damaged electrical wires, the main administration building of Huntington Park High School burned to the ground.

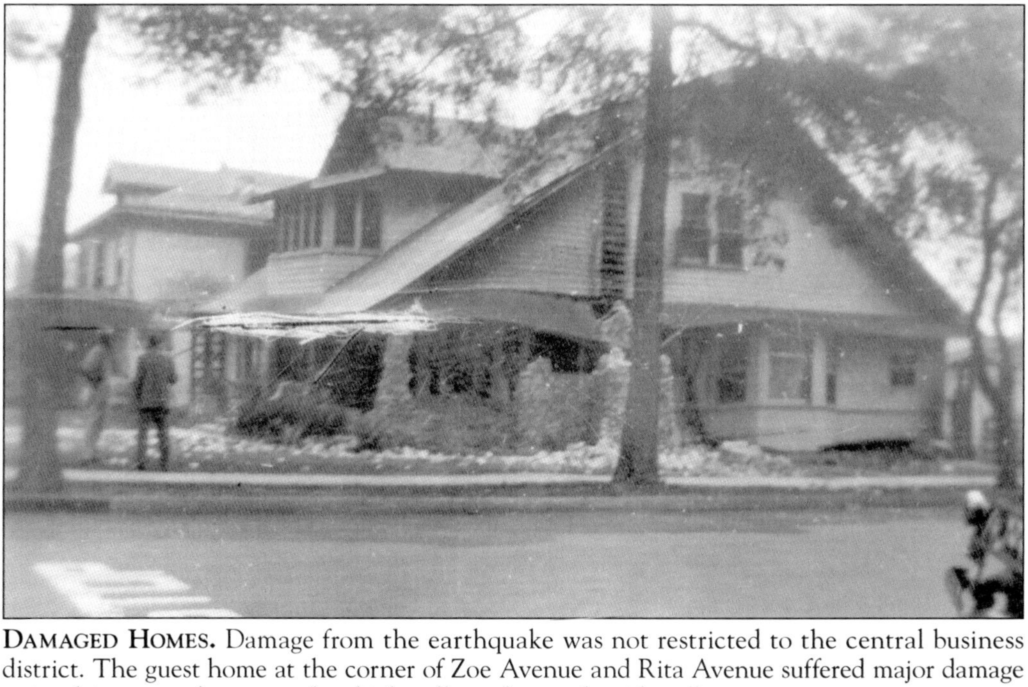

Damaged Homes. Damage from the earthquake was not restricted to the central business district. The guest home at the corner of Zoe Avenue and Rita Avenue suffered major damage to its chimney and stone work, which collapsed onto the sidewalk.

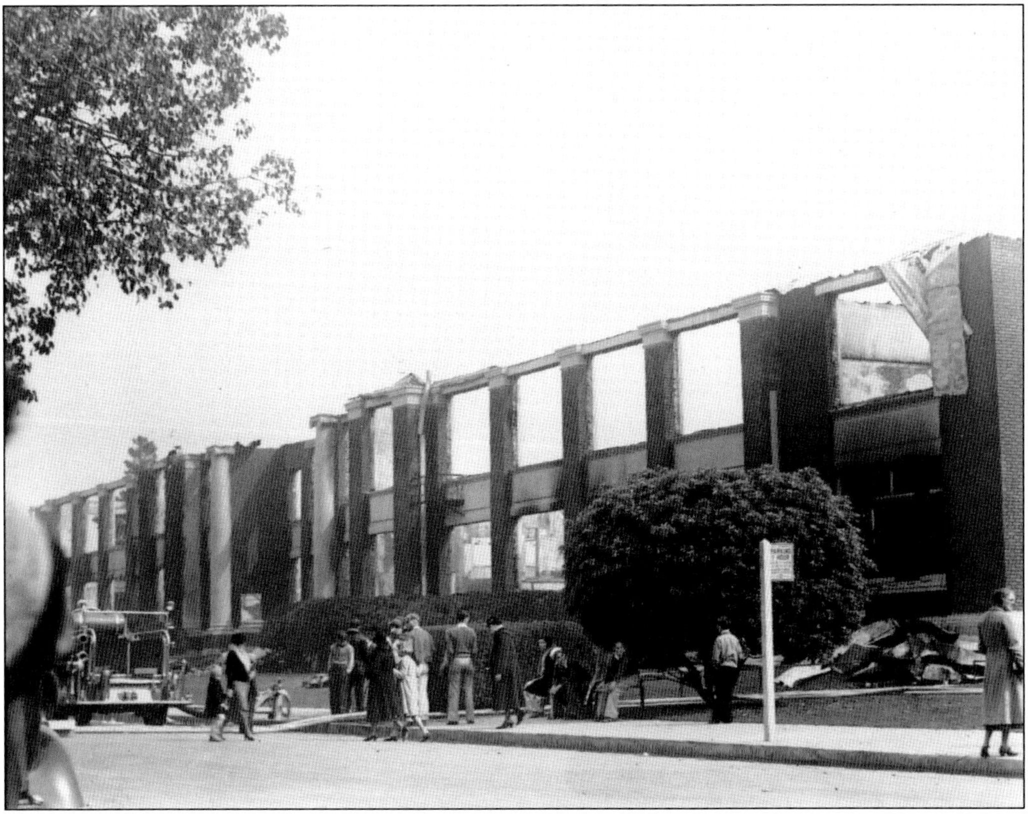

HUNTINGTON PARK HIGH SCHOOL. These two photographs, taken the day after the earthquake on March 11, 1933, illustrate the complete devastation to the school. Classes were held in local churches and a makeshift area of wooden structures known as "Bungalow Boulevard" from 1933 to 1935, when the school was rebuilt.

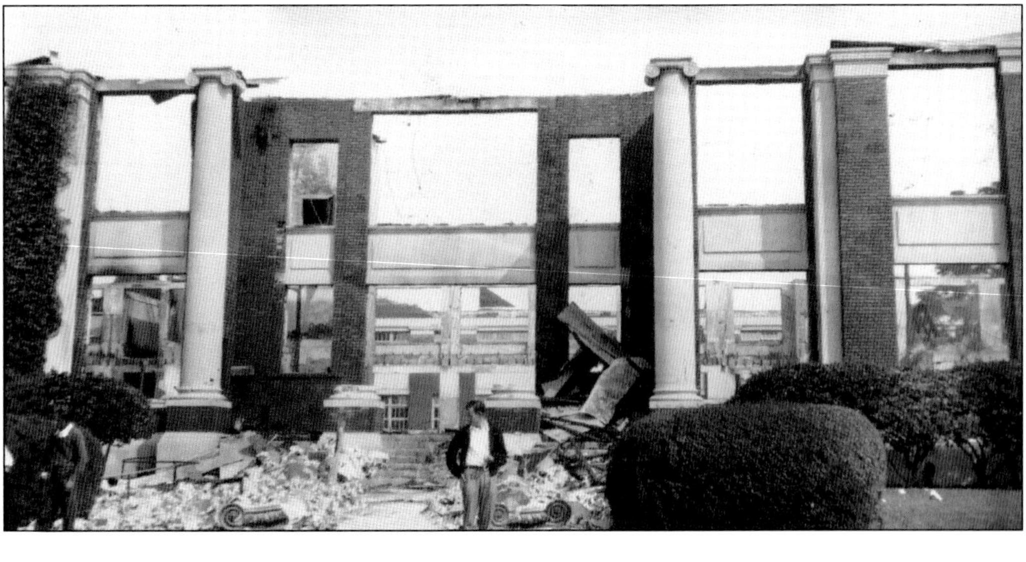

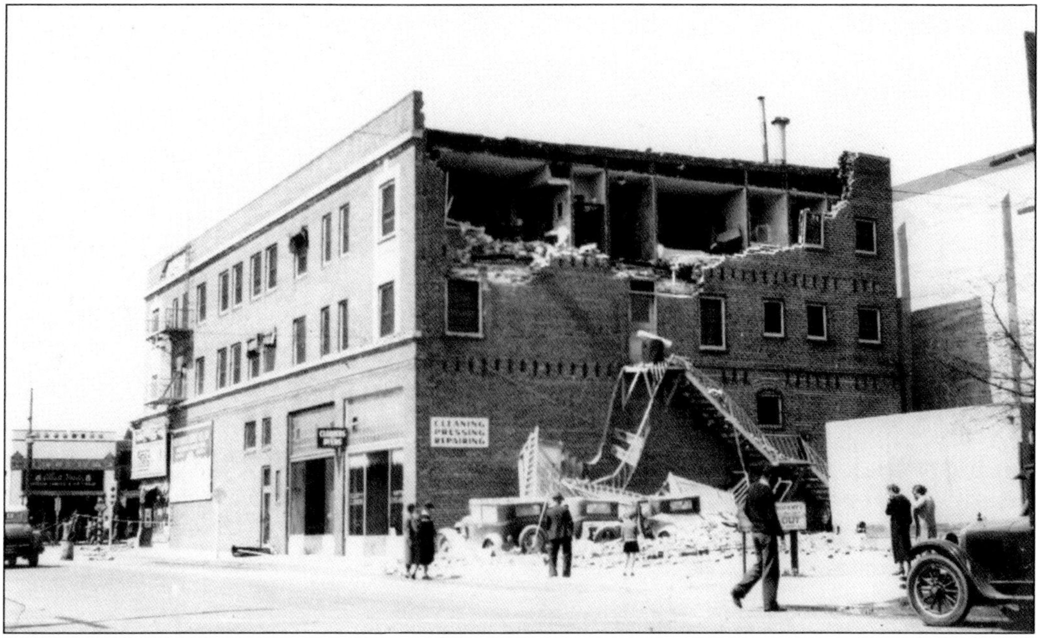

ZOE AVENUE AND PACIFIC BOULEVARD. This structure at the northeast corner of Zoe Avenue and Pacific Boulevard suffered major damage and buried several cars. These two photographs, taken on March 12, 1933, illustrate the danger of falling bricks. During this time, many of the buildings in Huntington Park were constructed of unreinforced masonry, which accounts for the amount of damage.

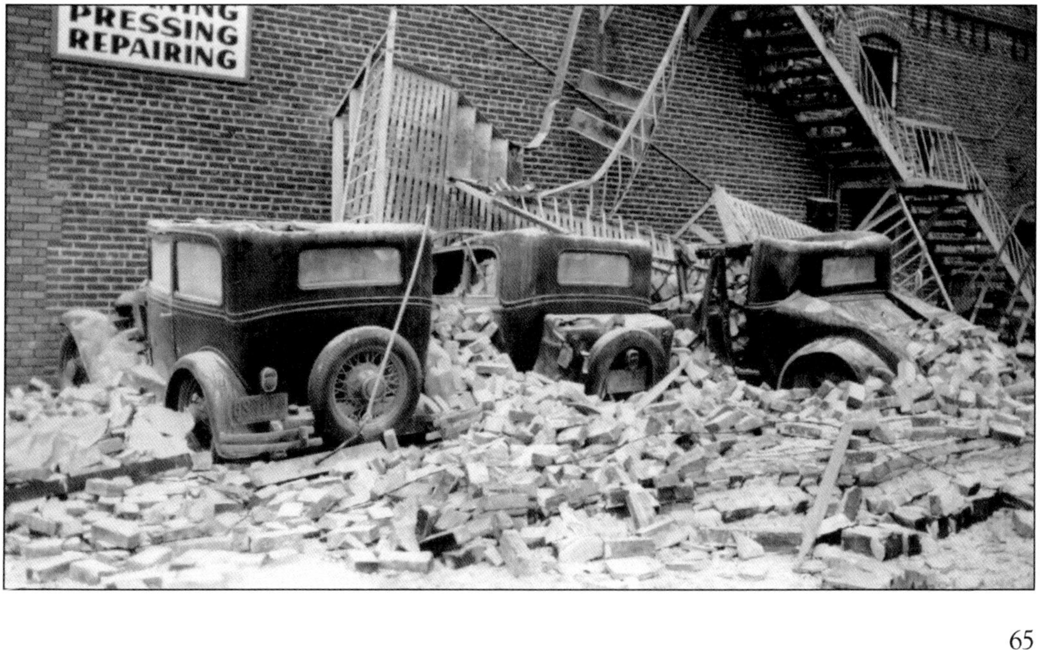

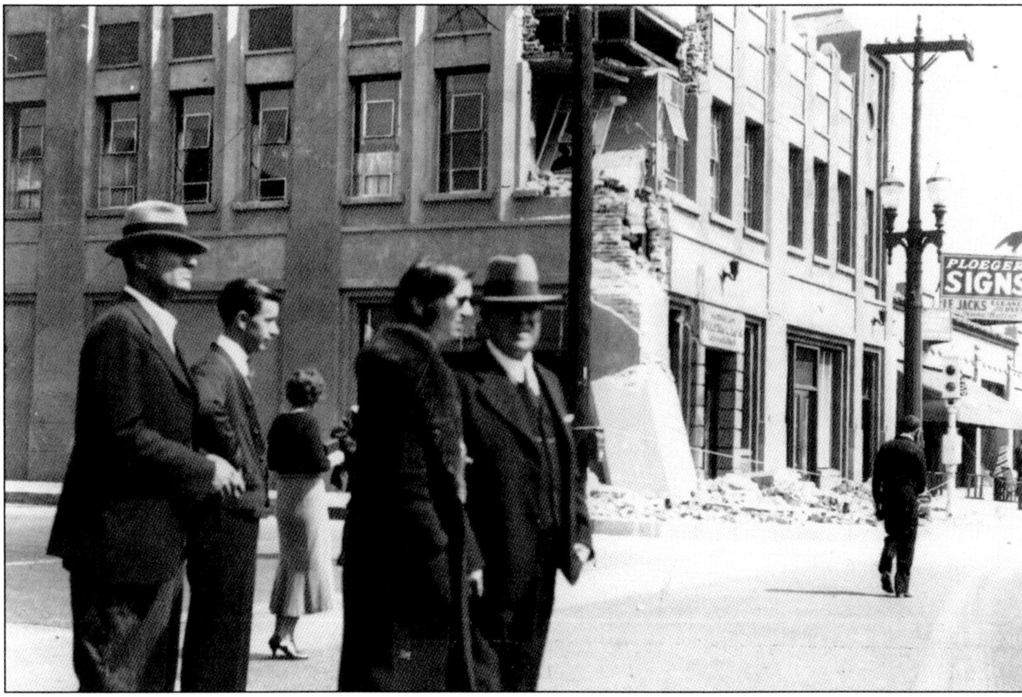

FLORENCE AND SEVILLE AVENUES. This photograph is of a building at the northeast corner of Florence and Seville Avenues. Many of those killed by the quake were struck and buried by falling debris as they fled from the crumbling buildings.

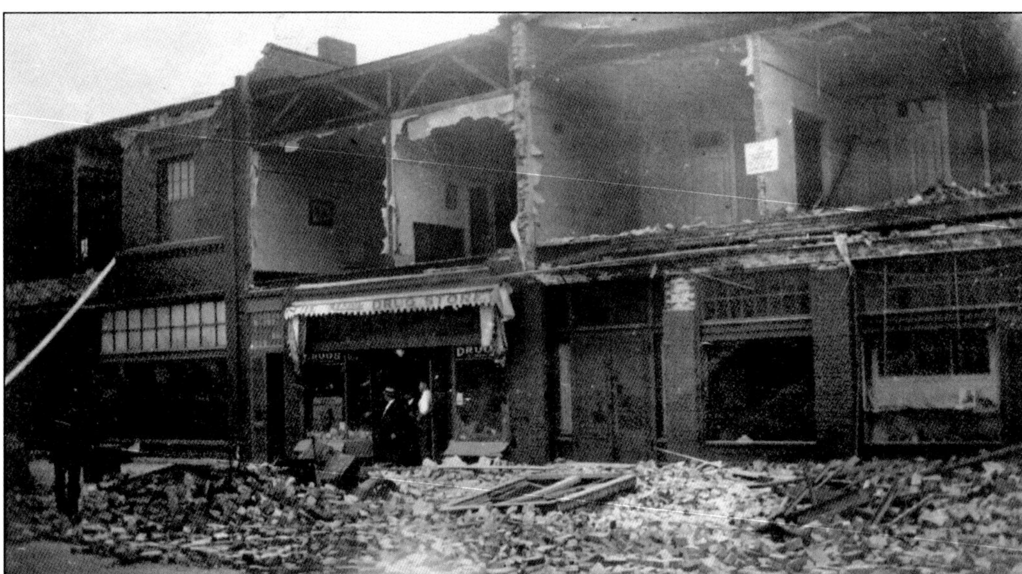

SCENES OF TRAGEDY. At the Boulevard Hotel, falling bricks killed Dotty Martyne as she fled the hotel she managed. Many more were injured throughout the city, most by the first of the tremors. The Rexall Drug Store (above) on Pacific Boulevard still appears open in spite of the surrounding devastation.

A CROSS-SECTION OF DESTRUCTION. This drug store located at the southwest corner of Cudahy Street and Seville Avenue in nearby Walnut Park, advertising "Under New Management," appears to have had a perfect slice taken out of it, leaving the interior of the second floor with a wider view.

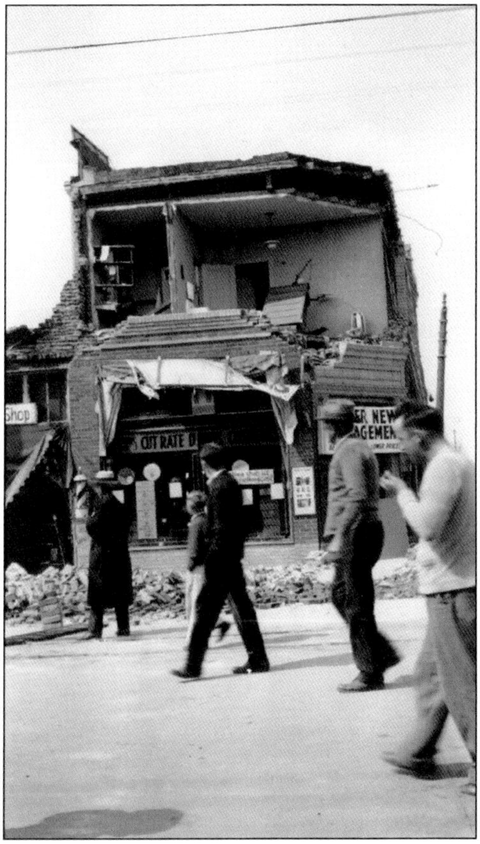

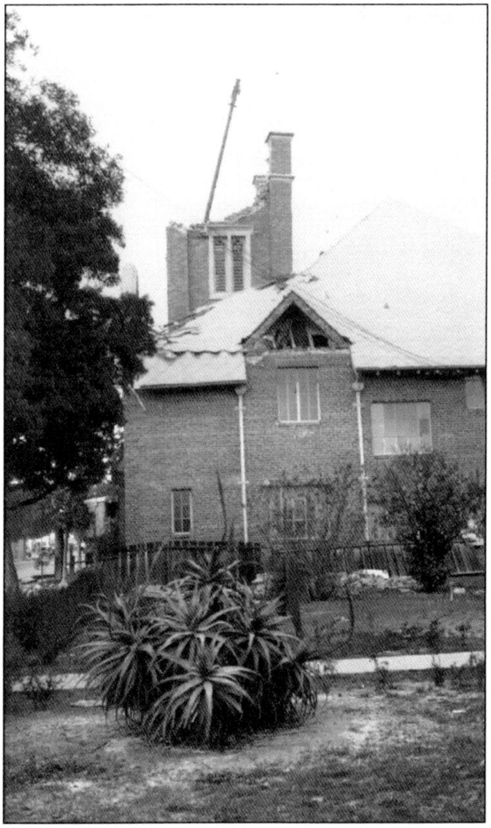

THE FIRST CHRISTIAN CHURCH. This photograph, taken on March 11, 1933, is of the First Christian Church on the northeast corner of Saturn and Rita Avenues. Accounts from the time related that the building was nearly completely destroyed. More than 1,000 people gathered in prayer in Miles Avenue Park on the Sunday following the quake, with the Reverend Kelly O'Neal, pastor of the First Christian Church, presiding.

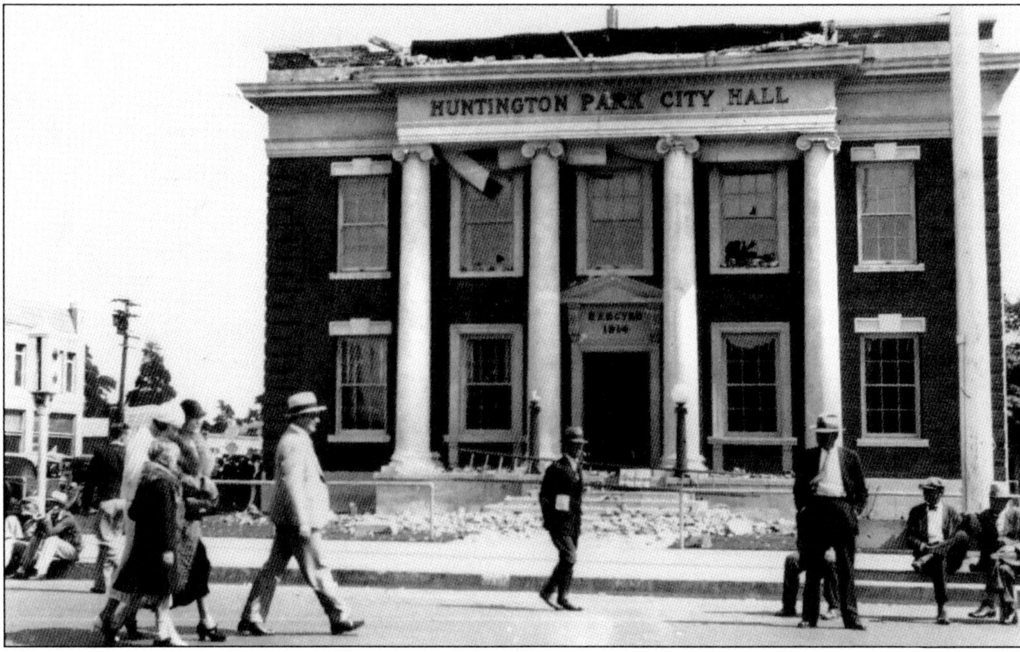

CITY HALL. Huntington Park City Hall was damaged to the point that it was uninhabitable as a result of the earthquake and was rebuilt. Following the quake, Mayor Richard Shultz declared a four-day holiday from March 11, 1933, through March 14, 1933, so that measures could be taken to safeguard lives and property. During this time period, the American Legion fed more than 2,500 people in a school cafeteria on the Saturday and Sunday following the quake. A portable food kitchen was loaned by Fox Film Company and was manned by the American Legion and the Boy Scouts.

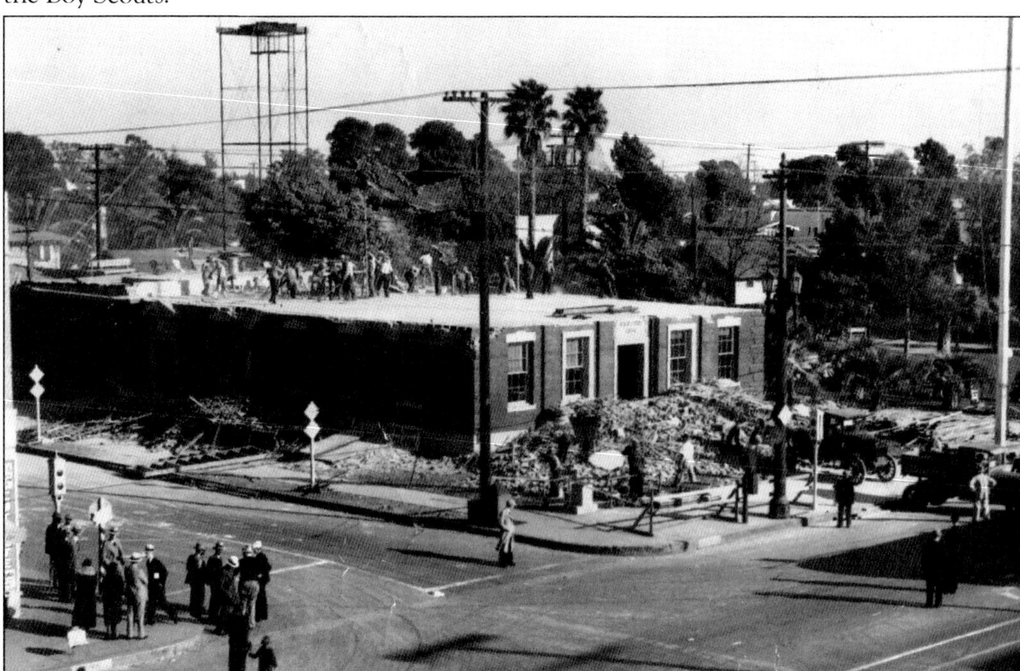

Four

The Fire Department
Gone but Not Forgotten

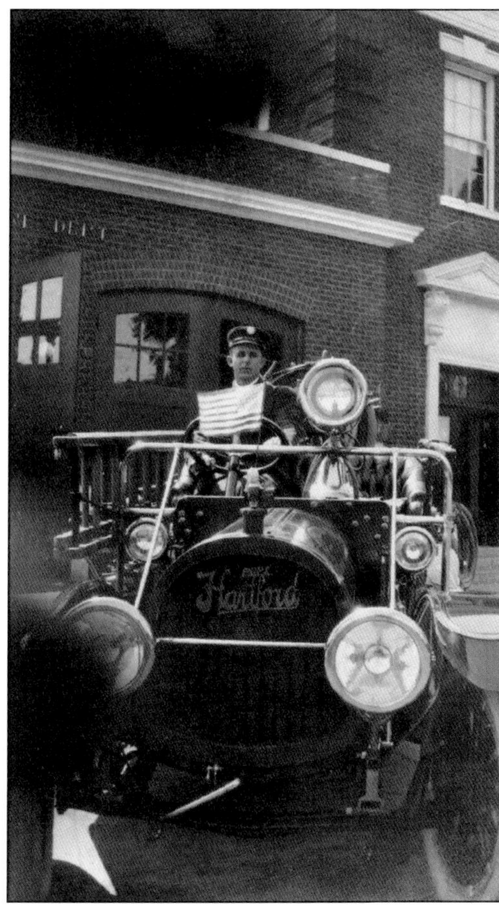

The First Fire Department. In 1907, the city approved the purchase of a 200-gallon chemical engine, 12 fire buckets, 4 pike poles, one 32-foot extension ladder, four 15-foot ladders, two 3-gallon fire extinguishers, 3 fire lanterns, and a wagon running gear for $327.25. The tank was mounted on the running gear and pushed or pulled around town. Herbert Woods was appointed the fire chief and firefighters were local volunteers who were paid $1 for each fire they responded to.

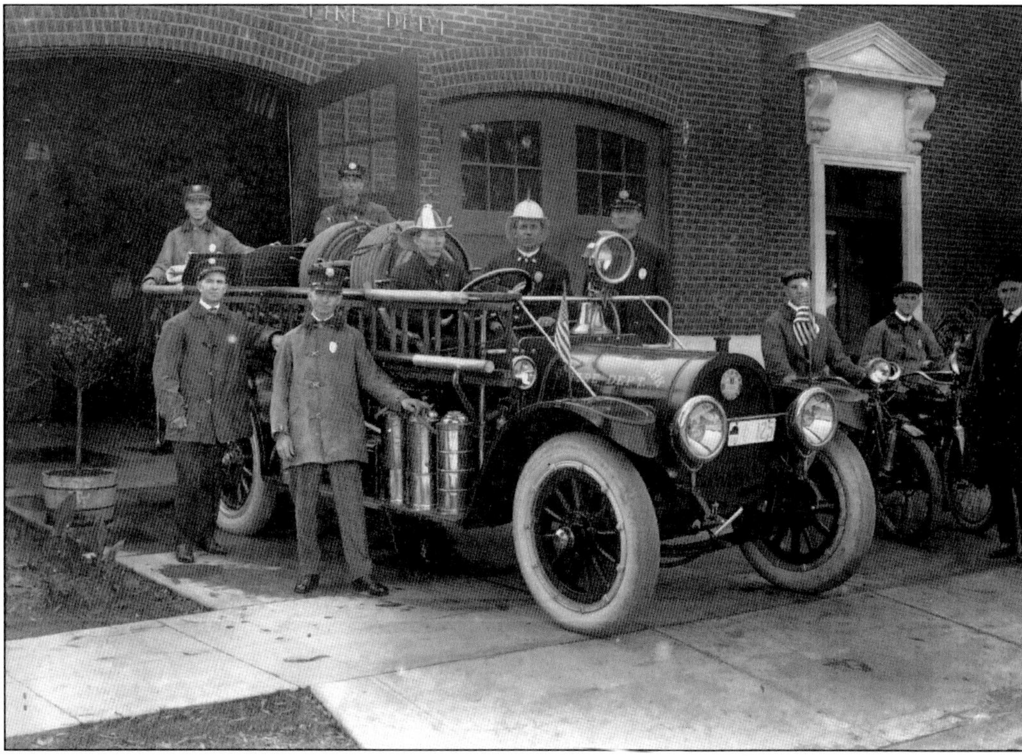

THE FIRST FIRE TRUCK. The first apparatus was housed in a shed built by Chief Woods. In 1909, the equipment was moved to a livery stable next to Buhles Store at Randolph Street and Pacific Boulevard. It was moved to city hall in 1914. Pictured is the fire truck and volunteer crew at the city hall station after 1914. Firefighter Bill Dixon used to race this vehicle up and down Pacific Boulevard to keep it in condition.

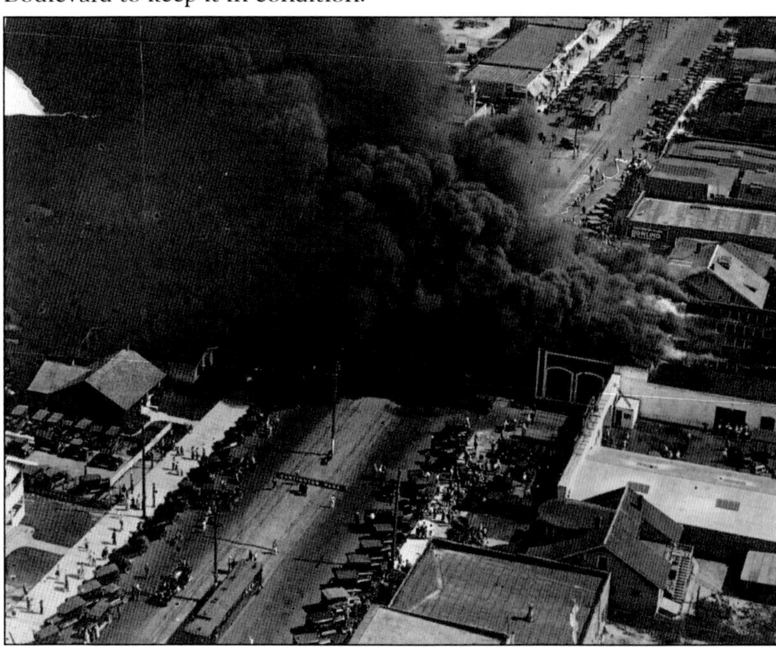

A PROFESSIONAL FIRE DEPARTMENT. In 1924, the City of Huntington Park employed a company of paid firefighters instead of volunteers. Bruce Hathaway was appointed as fire chief, where he served for many years. The paid department responded to the pictured fire on Pacific Boulevard on May 12, 1926.

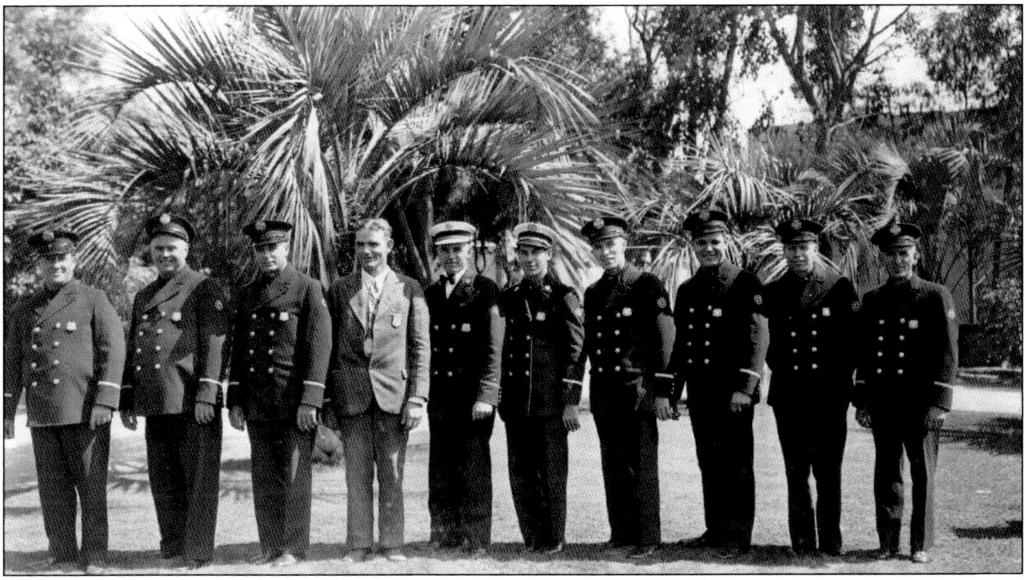

GROWING WITH THE CITY. As Huntington Park grew, so did the fire department. The above photograph was taken in the 1920s. The department photograph below, taken in 1934, illustrates that growth. In 1932, Engine House No. 2 was at Newell Street and Saturn Avenue, where Los Angeles County Station No. 165 is today. At this time, city fire equipment consisted of two large fire trucks, a ladder truck, and 6,000 feet of hose.

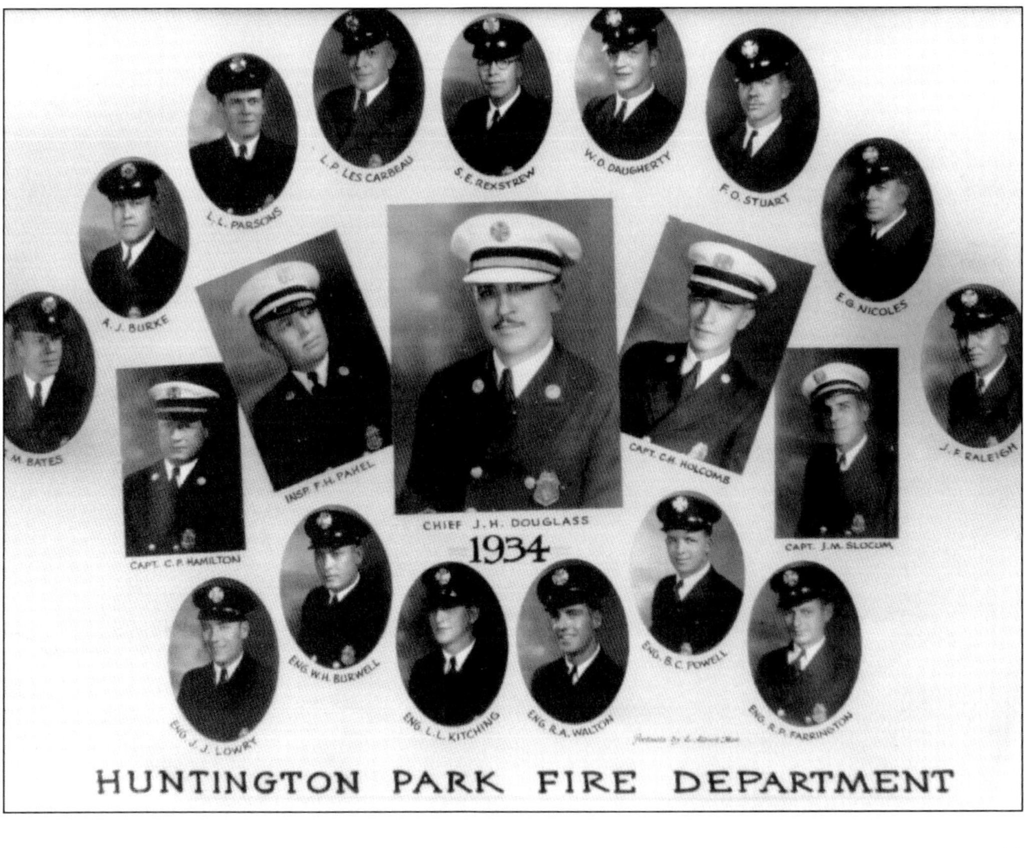

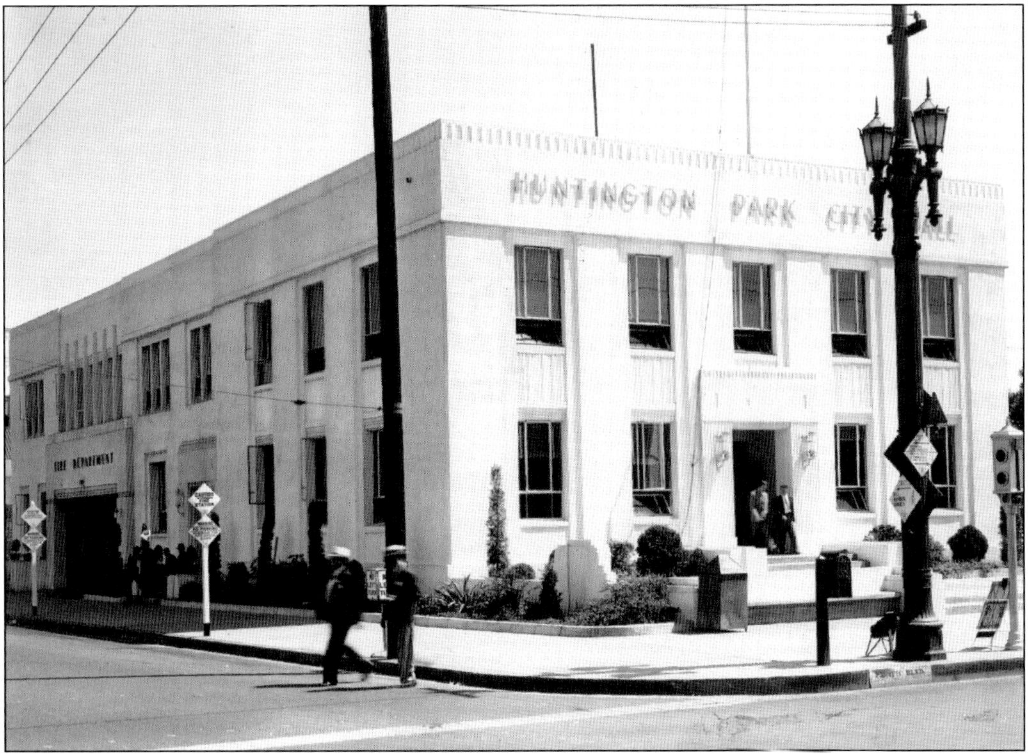

A NEW STATION. Following the 1933 earthquake, city hall was rebuilt and with it a new Fire Station No. 1. Additionally, Fire Station No. 3 was built on Gifford Avenue in an area referred to for many years as the Maywood Strip. Station No. 1 was later moved to Clarendon Avenue and Santa Fe where Los Angles County No. 164 is today.

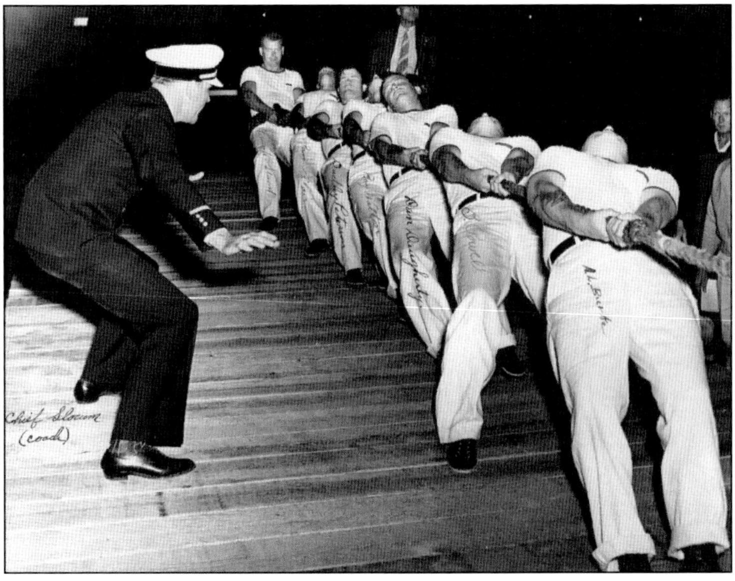

A PART OF THE COMMUNITY. On July 25, 1939, the Huntington Park Fire Department defeated American Concrete Pipe Company, two out of three, for the city tug-of-war championship. Pictured are Chief J. M. Slocum, left, the team coach, along with firefighters, from front to back Alfred Burke, Burl Powell, W. Dan Daugherty, Raymond Walton, Dudly Peterson, Raymond Blair, and Frank Stuart.

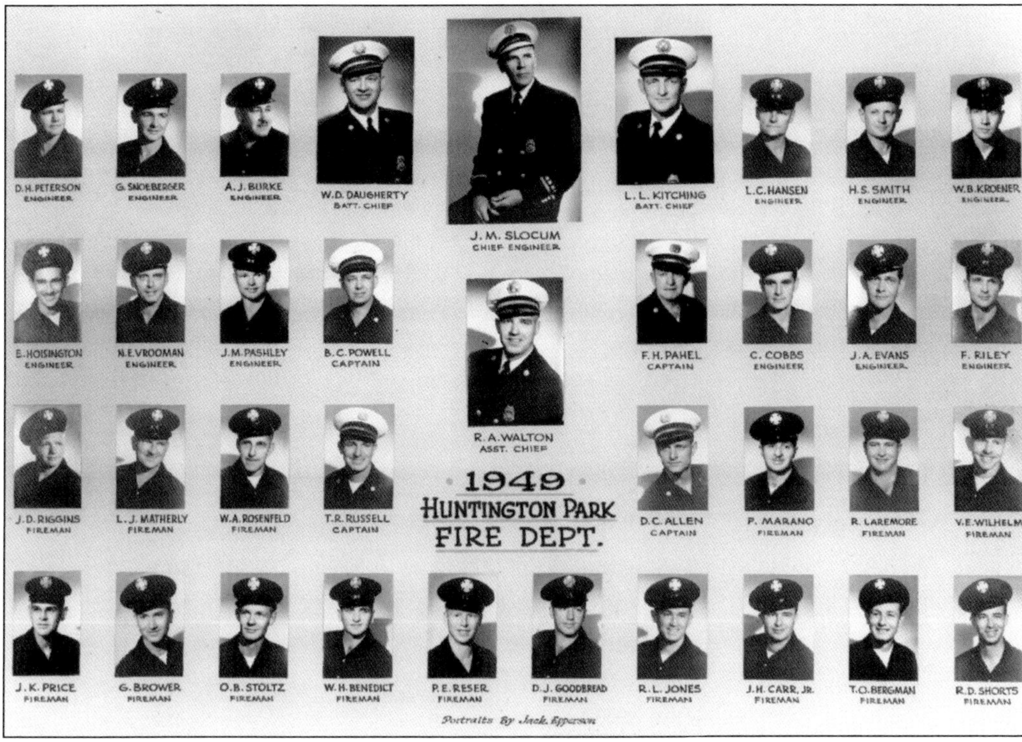

THE 1949 FIRE DEPARTMENT. By 1949, the Huntington Park Fire Department had grown to 36 men serving the three stations. J. M. Slocum remained chief until the department merged with the county in 1972.

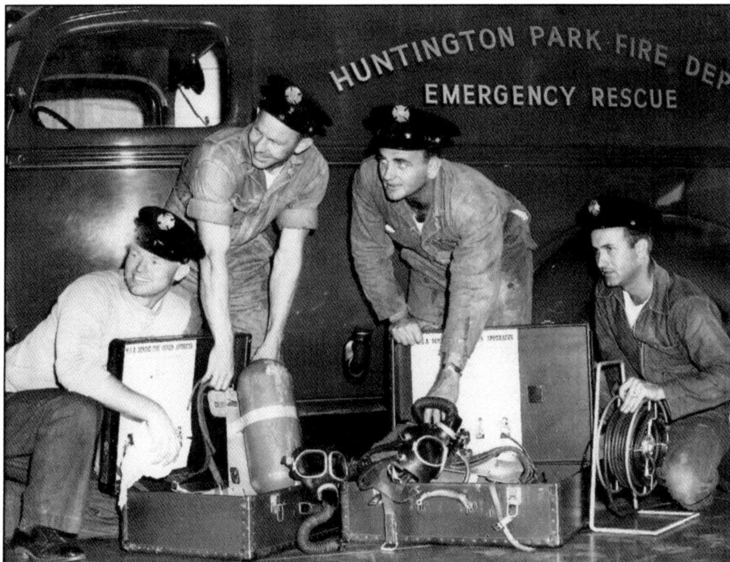

TO THE RESCUE. Pictured are firefighters Joseph Pashley, Victor Wilhelm, William Benedict, and George Brower on August 9, 1945. This rescue crew pulled an injured man out of a storm drain at Seville Avenue and Randolph Street after a gas explosion. Of note is their modern, at that time, rescue equipment.

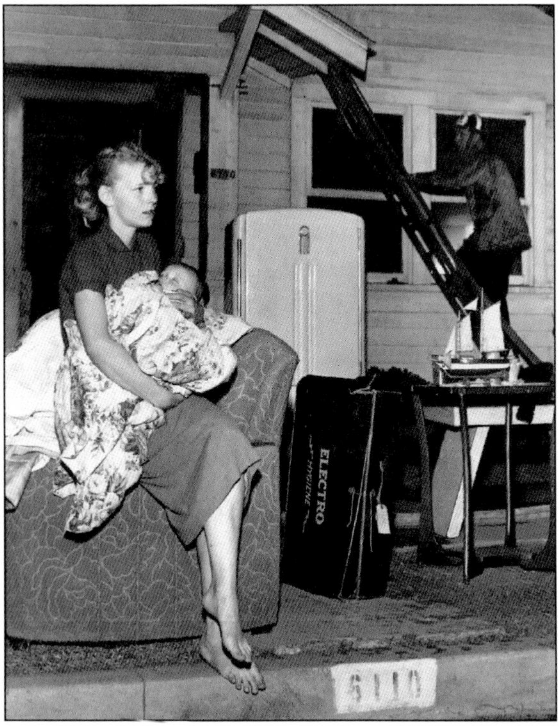

A House Fire. On November 11, 1956, Huntington Park firefighters responded twice to the home of Mr. and Mrs. F. E. Warden at 6110 Stafford Avenue. Pictured is Betty Warden with her few surviving belongings and her 10-month-old son Randy in her arms.

Fire On Carmelita Avenue. An electrical short in the television caused this fire at 6064 Carmelita Avenue, apartment B, in 1957. The house suffered minor damage, but the television was a goner. Ricky Galloway, age three, seems to have his fingers crossed, hoping for a picture.

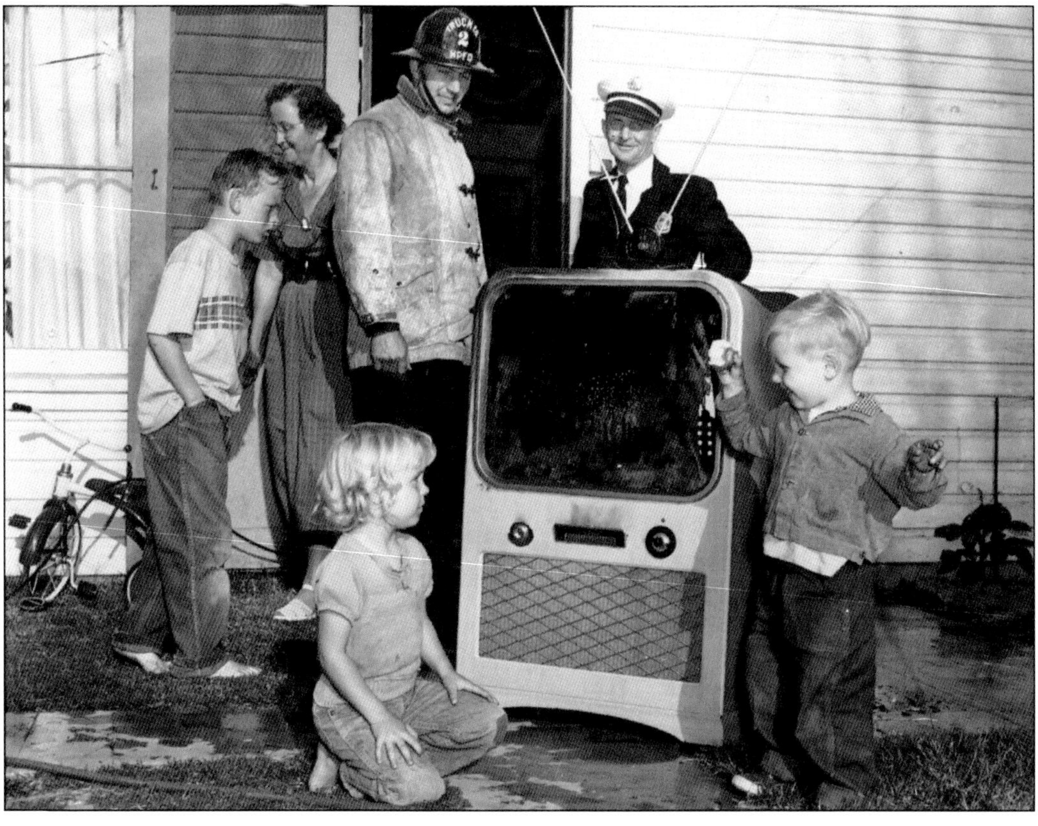

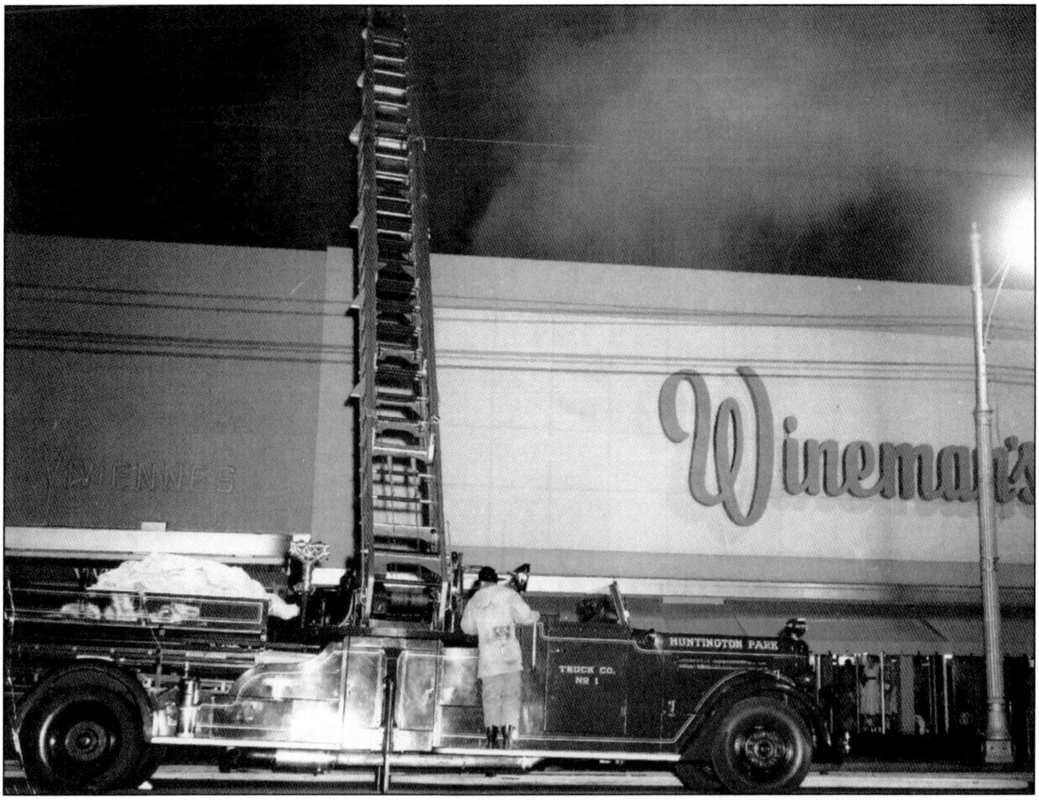

THE WINEMAN'S FIRE. On April 23, 1957, the Huntington Park Fire Department responded to a blaze at Wineman's Department Store on Pacific Boulevard (above). The store suffered major damage and required a large fire department response. The Wineman's fire was large and caused a great deal of damage. Huntington Park firefighters, Staples and Pashley (at right), administer oxygen to City of Vernon firefighter George Bass, who was assisting with the fire. Bass eventually became Vernon's fire chief and was a longtime councilman for the city of Bell. Fire departments, like law enforcement, often mutually aid each other by agreement when they require additional resources. Wineman's started as a dry goods store that developed into the city's largest independent department store and a cornerstone of Pacific Boulevard businesses.

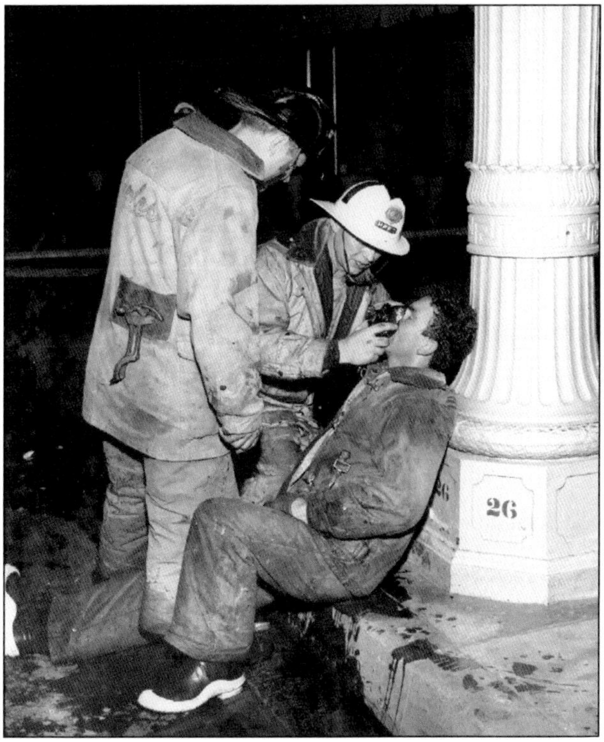

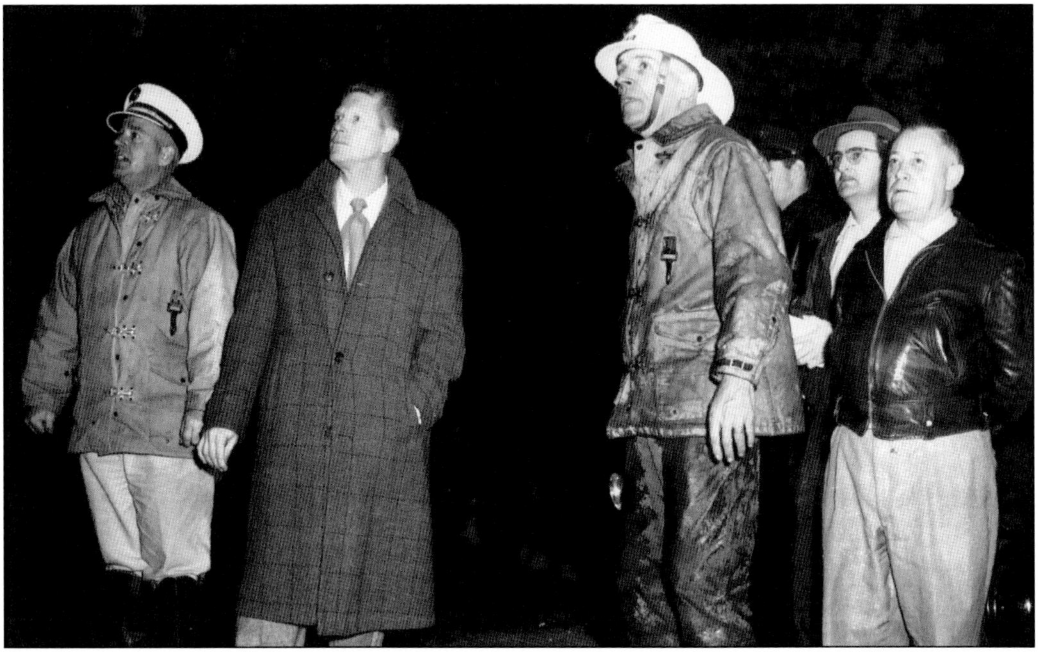

ANOTHER HIGH SCHOOL FIRE. On March 16, 1959, yet another fire occurred at Huntington Park High School, with the girl's locker room burning nearly to the ground. Here, from left to right, assistant fire chief Raymond Walton, school principal Richard Nida, Chief J. M. Slocum, *Huntington Park Daily Signal* editor J. Dennis, and high school custodian Norman Dietrich watch the blaze.

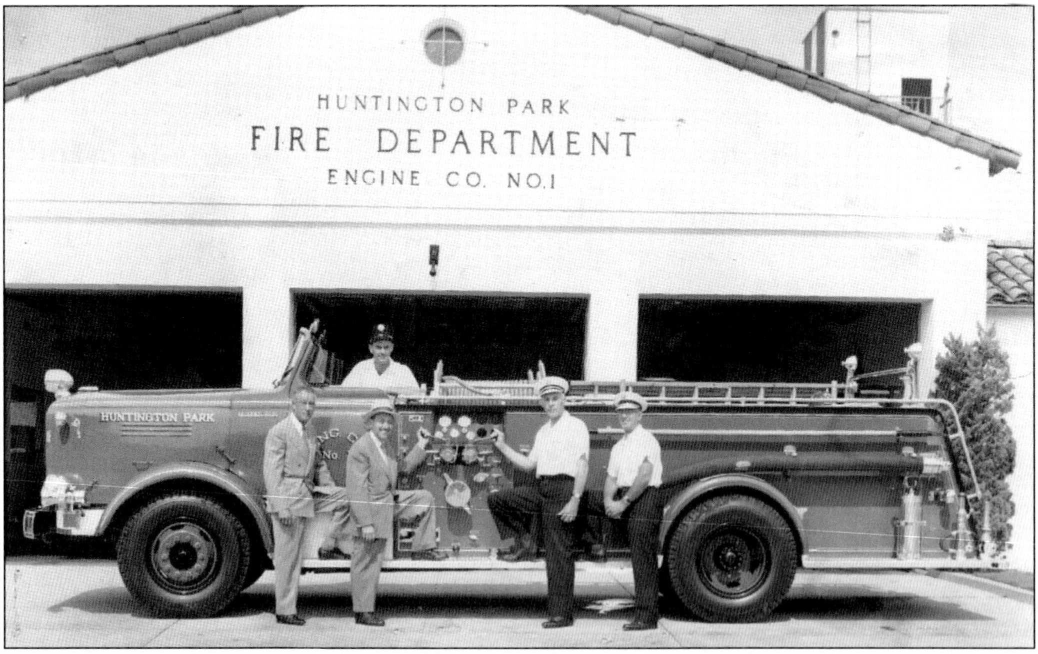

THE END OF AN AGE. Chiefs Slocum (second from right) and Walton (far right) pose for a photograph with supervisor Frank Bonnelli in front of Fire Station No. 1 in the late 1950s. The fire department was disbanded on January 1, 1972, when the city began contracting with Los Angeles County to save money. Most of the firefighters were absorbed by the county fire department.

Five

The Police Department

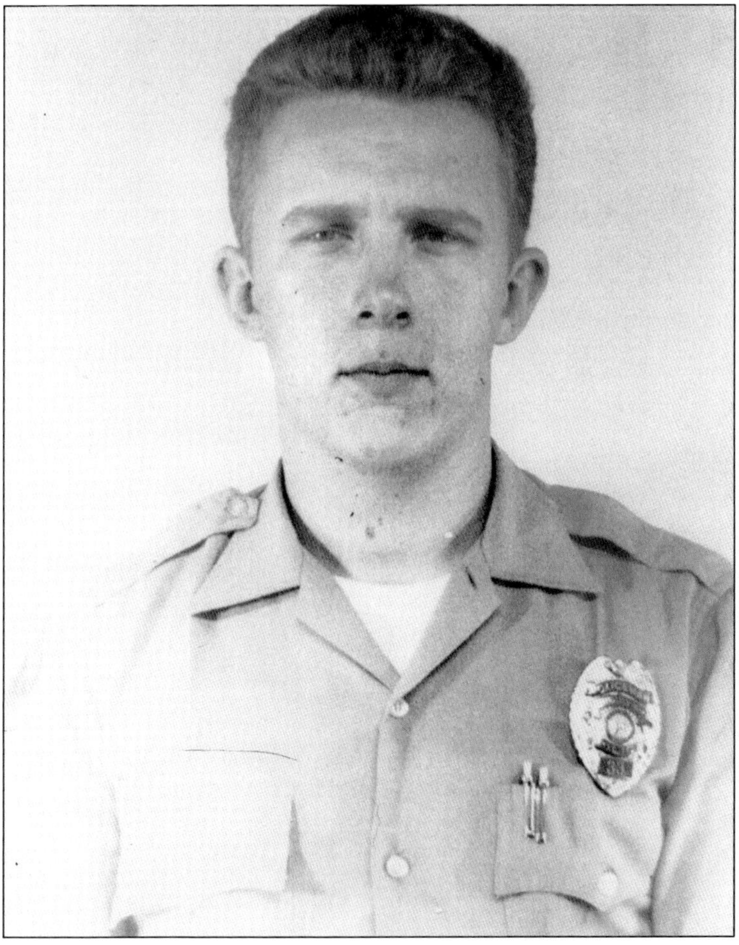

In Memory of Ofc. Robert Keller. On October 5, 1967, at 11:18 a.m., Ofc. Robert Keller responded to a silent alarm. While Keller was searching the business, a suspect who had entered through a skylight, leaped from a hiding place and fired at the officer, striking him in the heart. Keller fled the business but collapsed outside and died. The suspect was never identified. Officer Keller's name is listed on the California and National Law Enforcement Memorials. The investigation was reopened in 2007 and is ongoing.

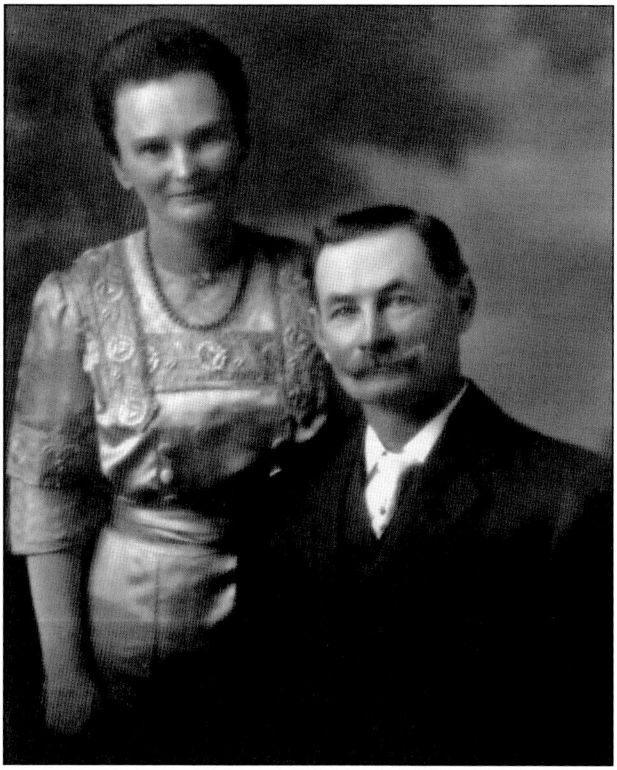

William E. Ford. Fred Cramer was the first city marshall, who served from August 20, 1907, to April 15, 1908. On April 15, 1908, William Ford, pictured here in his wedding photograph, was elected marshall. Marshall Ford served until April 18, 1910, when he retired as a result of injuries suffered while chasing "automobile bandits." He continued to serve the city of Huntington Park for a total of 37 years in other capacities, such as street superintendent, tax and license collector, tree warden, and fire chief. His salary as city marshall was $25 per month.

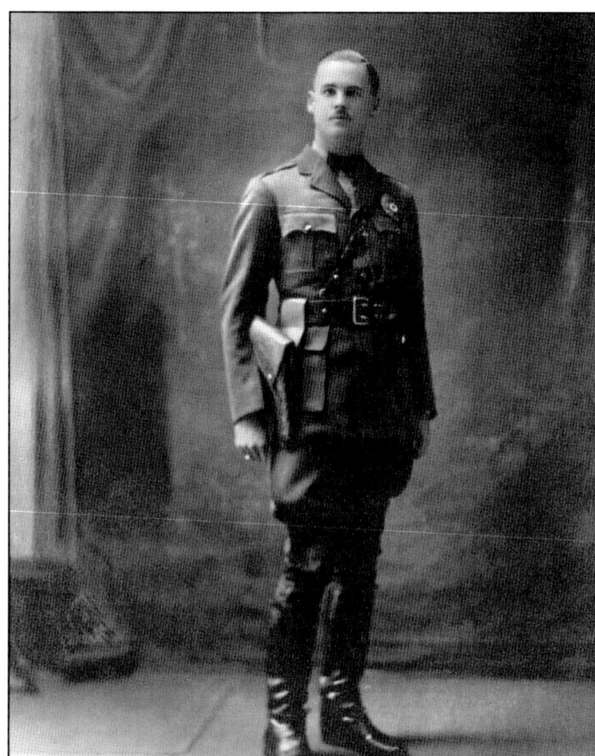

Early Huntington Park Law Enforcement. This is an undated photograph of an unidentified early Huntington Park motorcycle enforcement officer. Following World War I, the police department increased in size to a marshall and four deputies. New deputies wore their army uniforms for law enforcement duties. Officers remained deputies until 1932, when they were called policemen. Law enforcement was led by a city marshall until 1924, when a chief of police was appointed, the first being H. E. Leland.

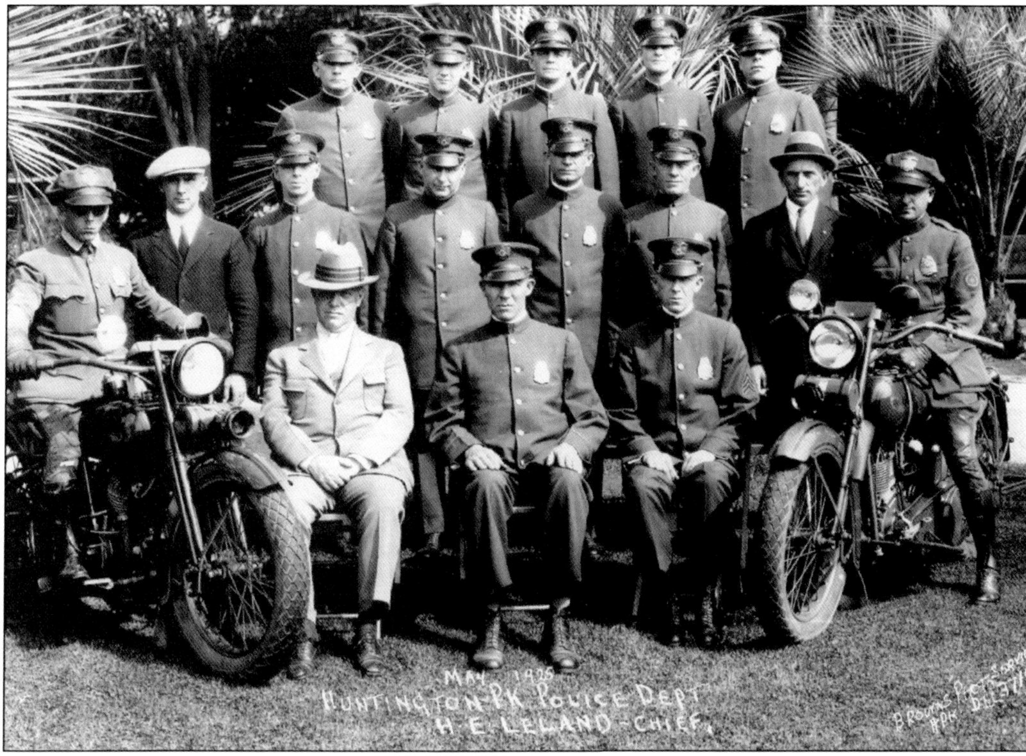

THE GROWING POLICE DEPARTMENT. By 1914, the police department had increased to 12 deputies and had a motorcycle officer. Pictured here is the 1925 department, under which new chief of police H. E. Leland had a total of 16 men with two motorcycle officers. During this time period, Prohibition was in effect and the police department was responsible for enforcement. A city ordinance, enacted in 1906, declared "spirituous, vinous, and malt or mixed intoxicating liquors shall be sold only upon prescription by a regular licensed physician."

THE MOTORCYCLE OFFICER. This is a photograph taken in 1927 of a Huntington Park Police Department motorcycle officer issuing a citation. When a motorcycle officer was hired, he was issued only a badge. He provided his own weapon, equipment, uniform, and even motorcycle. During this time period, police vehicles did not have radios, so several police boxes were positioned around the city topped by red lights. When a call for service was received by the station, the red light was activated. Once the red light was spotted, the officer would go to the call box and call the station.

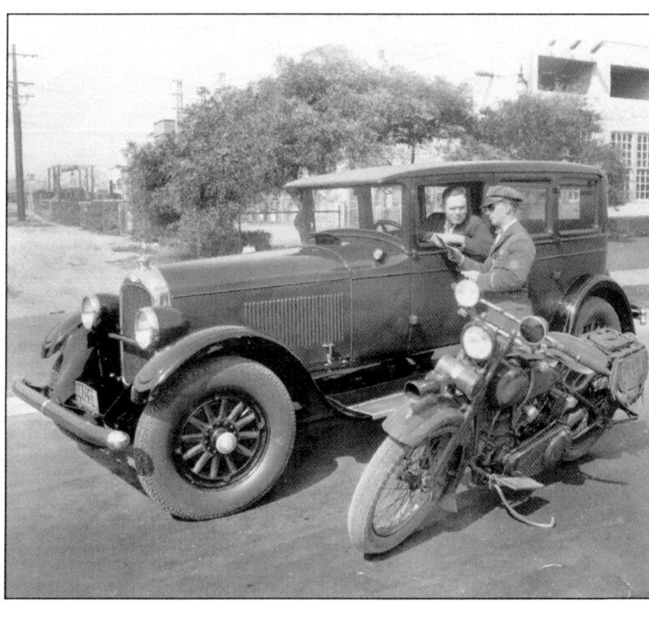

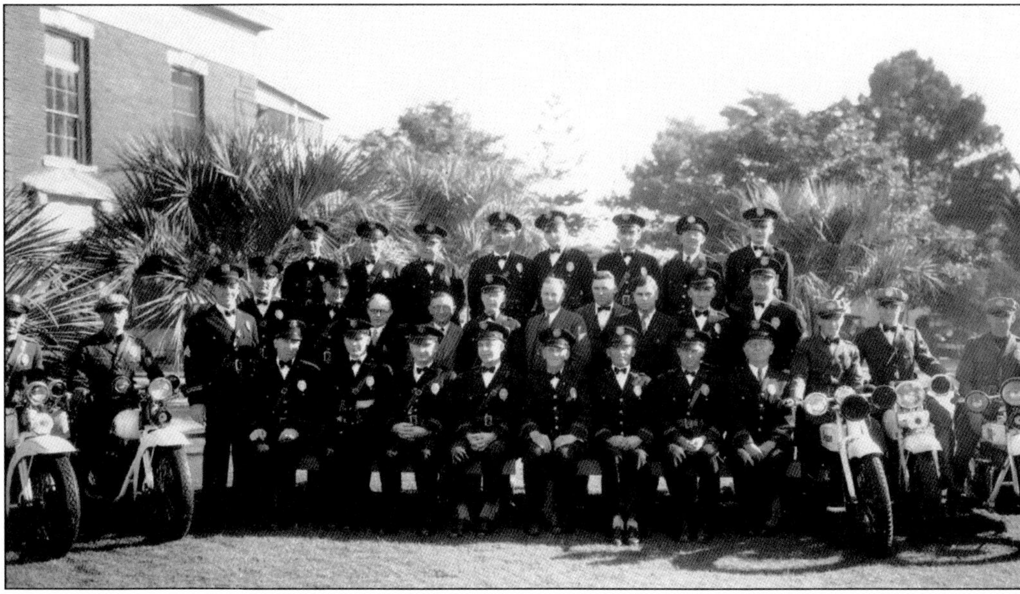

HUNTINGTON PARK POLICE DEPARTMENT, 1928. By 1928, the Huntington Park Police Department had grown to 28, including five motorcycle officers. In a police report from this time period, officers responded to "a funny looking animal in the street." The animal was found to be an opossum, which hid in a nearby vacant lot. A "Mr. Baker" ordered the officers off this property, and the report indicated, "We left the animal for him as he said it was good eating."

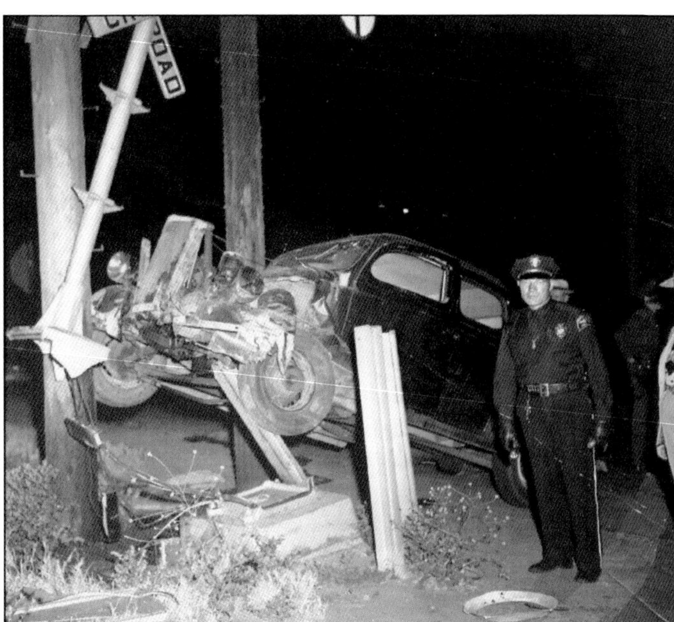

ACCIDENT INVESTIGATIONS. Aside from issuing citations, traffic enforcement officers also conducted investigations at traffic collisions. This 1947 photograph depicts an unidentified Huntington Park officer conducting an investigation at a serious accident on the Randolph Street railroad tracks.

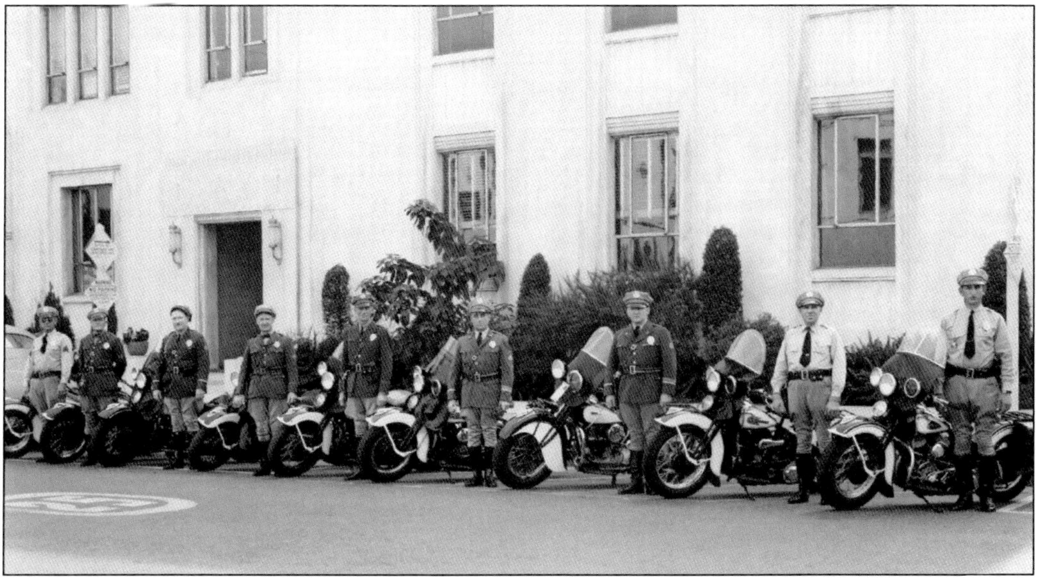

AN EMPHASIS ON TRAFFIC SAFETY. Traffic enforcement continued to be an increasing priority of law enforcement in the 1940s and 1950s, both for safety and for revenue. The 1956 annual report stated that 47,743 citations had been issued for the year. They investigated 618 accidents, with 187 injuries and three deaths. The above photograph was taken November 11, 1941, one month before Pearl Harbor. The photograph below was taken around 1947 in front of the new city hall building. Pictured from left to right are officers Laremore, Leavy, Jacobson, Collins, Markowitz, Waddell, Majewsky, Sanders, Beatty, and Costa.

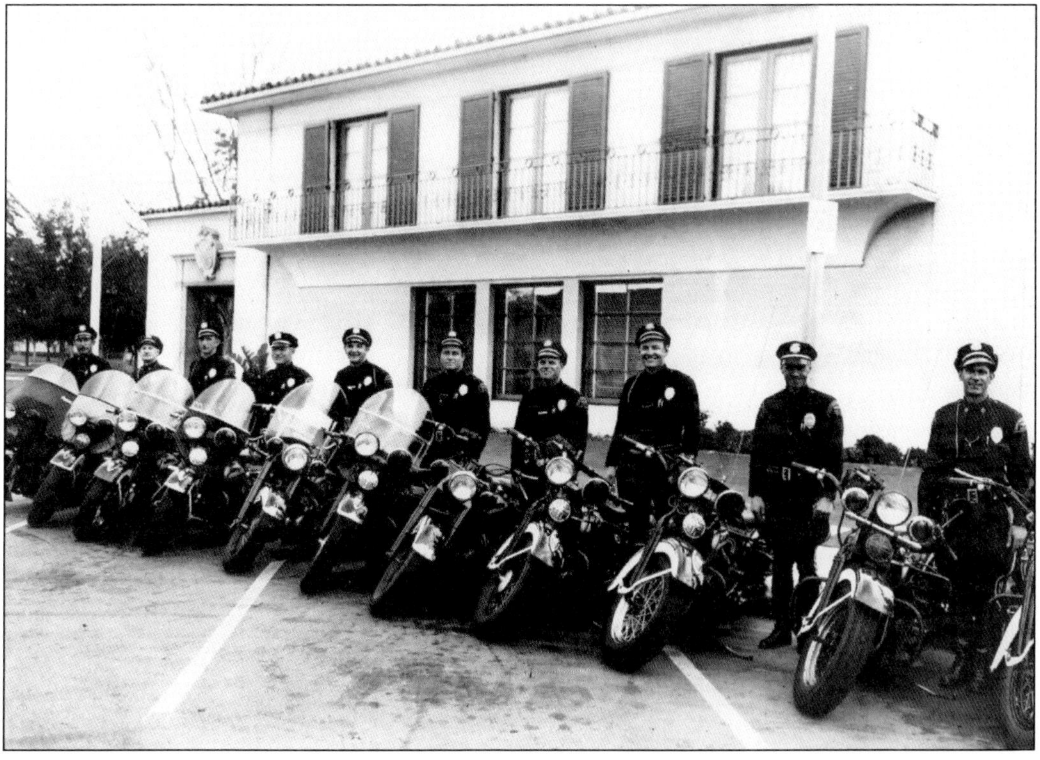

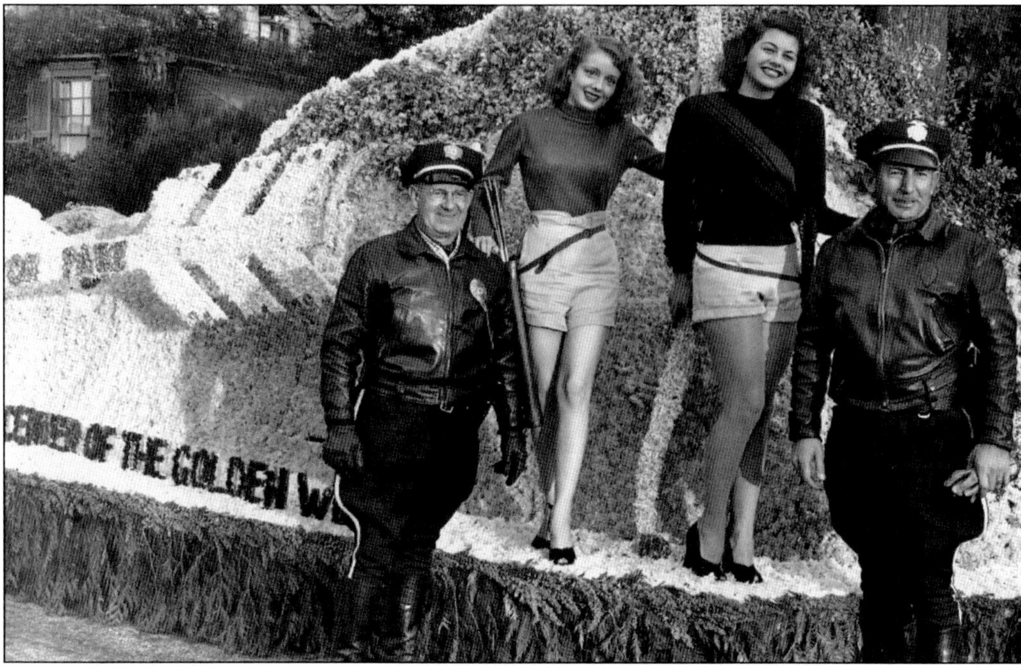

JANUARY 1, 1948. Officers Arthur Leavy and William Laremore are pictured here with the Huntington Park entry to the 1948 Rose Parade in Pasadena. The two beautiful unidentified Huntington Park ladies on the float are wearing quivers full of arrows.

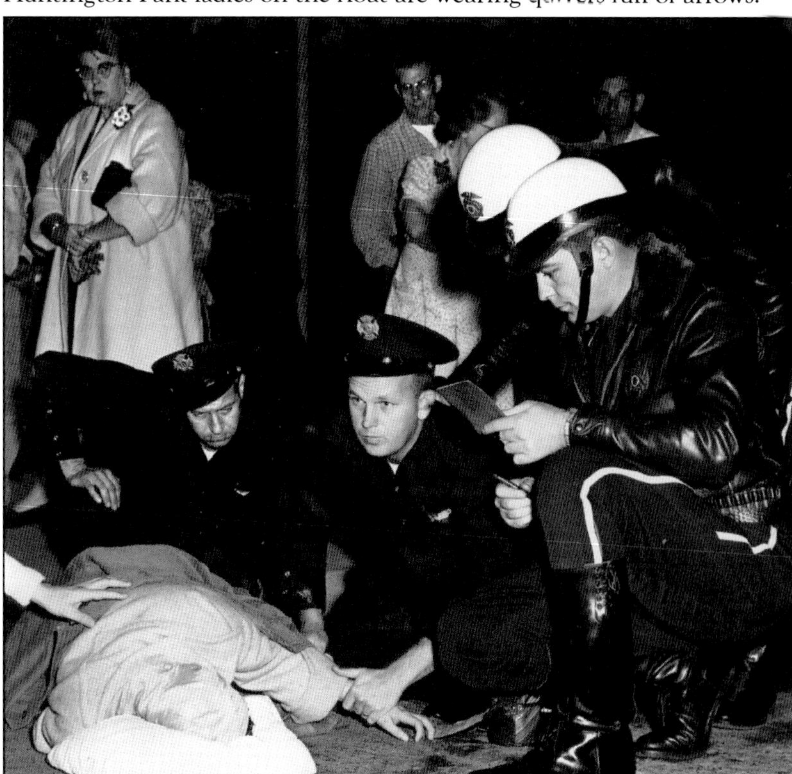

FIRE AND POLICE. Pictured are firefighters Cutter and Keene with Huntington Park police officers Blackburn and Thorton. The officers are assisting with the treatment of an injured person on January 1, 1956, at the intersection of Santa Fe Avenue and Mortimer Street. Like today, police and fire personnel work closely together.

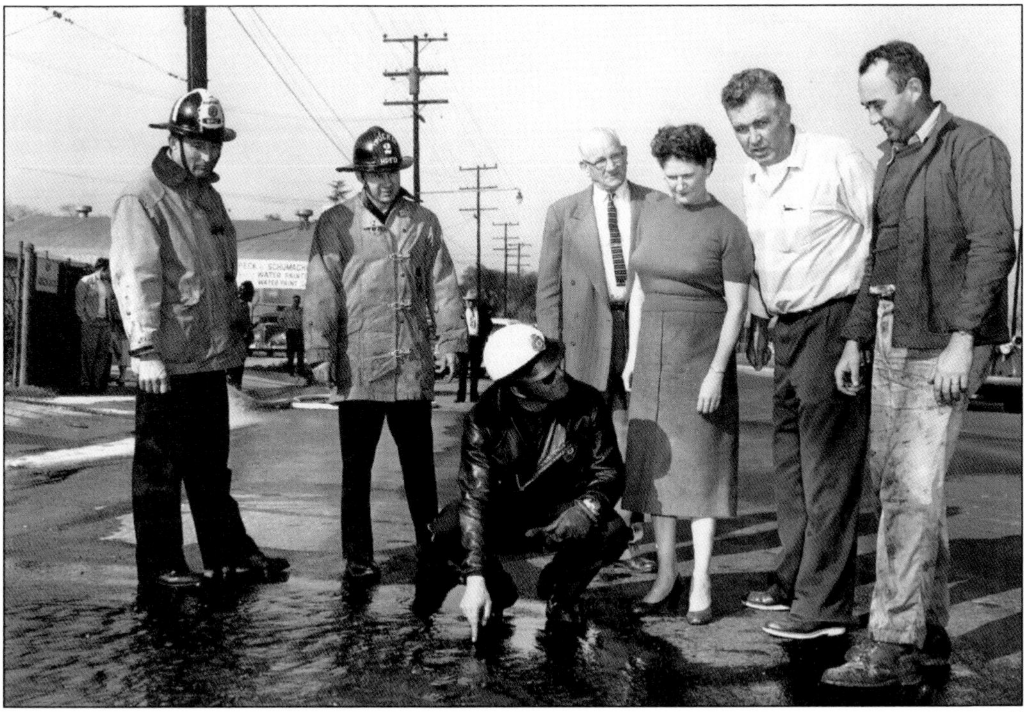

Gasoline Spill. In this photograph, Ofc. Walt Costa (crouched) investigates a gasoline spill on Salt Lake Avenue, which occurred on January 31, 1956. Also pictured, from left to right, are Captain Westreicher of the Bell Fire Department; Huntington Park firefighter Bill Staples; Bell chief of police Coones; Mary Clark, owner of the business where the leak occurred; Bell fire chief Tredor; and L. M. Morrissey of the Richfield Oil Company.

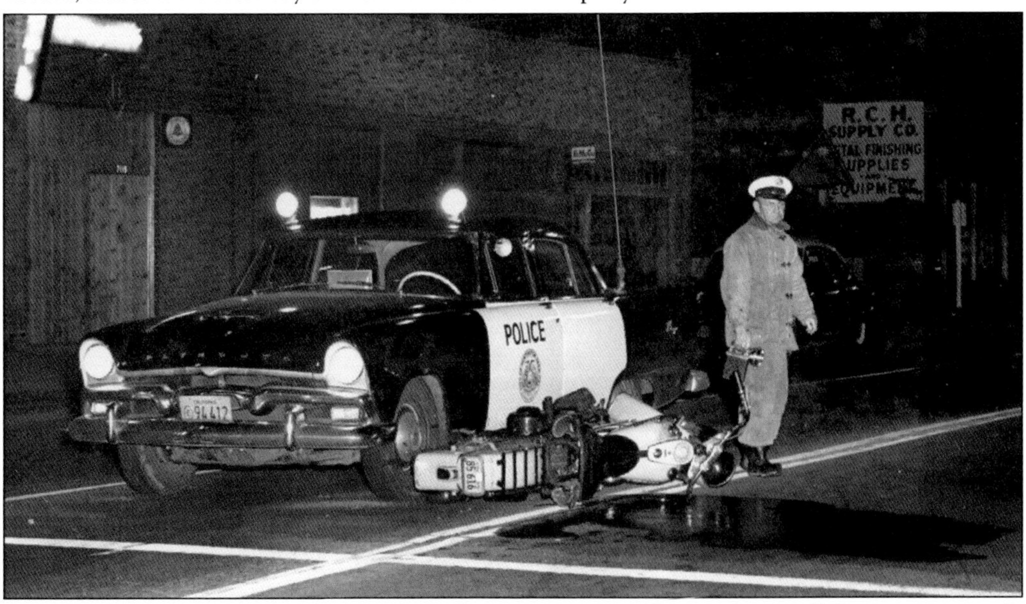

Accident, 1958. Assistant fire chief Ketching investigates the gasoline spill from a motorcycle that struck a Huntington Park police car in 1958. There were no additional details about this accident, but the motorcycle was not a police bike.

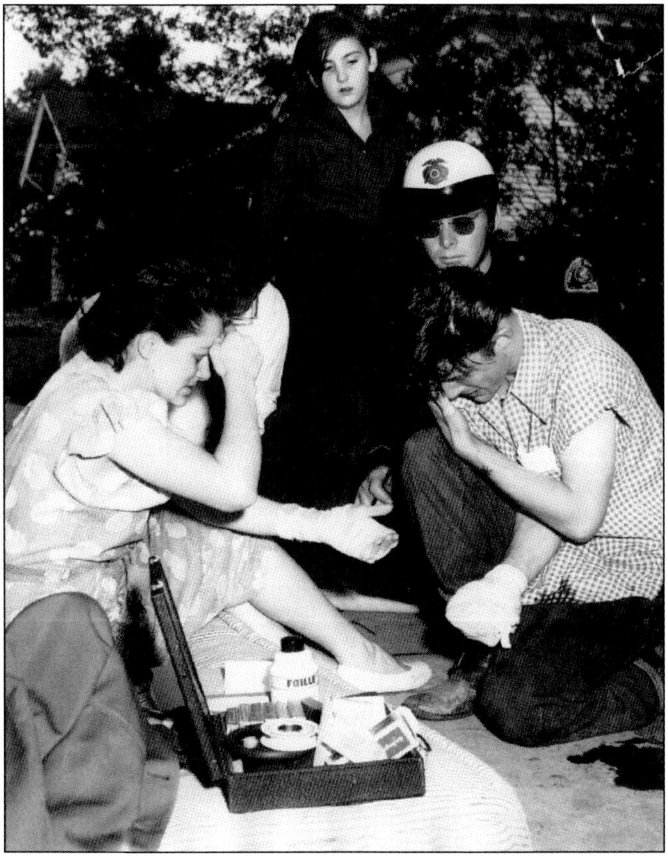

FIRE INVESTIGATION. In this graphic and emotional photograph, Huntington Park police officer Vukasovic investigates and gives aid to the victims of a fire in the 2500 block of Fifty-seventh Street on May 21, 1959.

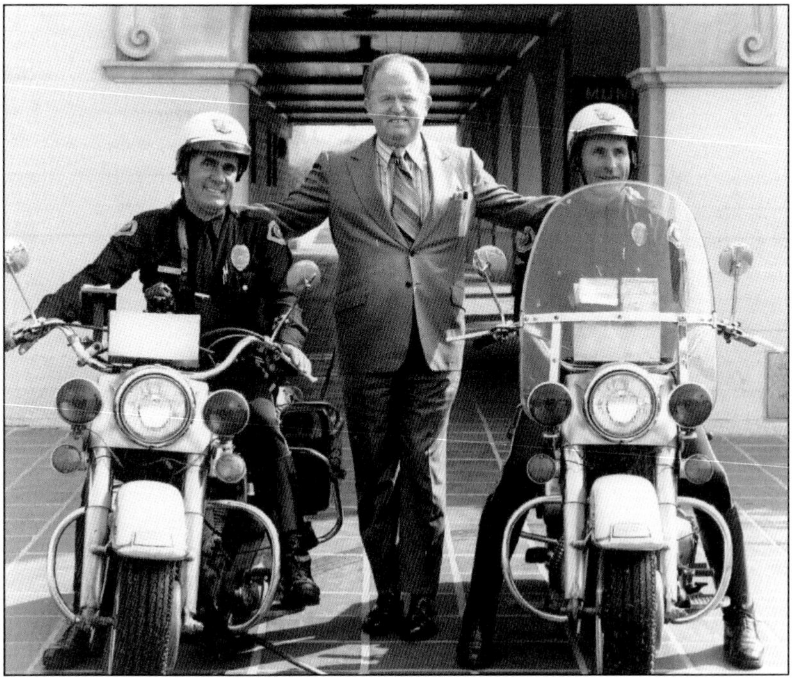

CHIEF OF POLICE HENRY FERTIG. Chief Henry Fertig (center) was the longest-serving chief of police in the history of the Huntington Park Police Department. He served as chief for 15 years, from 1958 until he retired in 1976, when Chief Loren Russell succeeded him. He is pictured here in 1972 with Ofc. Walter Costa (left) and Ofc. Buck Buchanan (right).

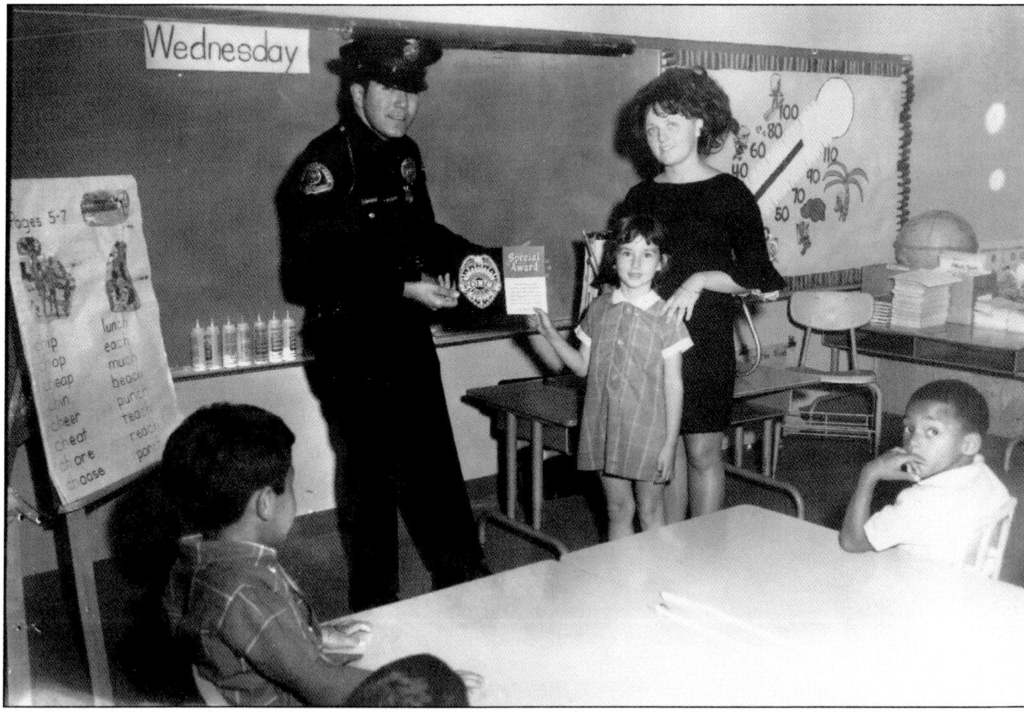

CHIEF OF POLICE GENO CONTESSOTTO. Ofc. Geno Contessotto is pictured above in the 1960s or 1970s presenting a special award to a schoolchild in front of her class and below giving a class a tour of a police car. Contessotto served as chief of police from June 17, 1983, to July 24, 1987. The modern Huntington Park Police Department continues its involvement with children in the community today through station tours, speaking engagements, the Police Activity League, Drug Abuse Resistance Education (DARE), and Juveniles at Risk.

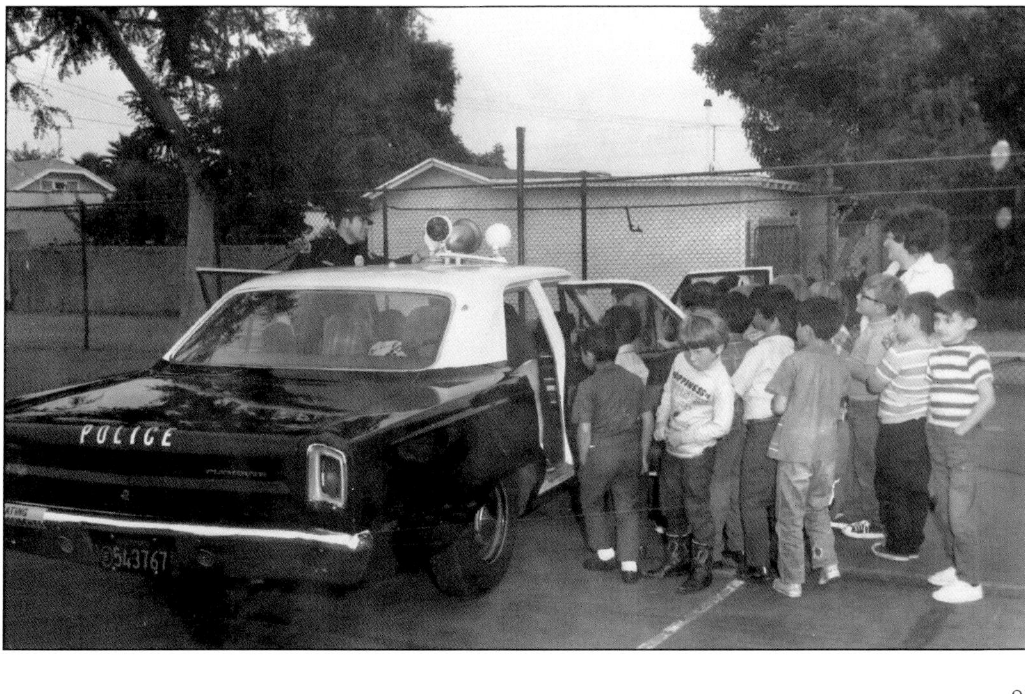

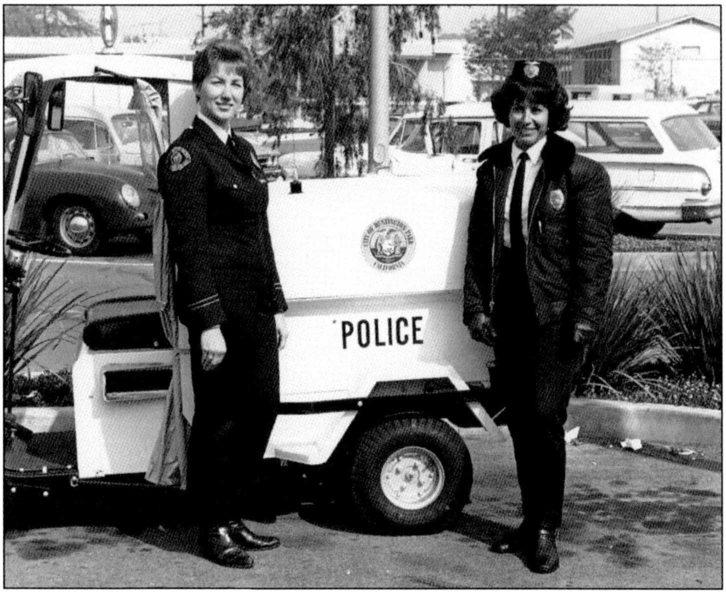

PARKING ENFORCEMENT. Not to be referred to as "Meter Maids," parking enforcement officers Connie Prentice and Rachal Anthony are pictured here in 1972. Non–sworn in personnel such as these women freed officers to conduct other enforcement duties.

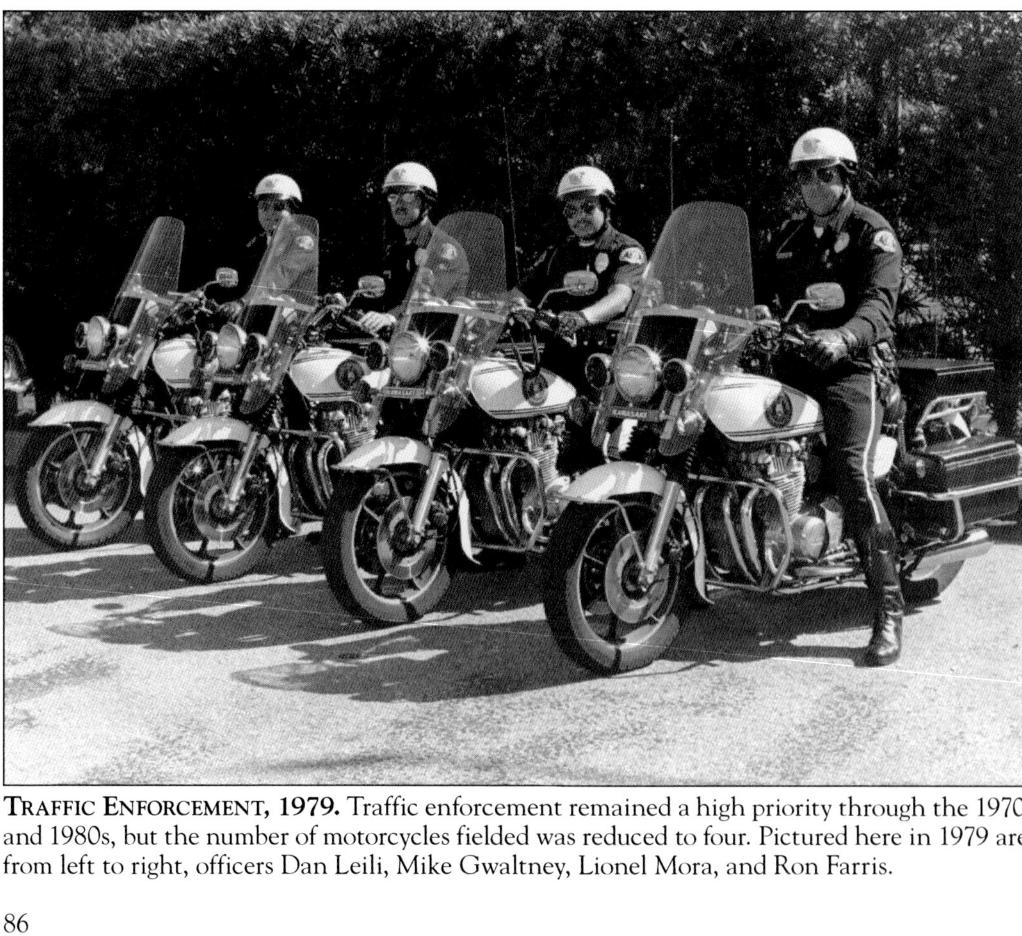

TRAFFIC ENFORCEMENT, 1979. Traffic enforcement remained a high priority through the 1970s and 1980s, but the number of motorcycles fielded was reduced to four. Pictured here in 1979 are, from left to right, officers Dan Leili, Mike Gwaltney, Lionel Mora, and Ron Farris.

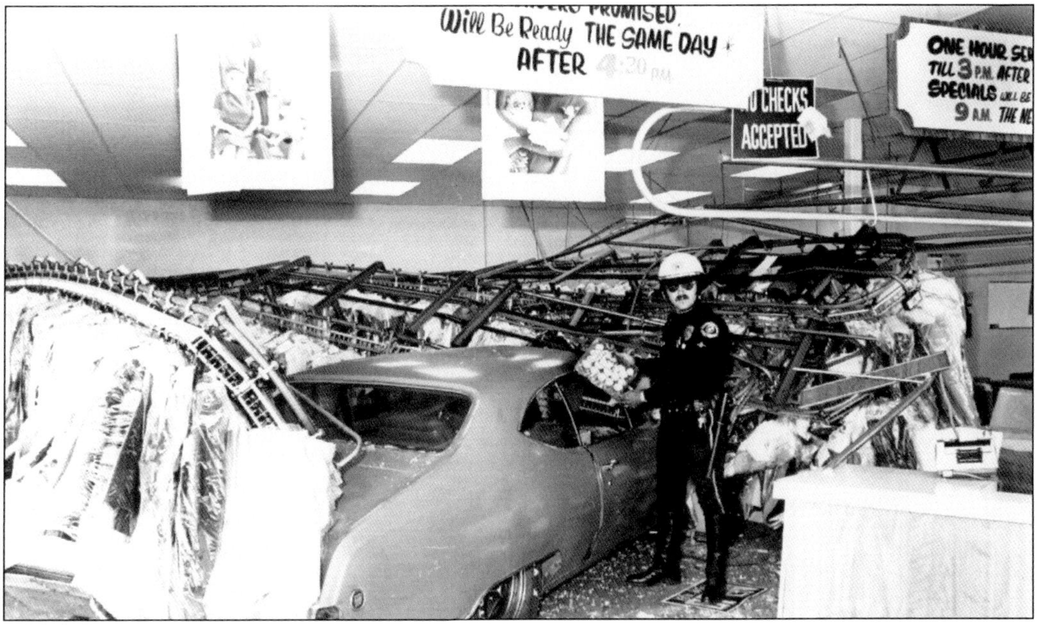

THE EGGS WEREN'T BROKEN. In this entertaining 1979 photograph, a car had plunged through the front window of a dry-cleaning business at Gage and Santa Fe Avenues. Ofc. Mike Gwaltney conducted the investigation and was surprised to find that, in spite of the damage, the eggs taken from the vehicle weren't broken.

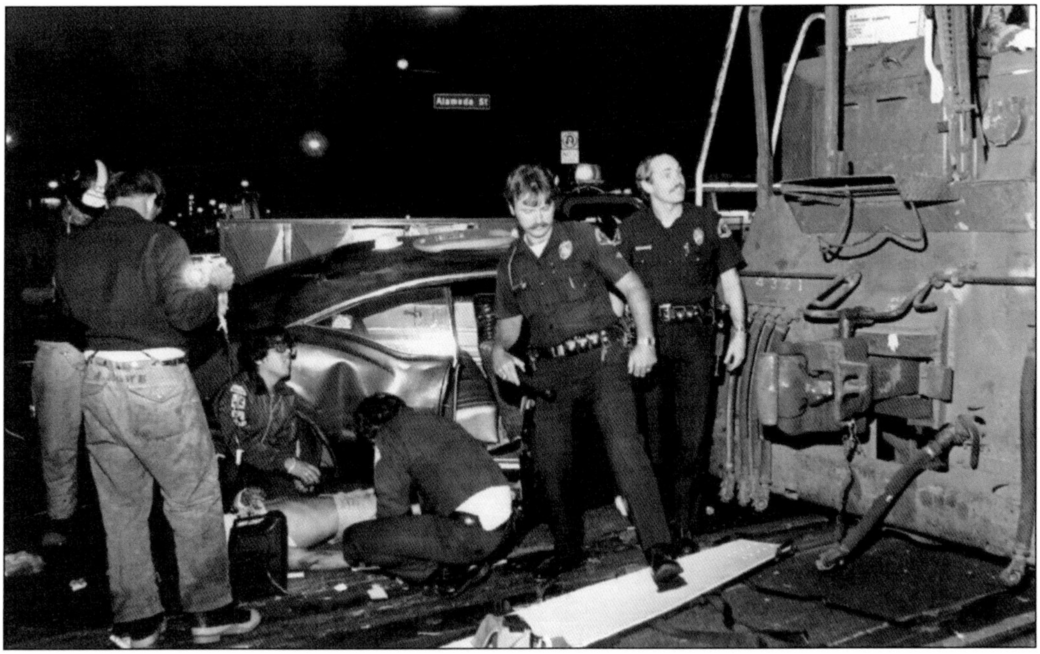

AUTO VERSUS TRAIN. Officers Mike Gwaltney and Bryan Poland conduct an investigation at the scene of this 1979 traffic collision between a train and an automobile. The collision occurred on Gage Avenue at Alameda Street. At least one person was injured and was being treated by paramedics. Those railroad tracks are now underground as part of the Alameda Corridor. The remainder of the railroad tracks are now rarely used, also as a result of the Alameda Corridor.

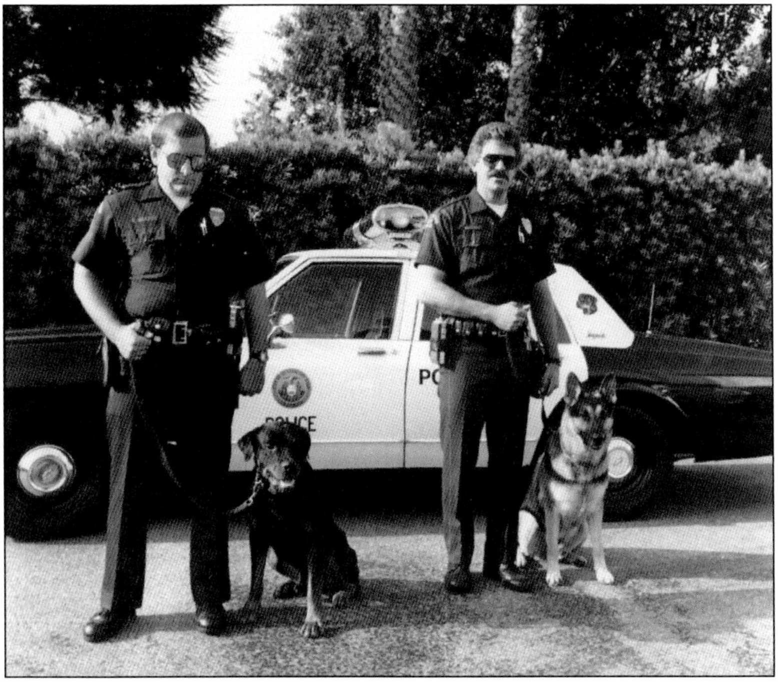

K-9 TEAMS. This c. 1985 photograph depicts the Huntington Park Police Department K-9 team. Pictured is Ofc. Ron Beason with his K-9 partner, Arno (left), and Ofc. Jon Nerlinger and his K-9 partner, Cody (right). Police dogs have become an increasingly valuable asset to law enforcement as they can much more efficiently conduct searches while reducing the risk to officers' lives.

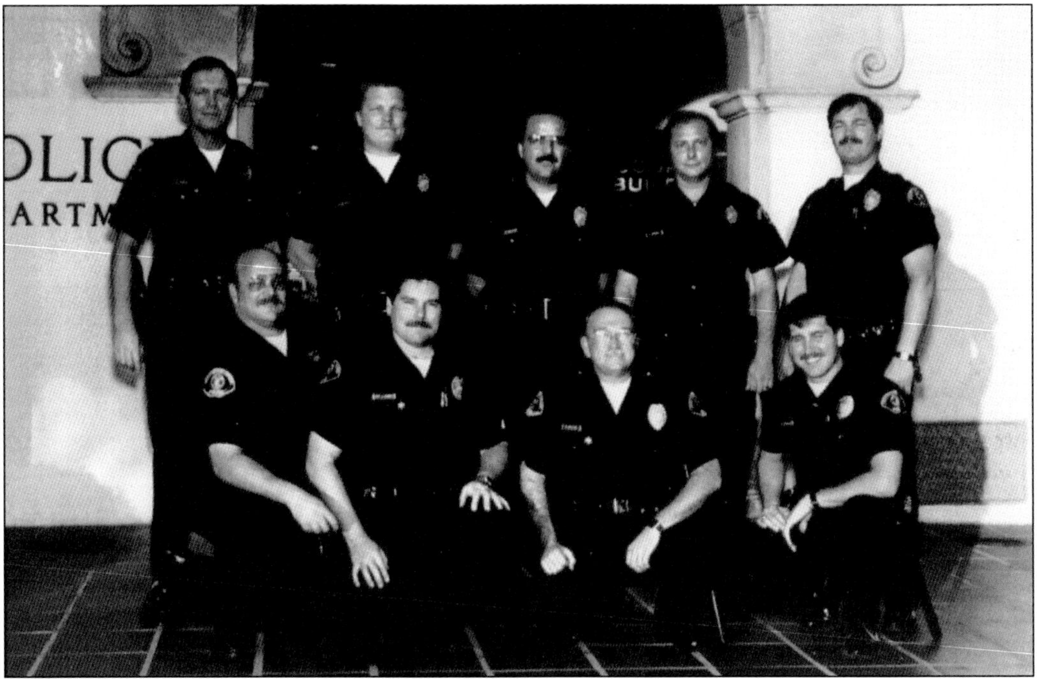

RESERVE OFFICERS. Reserve officers are also valuable assets to the Huntington Park Police Department. Reserves conduct the same duties and take the same risks as regular officers, but they do it without pay. Pictured here in 1987 from left to right are (first row) James Sanceri, James Kinsey, Robert Ragland, and Neal Mongan; (second row) Carl Reese, Scott Robison, William Pastor, John Heinlen, and David Sanford. Officers Sanford, Kinsey, and Mongan went on to become paid officers and are all sergeants in 2007.

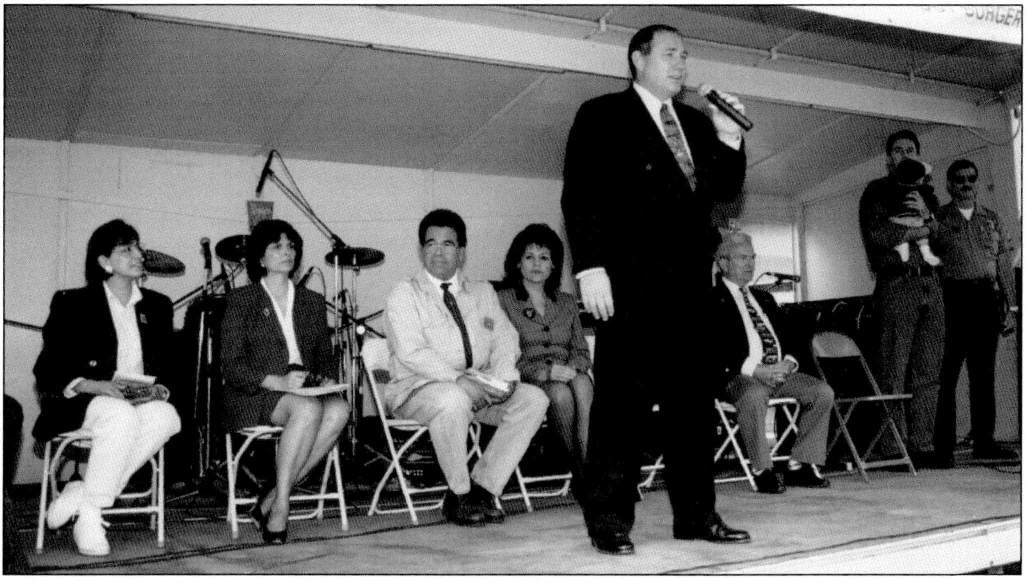

CHIEF OF POLICE RANDY NARRAMORE. Randy Narramore was chief of police from 1995 to 2006. Chief Narramore was responsible for the modernization of the police department. During his tenure, the entire Police Building received a much needed remodeling. The entire project was paid for out of asset forfeiture funds, not costing the taxpayers anything. He was also responsible for the formation of the tactical unit, the mobile command post, the helicopter program, the Juveniles At Risk Program, and equipping officers with the most modern tools.

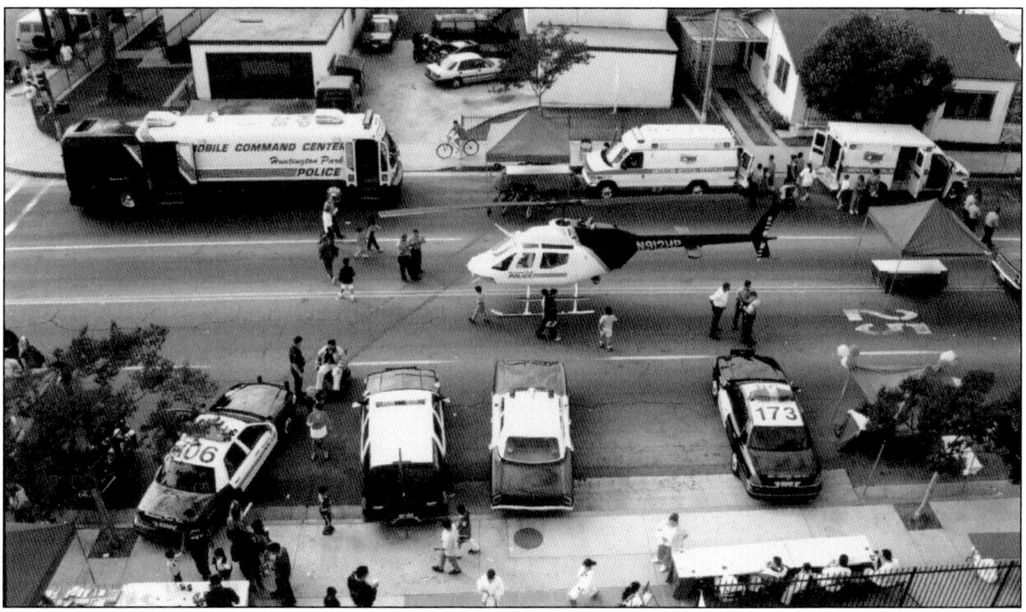

NATIONAL NIGHT OUT. This *c.* 2000 photograph was taken from the police department clock tower. At the upper left is the state-of-the-art mobile command post, Goliath, and at center is the helicopter; the bus and helicopter were donated. The police department celebrates National Night Out Against Crime, held in August of each year. The event, for which Huntington Park has received several awards, features free snacks, safety booths, police car rides for kids, and a solidarity march that about 500 people participate in.

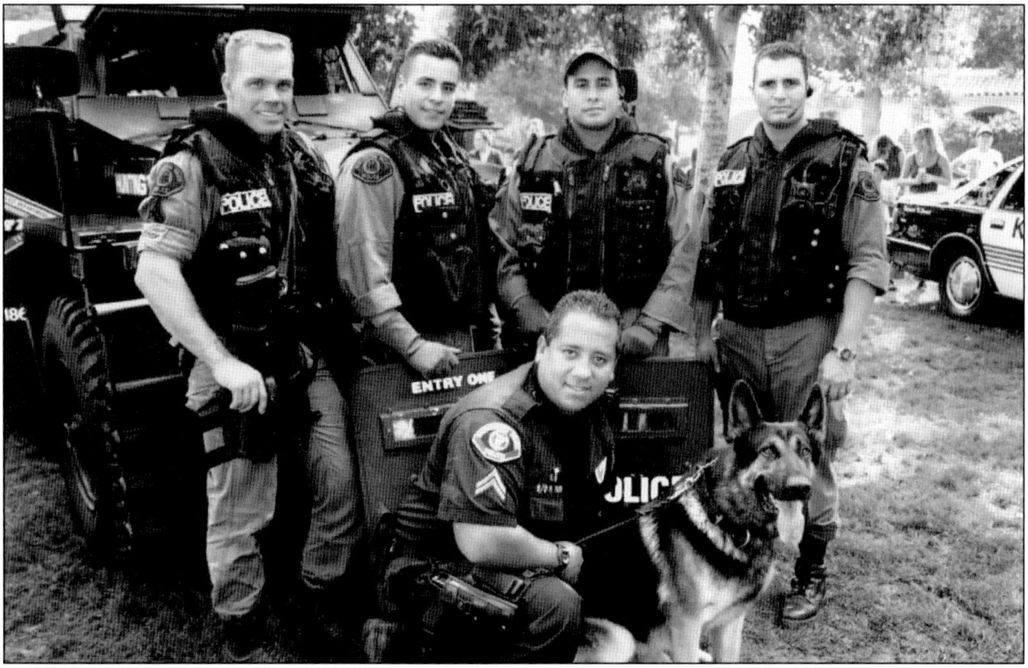

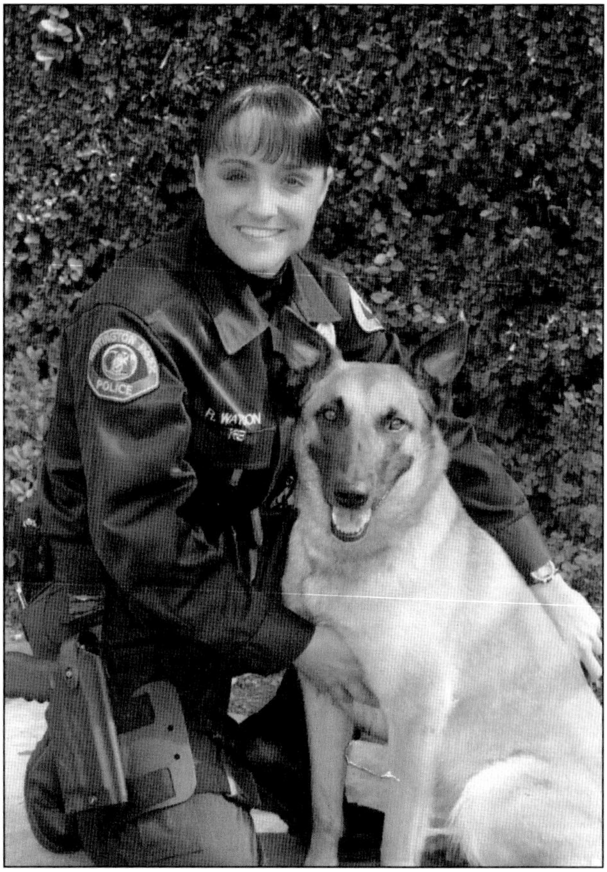

SERT. This *c.* 2000 photograph shows members of the SERT: officers Erik Degn, Frank Garcia, Gary Couso, and Neil Castelli. Kneeling is senior officer Mac Marin and his K-9 partner, Niko. In the background is SERT's "Hummer Pig," a donated armored vehicle.

OFC. RONDA WATSON. Ofc. Ronda Watson was the department's first and only female K-9 handler. She is pictured here with her partner, Andy. Ofc. Ronda Watson, injured in an on-duty traffic accident, is retiring as of 2007. She was also a recipient of the department's Life Saving Medal.

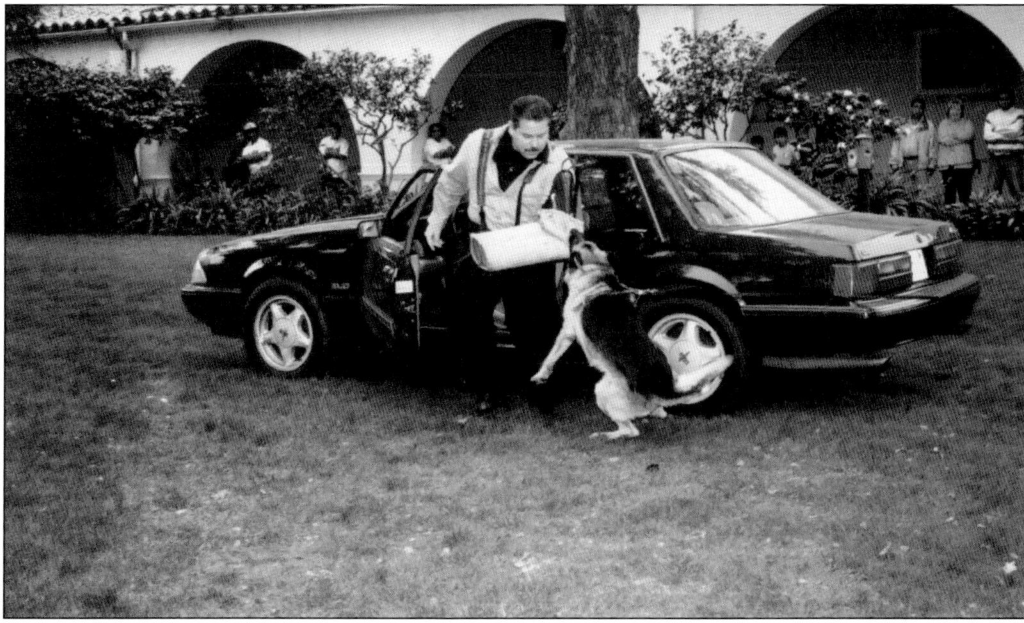

Sgt. James Kinsey. Pictured here is Sgt. James Kinsey, author of this book and supervisor of the department's K-9 program during the late 1990s. During this public demonstration, K-9 Baro, handled by Ofc. Neal Mongan, extracts Sergeant Kinsey from a vehicle.

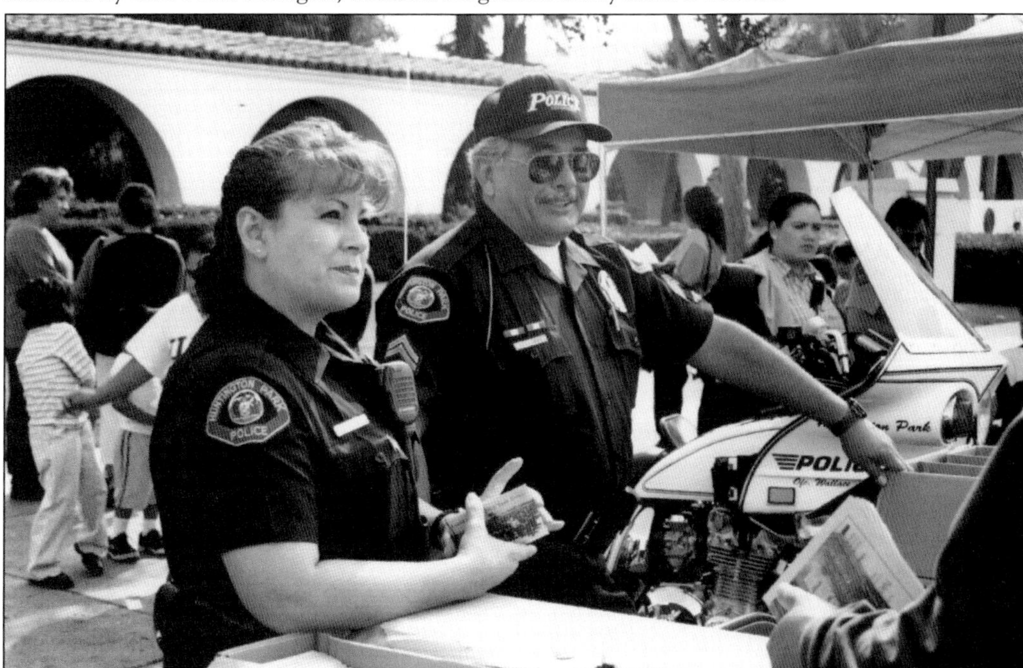

Reserve Ofc. Norma Villa. Ofc. Norma Villa, pictured here in 2000, was a reserve officer with the Huntington Park Police Department. Officer Villa's regular employment was as a vice president of Community Bank, which began operating in Huntington Park in 1945. To the right of officer Villa is 30-year-veteran senior officer Lionel Mora. Most of officer Mora's career was spent on a motorcycle.

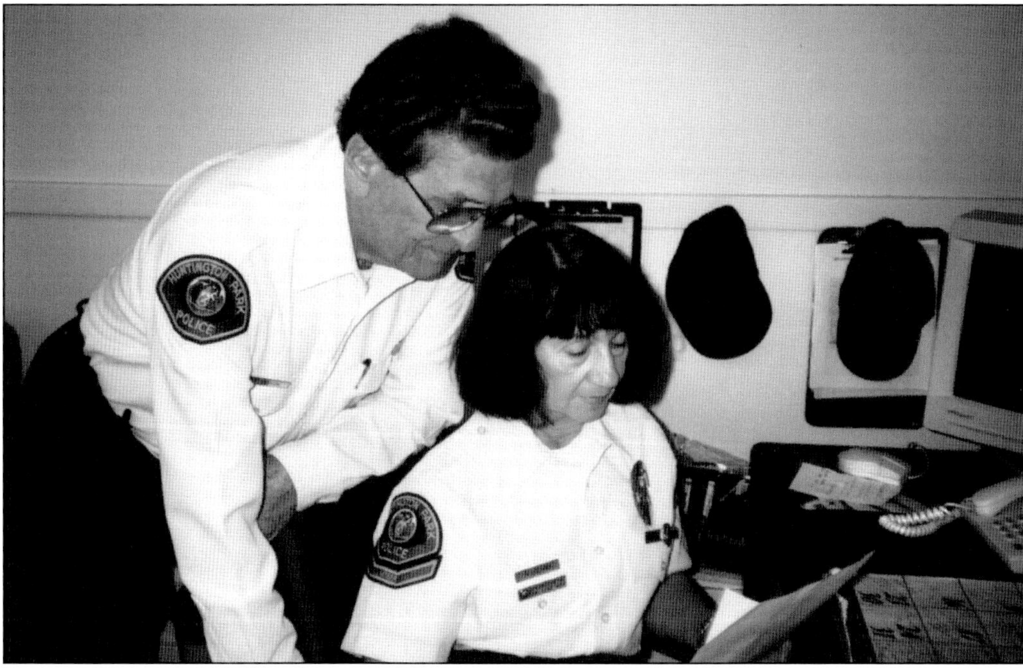

VOLUNTEERS. One of the programs initiated by Chief Narramore was Citizen's Volunteers. Pictured here are volunteers Manual Gascon and Nancy Lozano; both emigrated from Cuba. Police volunteers are people who have taken personal responsibility to make a difference in the community by providing support functions. Volunteer Lozano was the first in Huntington Park's program.

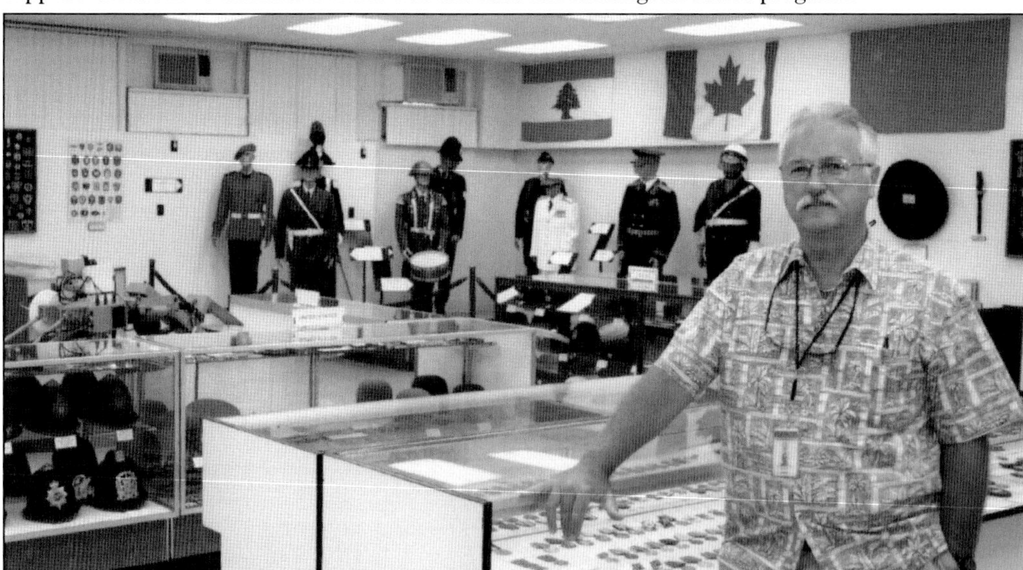

THE INTERNATIONAL POLICE MUSEUM. Founded by Huntington Park police captain Michael Gwaltney, the museum opened in the old health department building following Gwaltney's retirement in 2004. The museum boasts police, military, and holocaust memorabilia from all over the world. Captain Gwaltney displays only about 20 percent of his collection and may have the largest police hat collection in the world. The museum entertains residents, schoolchildren, and visitors from all over the world.

Six

Places and Faces

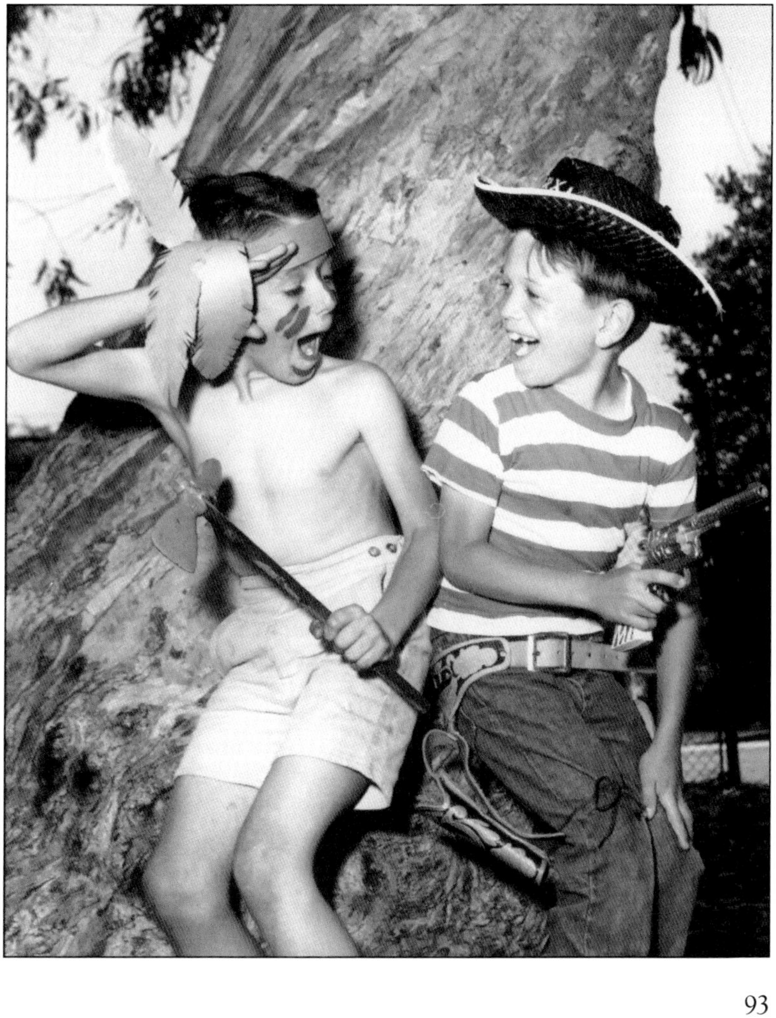

It Is the People. What makes a city is not its buildings, businesses, and roadways; its the people who occupy them. Huntington Park has 100 years of faces and places that distinguish its colorful history. This chapter captures some of the city's century of personalities. Only identified as two Huntington Park boys, this image illustrates the childhood of many who will read this publication. The photograph may have been taken at one of the many day camps held at Municipal Park in the 1950s.

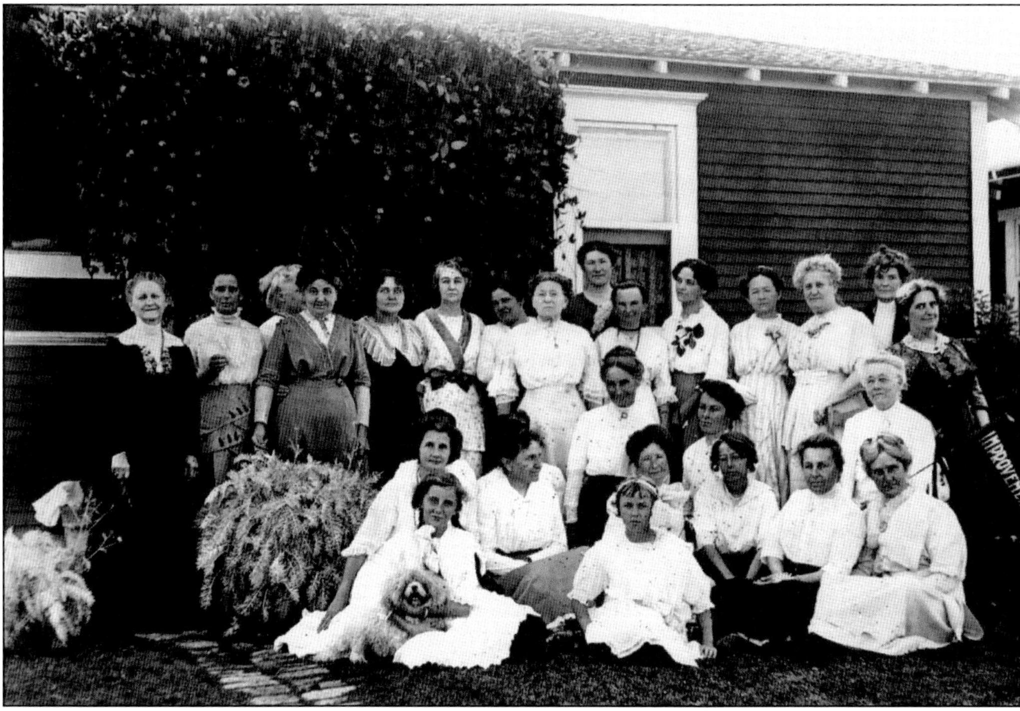

WOMAN'S IMPROVEMENT CLUB, 1911 AND 1924. As stated in the 1935 history of Huntington Park, "To the woman of a new city falls the task of bringing refinement to the new home place. As individuals they beautify and improve their homes. In groups with unified purpose, they multiply their contribution to good living in the community by beautifying the city in which they live." The women pictured here accepted that mission; in 1911 (above) and in 1924 (below), in front of their new building on Clarendon Avenue, are members of the Woman's Improvement Club or EBELL Club.

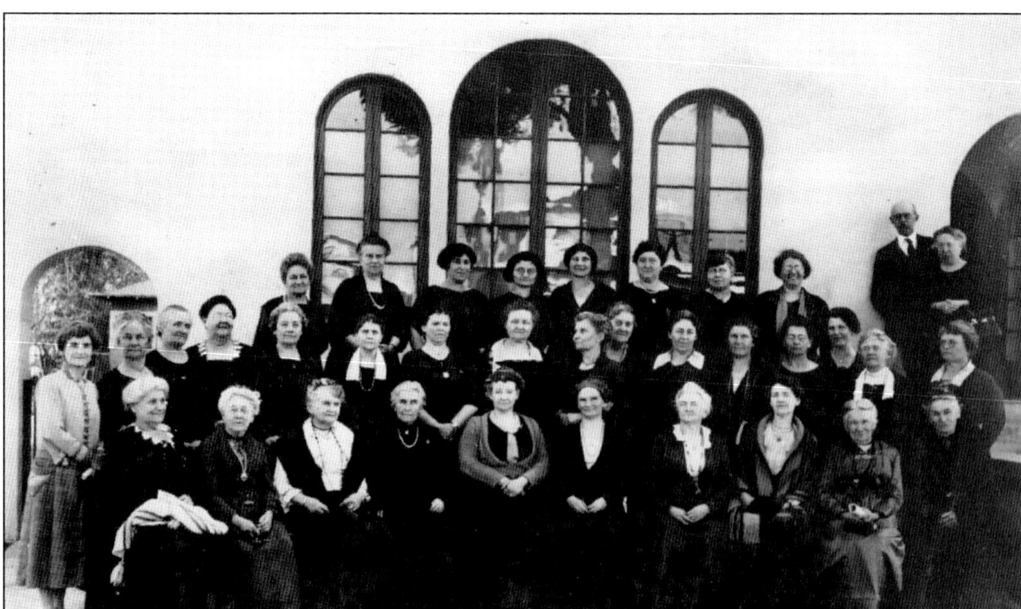

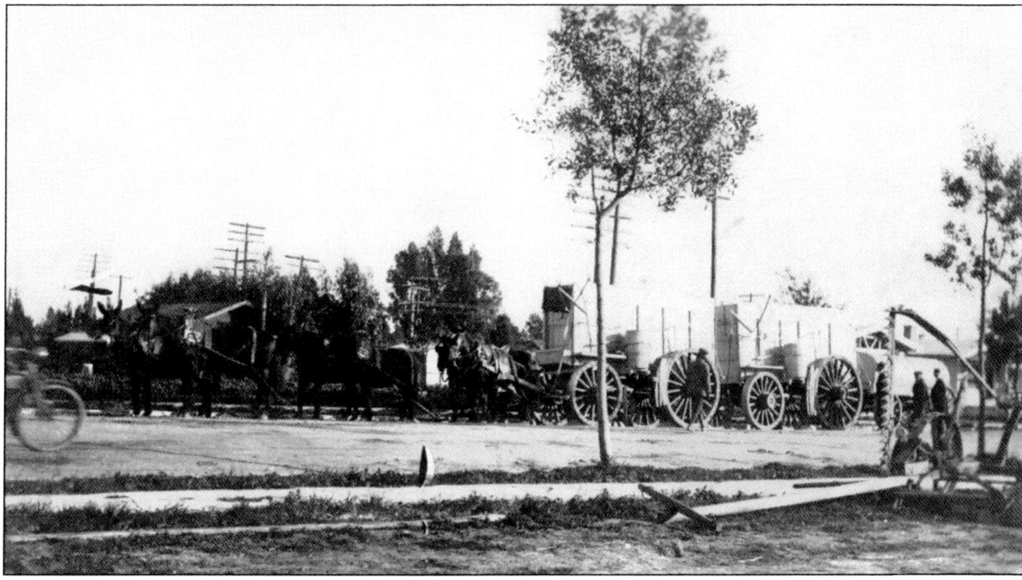

TWENTY-MULE TRAIN BORAX. In 1916, as part of a promotion for a soap product, this mule train started a cross-country trip from Huntington Park. Pacific Coast Borax Company owned the symbol whose origins were from the mule-powered wagons used to transport borax out of Death Valley to the rail spur between the years of 1883 and 1889.

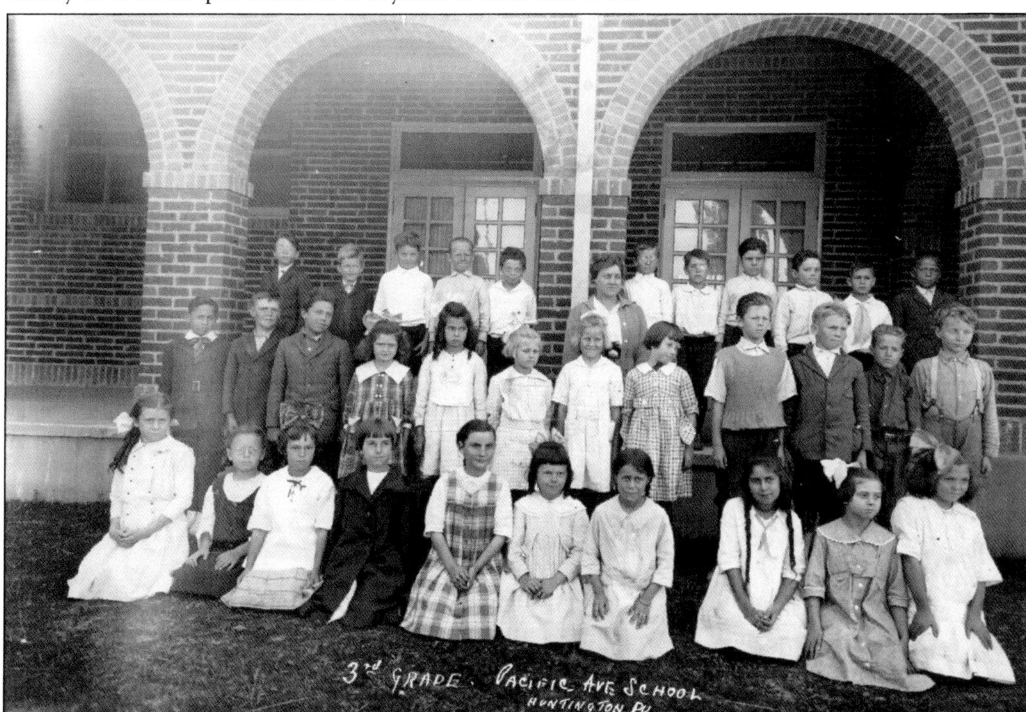

PACIFIC AVENUE SCHOOL. This photograph depicts the third-grade class of Pacific Avenue School and teacher Miss Langloh in 1918 as the United States entered Word War I. Pacific Avenue School was, and still is, located on Pacific Boulevard between Fifty-seventh and Fifty-eighth Streets. It has serviced disabled children in recent years.

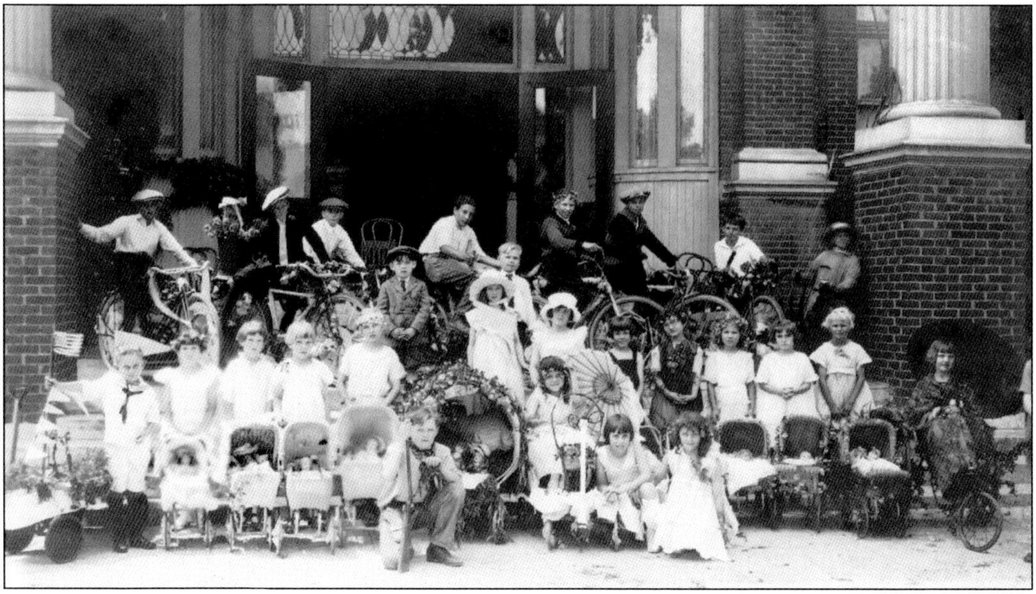

THE MAY DAY PARADE. This photograph of Malabar Street School was taken in 1925, the same day of the cover photograph. A tradition associated with the May Day celebration was a parade in which children decorated their bicycles, wagons, and carriages in bright ribbons and flowers and paraded around the schools.

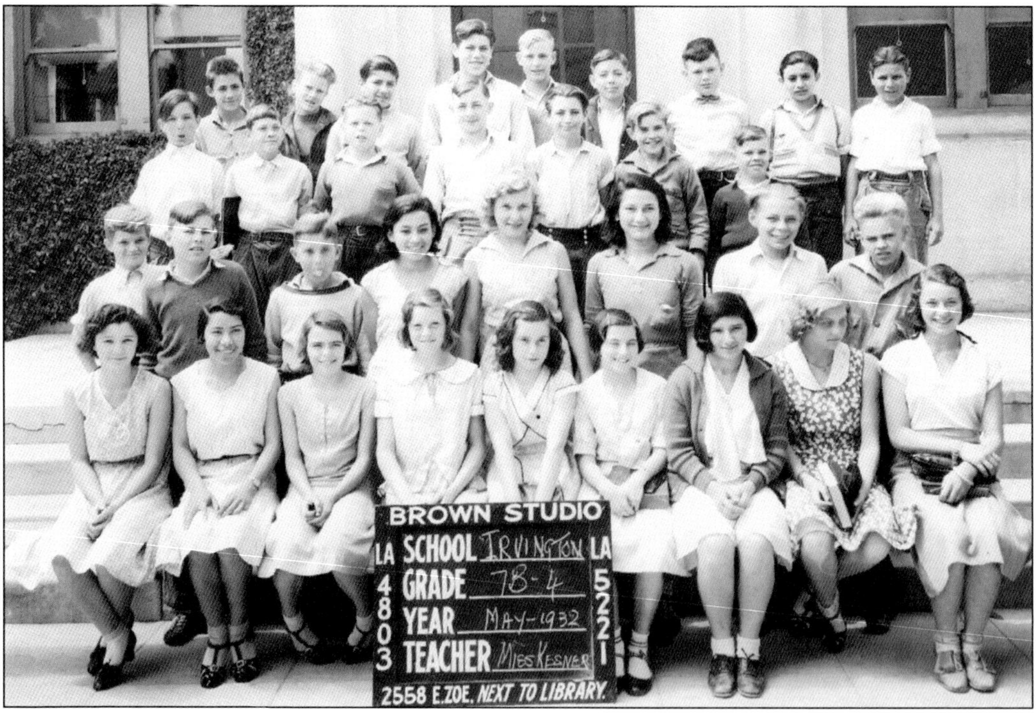

IRVINGTON MIDDLE SCHOOL, 1932. This 1932 photograph of the third-grade class at Irvington Middle School, taken by Brown Studio, a local business, illustrates the old axiom "boys will be boys" with the expressions given at the left. Brown Studio was responsible for many of the city's early photographs.

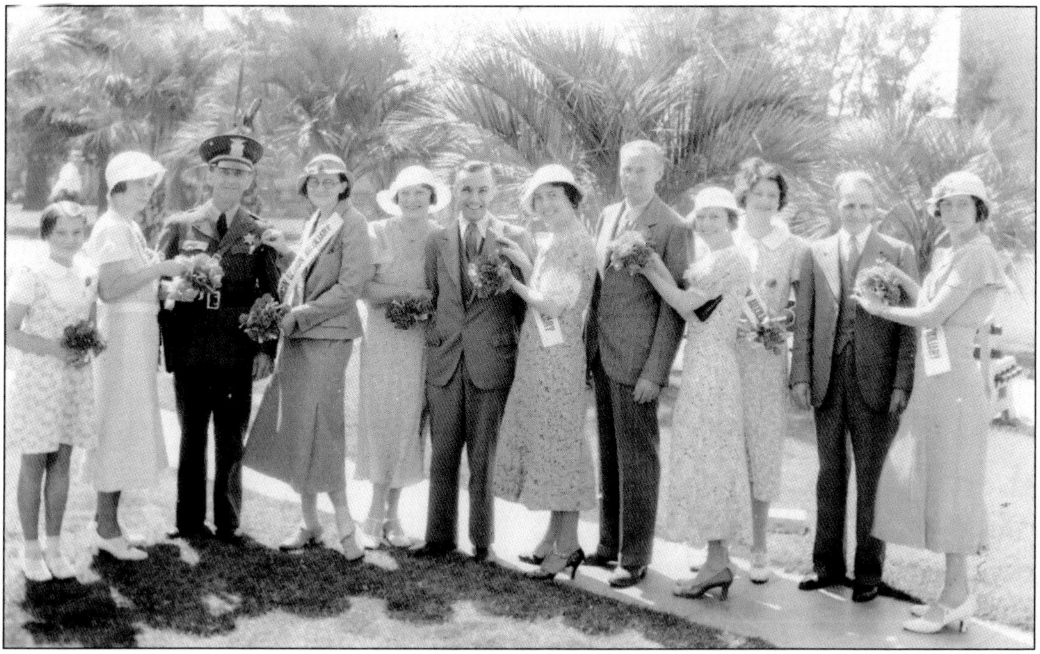

LADIES OF THE AMERICAN LEGION AUXILIARY. The American Legion is an organization of American veterans that was founded in 1919 after World War I. The American Legion Auxiliary is an organization of women dedicated to past and present American war veterans, children, and the communities of these people. Pictured are American Legion and Auxiliary members in Huntington Park around 1930. The legion was very active in the Huntington Park community.

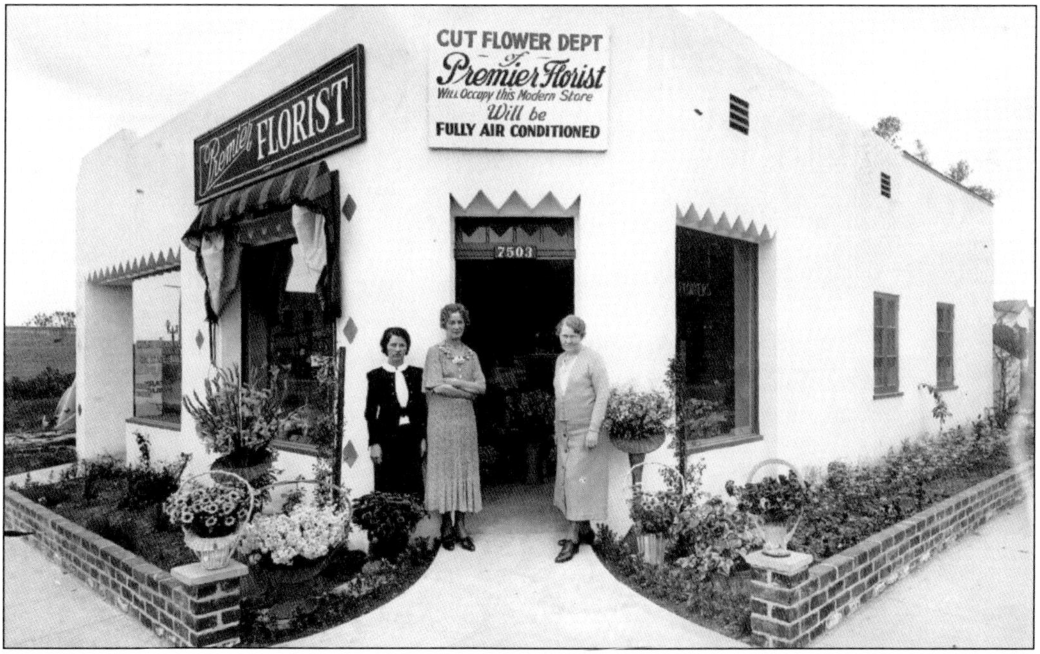

PREMIER FLORIST. Premier Florist was a woman-owned business established in 1936 at the corner of State Street and Live Oak Avenue. Pictured are proprietor Inez Johnson with assistants Jeanette Roberts and Clara Barry. The building is now occupied by an insurance company.

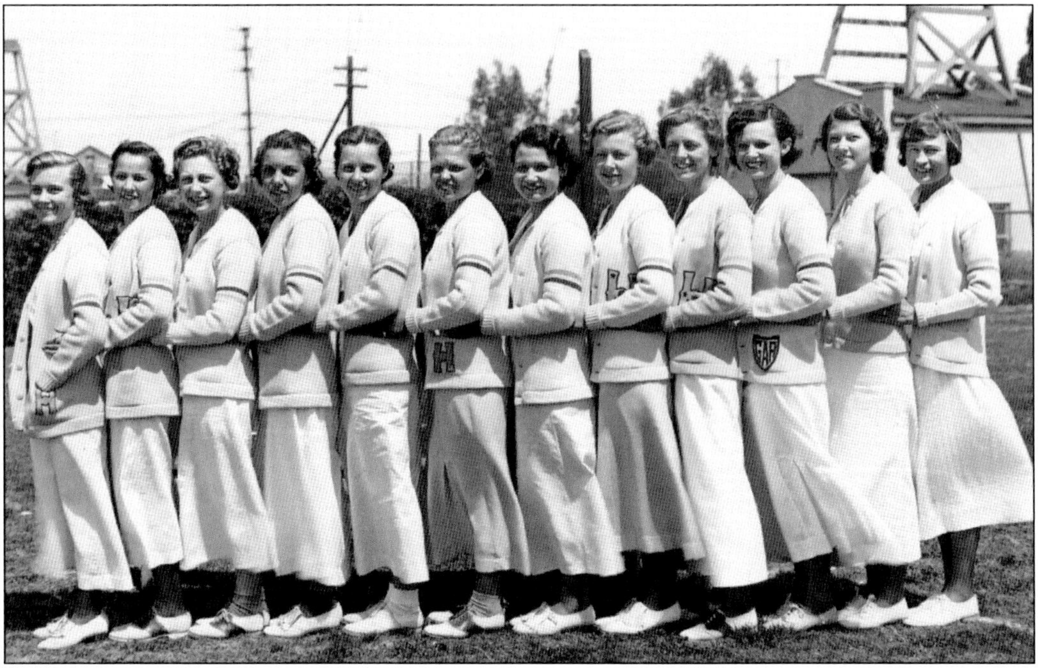

THE GIRL'S ATHLETIC ASSOCIATION. Pictured are the members of the 1935 Huntington Park High School Girl's Athletic Association. The association is similar in nature to a group of lettermen. Athletics played an important part of Huntington Park High School's past. The first year of organized athletics at the school was in 1915, where 23 monograms or "letters" were given. In 1929, the school's athletes were presented 125 of these awards.

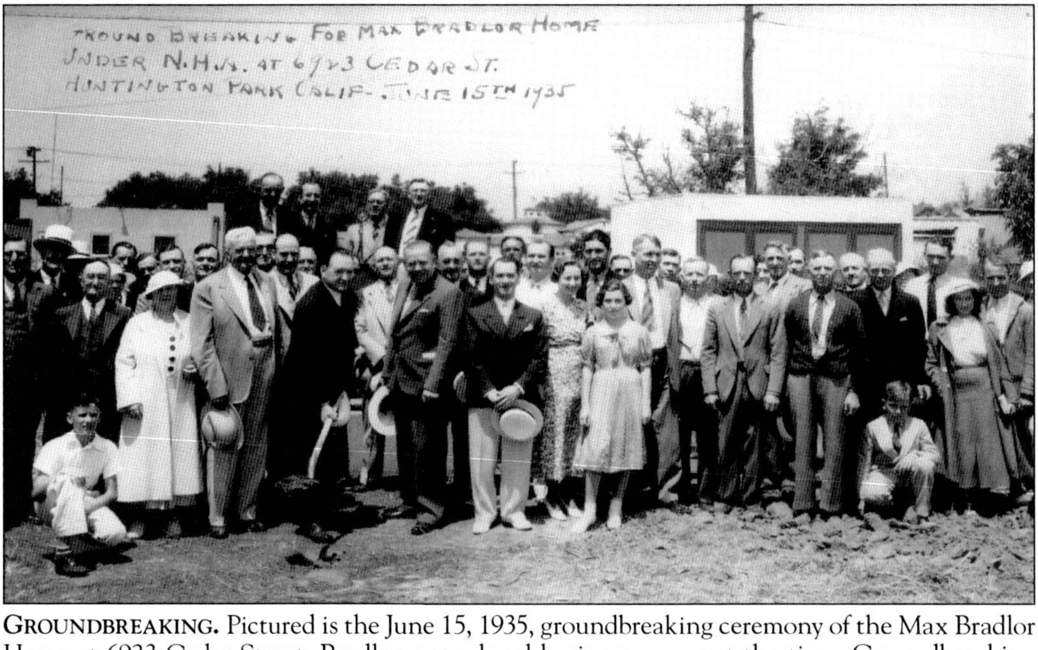

GROUNDBREAKING. Pictured is the June 15, 1935, groundbreaking ceremony of the Max Bradlor Home at 6923 Cedar Street; Bradlor was a local business owner at the time. Groundbreaking ceremonies for both businesses and new houses during this time period were often extravagant events with many attending.

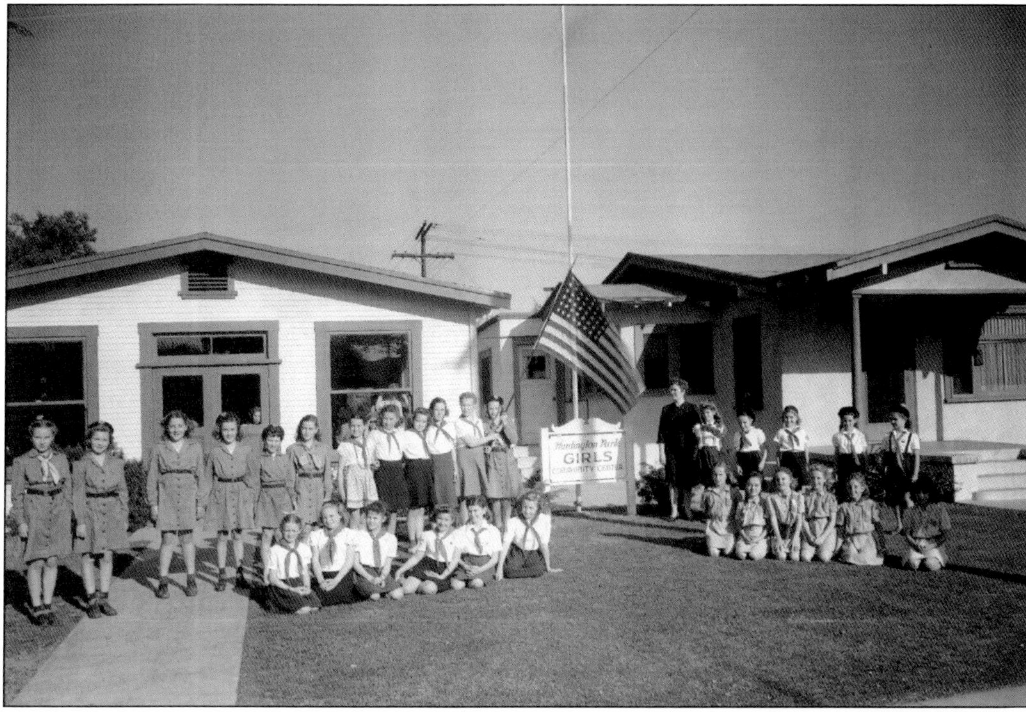

GIRL'S COMMUNITY CENTER. Pictured is the Girl's Community Center in 1943, located at 6918 Miles Avenue. The center was opened to support the various female youth groups in Huntington Park at the time. An open house was held on May 16, 1943, and featured participants from the Girl Scouts Troop No. 10, the Campfire Girls, the Junior Catholic Daughters of America, the Gage Junior High School Glee Club, and the American Legion Auxiliary.

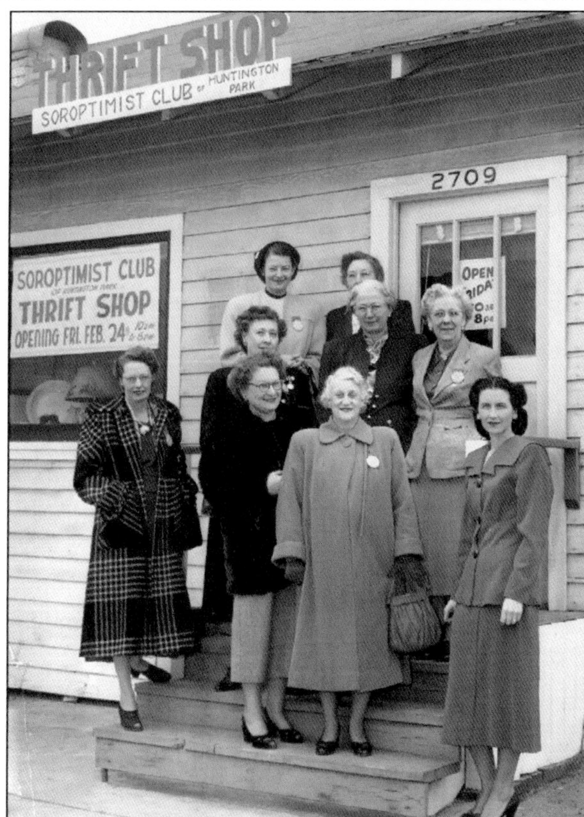

THE SOROPTIMIST CLUB. Founded in 1921, the Soroptimist "Best for Women" Club is a business and professional women's organization dedicated to improving the lives of women in the community. Included in this picture of the group outside their fund-raising thrift shop are Dela Doyle, Dr. Bett Wright, Helen Heafield, Irene Scoggin, Dr. Elsie Shildwachter, Mildred Johnson, Agnes Platt, and Bea Haller. Agnes Platt was a Huntington Park city clerk.

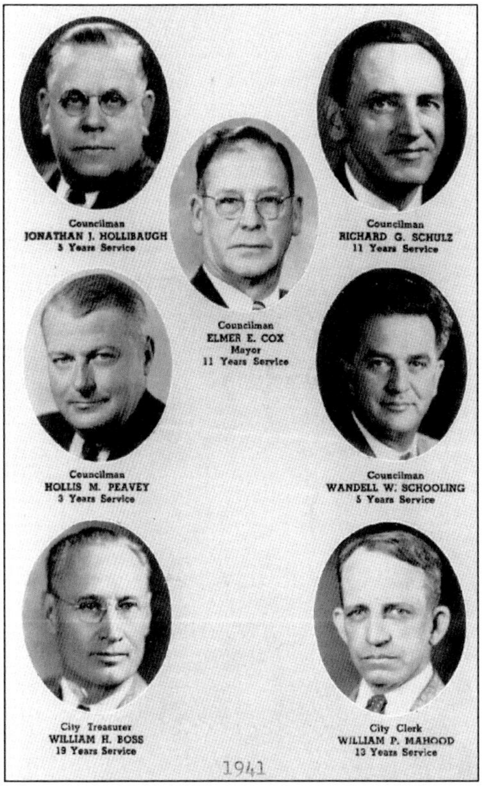

HUNTINGTON PARK GOVERNMENT, 1941. This photograph shows members of Huntington Park's 1941 government and the years of service attained by that point in time. Councilman Wandell Schooling's son, Russell, was also mayor and went on to serve many years as a judge in the Southeast Municipal Court in Huntington Park.

PATRIOTIC HALL IN MUNICIPAL PARK. Many Huntington Park citizens proudly served in both world wars. A memorial in Miles Avenue Park lists the names of Huntington Park veterans of World War I. Robert Trusten McColley, the only Huntington Park resident to be killed in that war, died in the battle of the Argonne Forest. This photograph was taken in Patriotic Hall, and even though all patriotic groups could use it, in all probability this is the American Legion in the 1930s or 1940s.

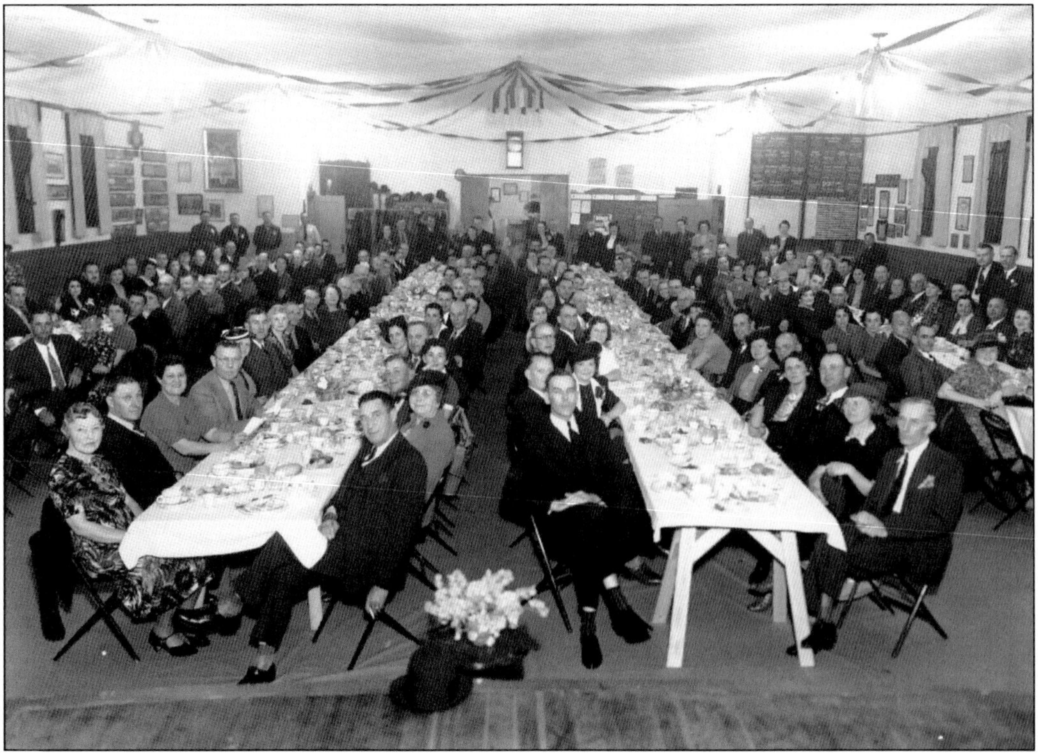

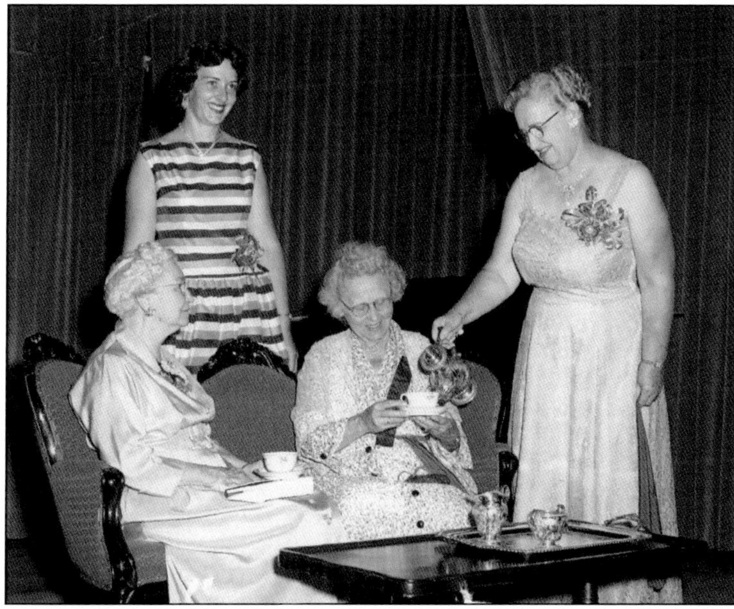

HONORING WOMEN PIONEERS. During the 1950 golden anniversary celebration, women of the Huntington Park Pioneers and founders of the EBELL/Woman's Improvement Club were recognized. Pictured are Mrs. Marjorie Ford (seated left), wife of Marshall William Ford, and Anna Geck (seated right), an educator and city historian. The other women are unidentified.

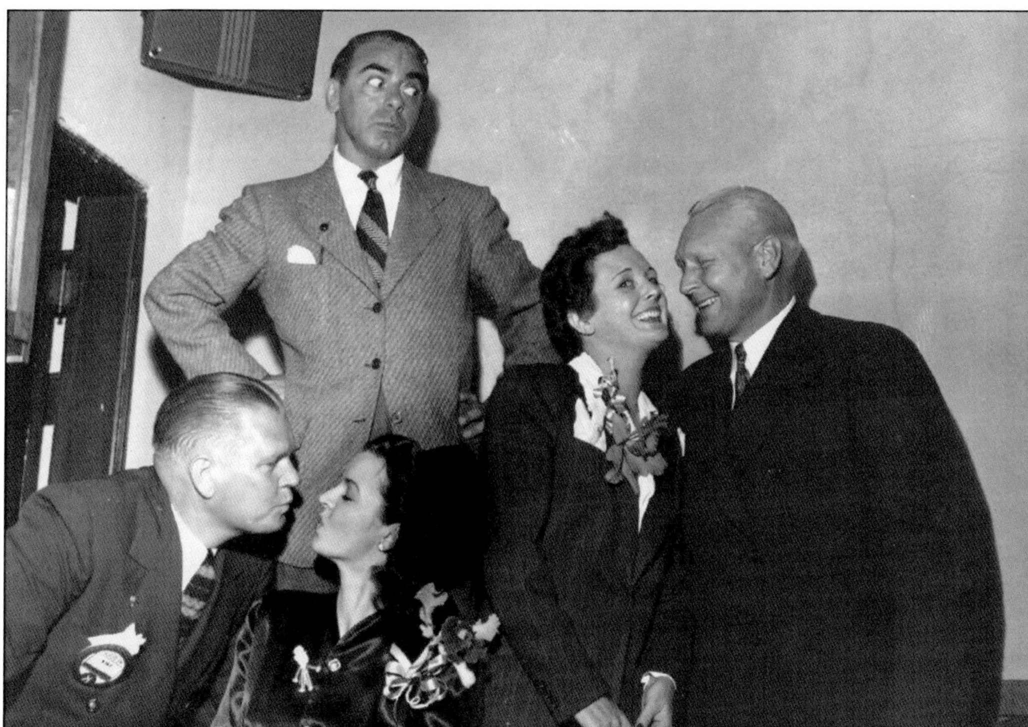

THE KIWANIS CLUB. Pictured during an undated Kiwanis Club event is comedian and radio and television personality Eddie Cantor in the back and actress Mary Astor, of *The Maltese Falcon* fame, on the right. Kiwanis Club member Art Sanders is wearing the badge. The Kiwanis were chartered in Huntington Park in 1924 with a membership of 24 local businessmen. Maurice Sopp, of Sopp Chevrolet, was one of them. The Huntington Park Kiwanis Club, which is still active, has dedicated more than 75 years to the community with an emphasis on youth.

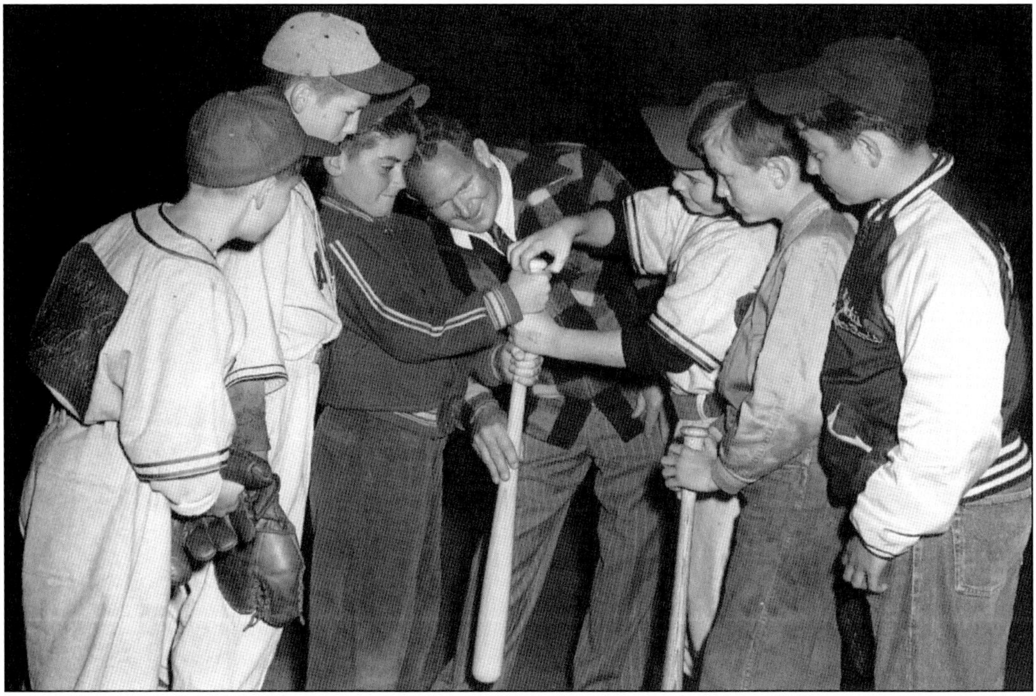

LITTLE LEAGUE. These boys are participating in an age-old little league tradition to determine who's up first. This photograph of Huntington Park ballplayers, taken in the 1940s or 1950s, illustrates how sponsors were a part of the tradition. The uniform on the boy at left advertises Brown's Sporting Goods, a shop on Pacific Boulevard. Baseball is still a very popular sport in Huntington Park with leagues for all ages.

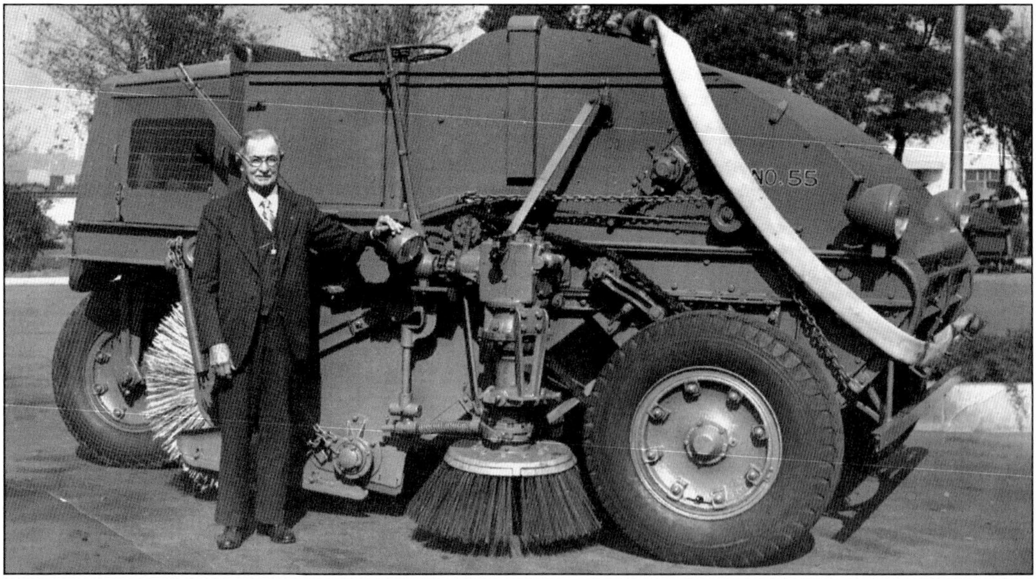

W. E. FORD. Street superintendent and former marshall William (Uncle Billy) Ford is pictured in front of one of his modern street sweepers in the 1940s shortly before his retirement. Ford Lane, behind city hall, was named after him in the 1930s in honor of his long service to the City of Huntington Park.

GENERALS IN HUNTINGTON PARK. In mid-1945, during a War Bond Drive, Gen. George S. Patton (left), famous for the Battle of the Bulge, and Gen. Jimmy Doolittle (center, facing camera), famous for the bombing mission over Tokyo early in World War II, addressed Huntington Park citizens from the bandstand next to city hall. Mayor Schooling is next to the generals with councilmen Cox and Hollibaugh looking on. The Huntington Park Youth Band, led by Phil Moore, is also on stage.

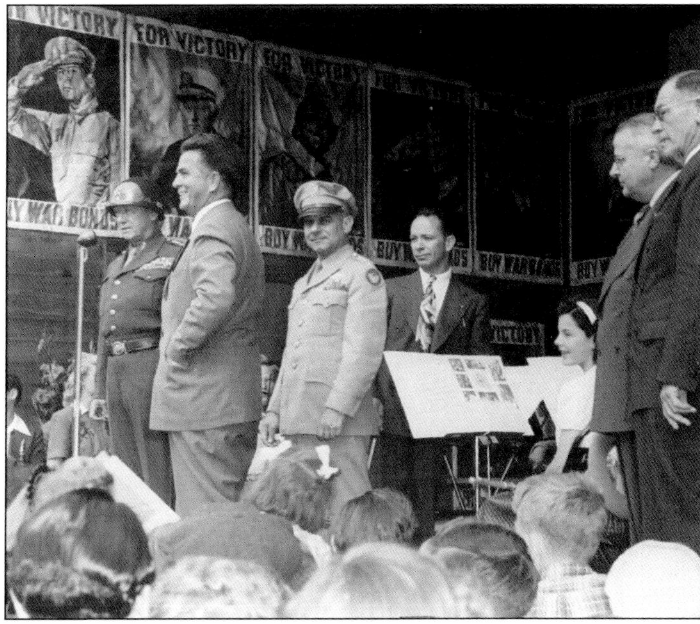

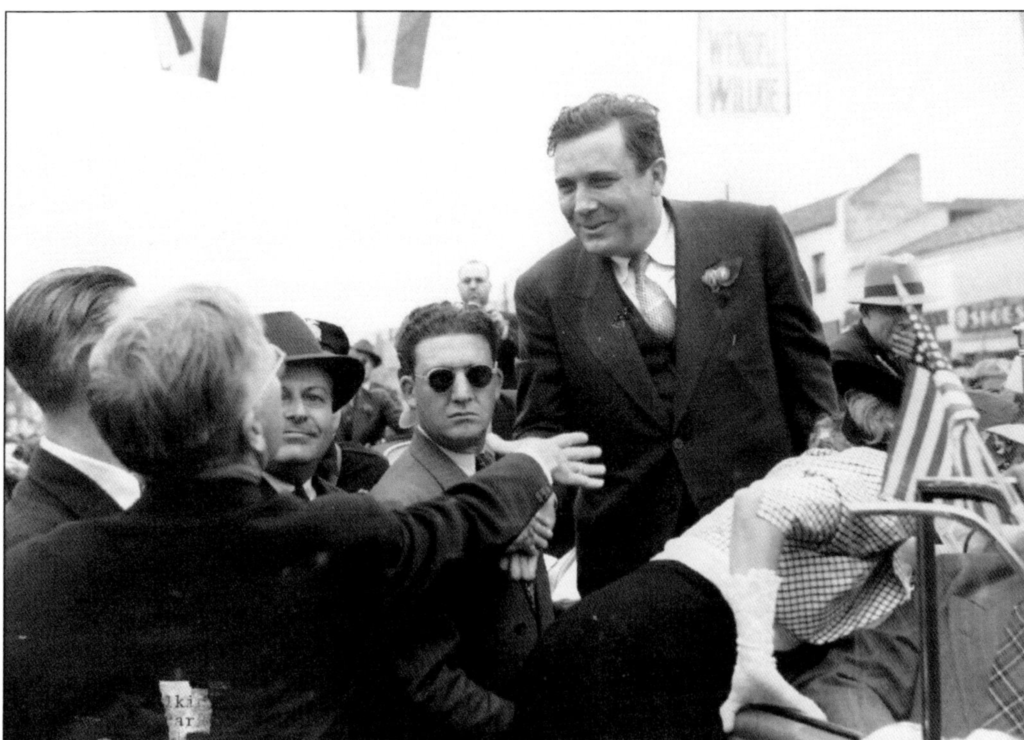

WENDELL WILLKIE. Presidential candidate Wendell Willkie passed through Huntington Park during his unsuccessful bid for president of the United States. In 1940, Willkie was the republican nominee and lost to Franklin D. Roosevelt, although he was surprisingly a strong supporter of Roosevelt during World War II. Note how one of Willkie's supporters is very enthusiastic and apparently climbing into the car.

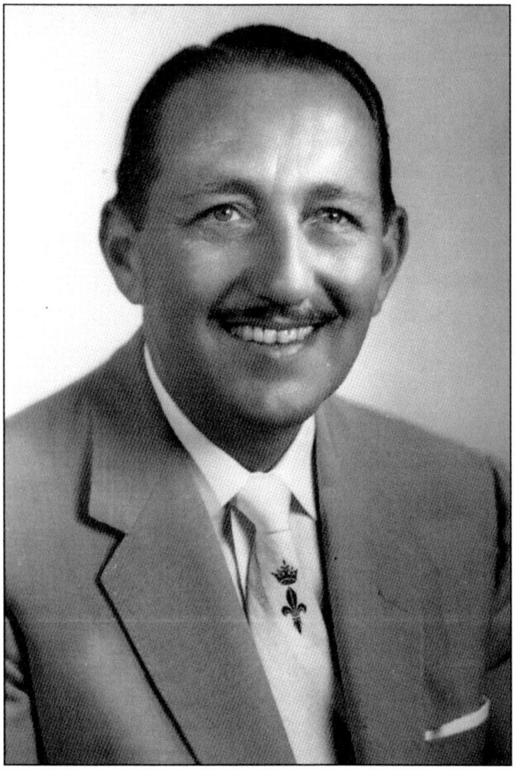

FRANK BONELLI. Frank Bonelli, at left, was a figurehead in state, county, and Huntington Park politics from June 20, 1946, when he was appointed to the Huntington Park City Council, until 1956. Bonelli served two one-year terms as mayor of Huntington Park in 1948 and 1952, and he also served in the state assembly from 1952 to 1958—two years in both offices at the same time. He served as a supervisor for Los Angeles County from 1958 to 1970, and a county park is named after him. In the photograph below, Bonelli appears with T. N. Lord, chief of police William Salvin, Herman Shultz, and fire chief John Slocum.

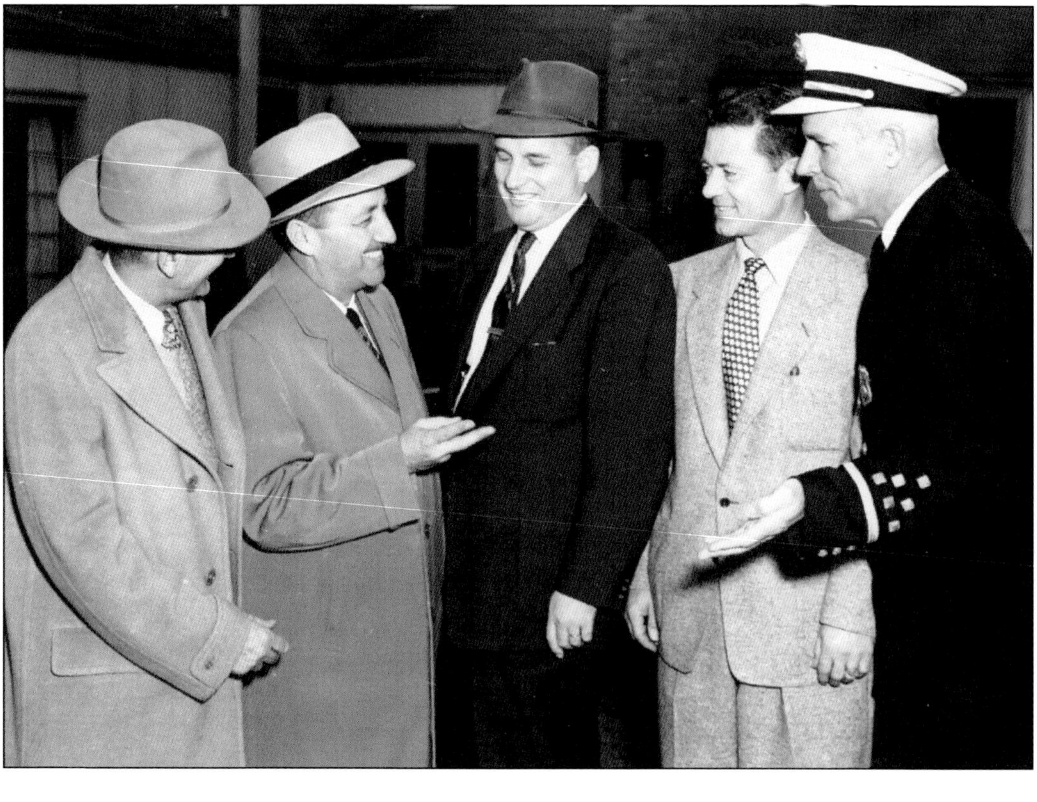

GIRLS DAY. Like Boys Day in Government, for many years the ladies had their day too. This 1962 photograph depicts students Pamela Schmoltz (left) and Karen Lancefield (right) on Girl's Day with Verne Tinnerstet of the chamber of commerce.

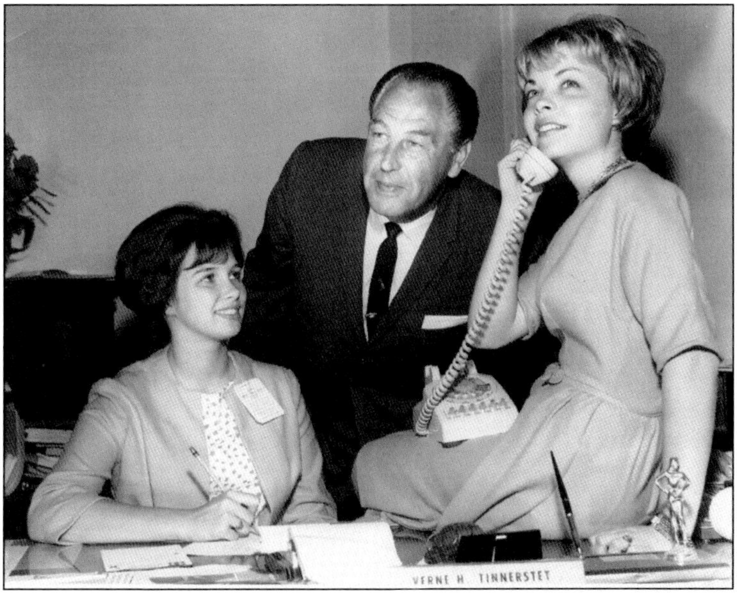

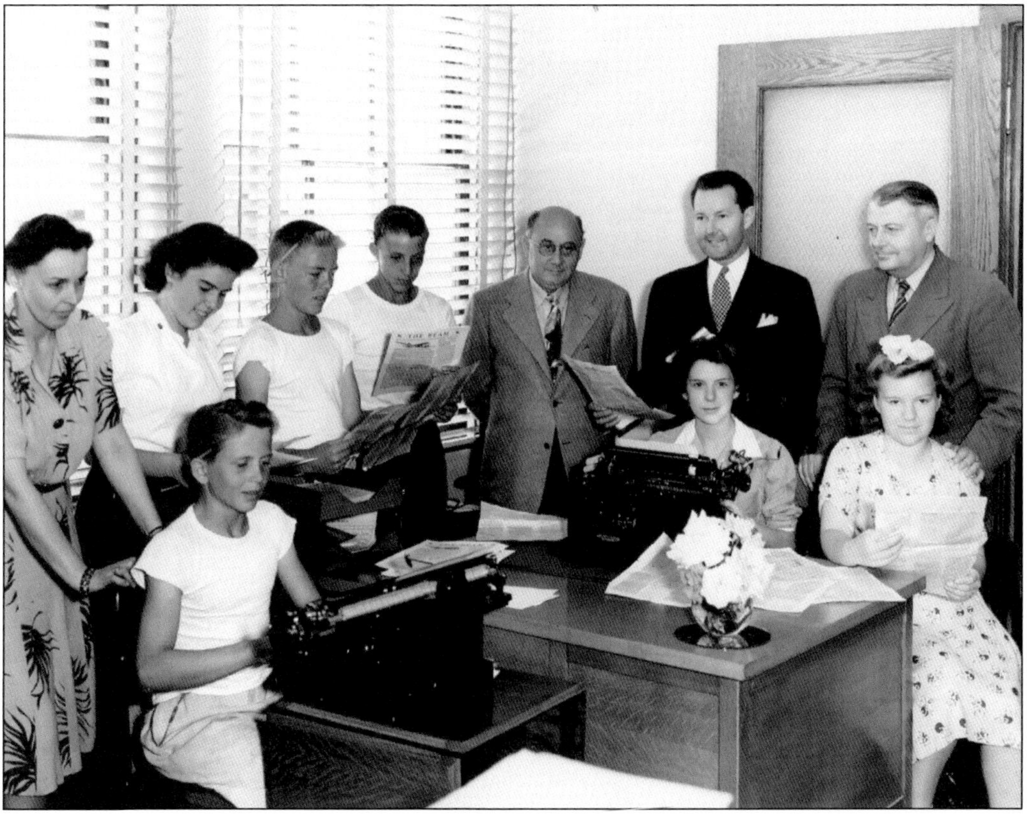

GAGE STUDENTS. This 1950 photograph depicts several Gage Junior High School students learning journalism. The students are reading a publication called the *Beam*. Mayor Hollis Peavy, at the back right, is standing next to Gage Junior High School principal Meldrim Burrill.

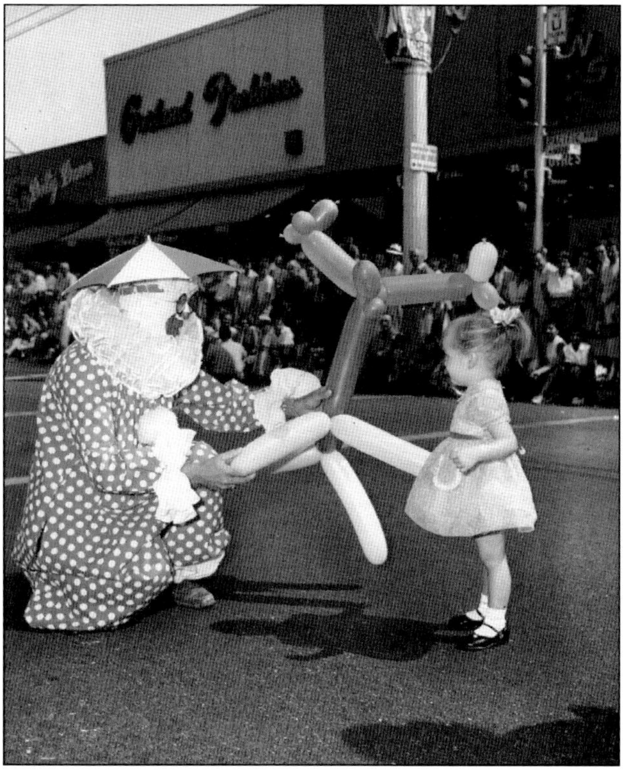

THE GOLDEN ANNIVERSARY CELEBRATION. The Huntington Park golden anniversary parade (left), entitled "50 Years of Progress," was held on September 15, 1956. The parade route traveled south on Pacific Boulevard from Slauson Avenue and east on Florence Avenue to Municipal Park (Salt Lake Park). Queen Glenda McQueen (below), astride a horse for one of her many Golden Anniversary photographs, rode a float in the parade with the other members of the court.

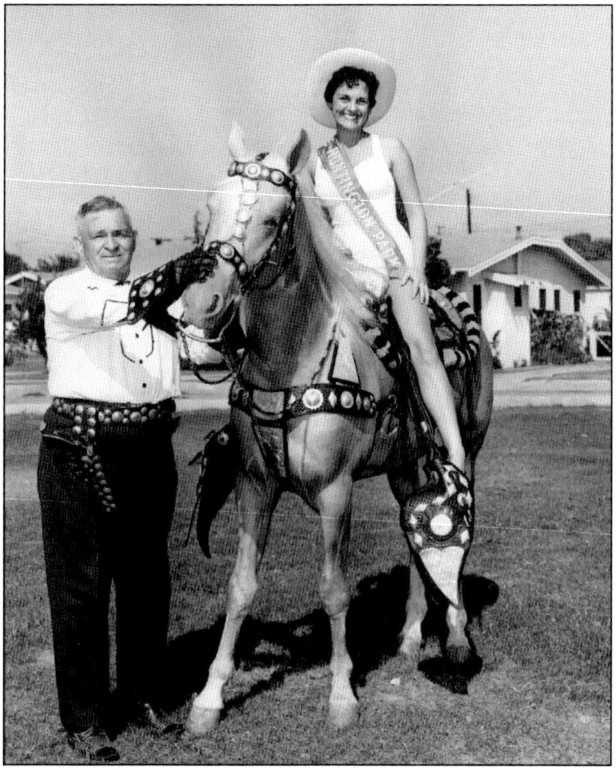

THE WARNER BROTHERS THEATER. The beautiful Warner's Theater at 6714 Pacific Boulevard opened on November 18, 1930 and featured Jack Warner Sr. himself. Movie stars in attendance included Noah Berry, Barbara Stanwyck, Joan Blondell, Walter Pidgeon, Douglas Fairbanks Jr., and Loretta Young among others. The plaque honoring Huntington Park World War I casualty Robert McColley, now on the front of city hall, was presented by the American Legion. The theater has fallen into disrepair and is now closed. Efforts are underway by a local historical group to save it.

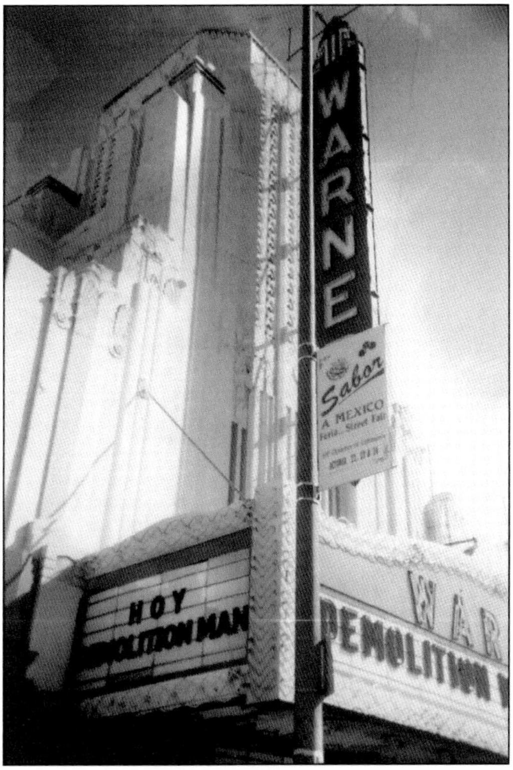

THE STAFF AT RAFFS. The staff at Raffs Jewelry in the 6300 block of Pacific Boulevard are preparing for their first "Midnight Sale" in Huntington Park. Owner Gerald Raff is on the right. Of note are the red polka dots and the man burning the midnight oil.

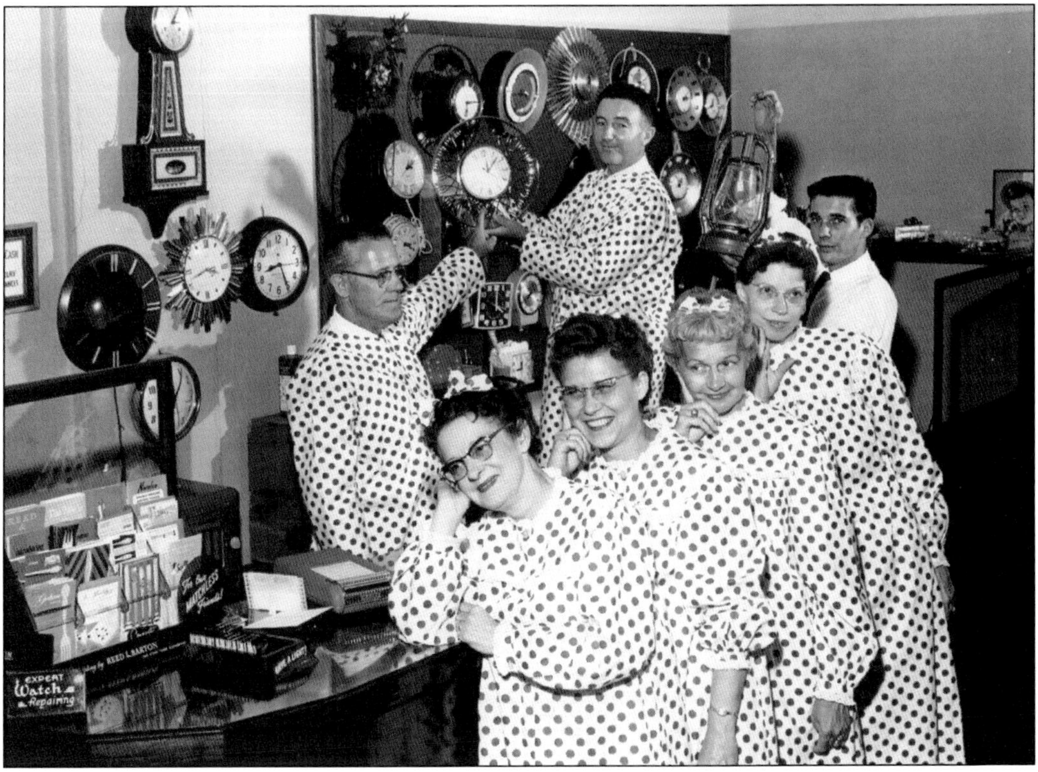

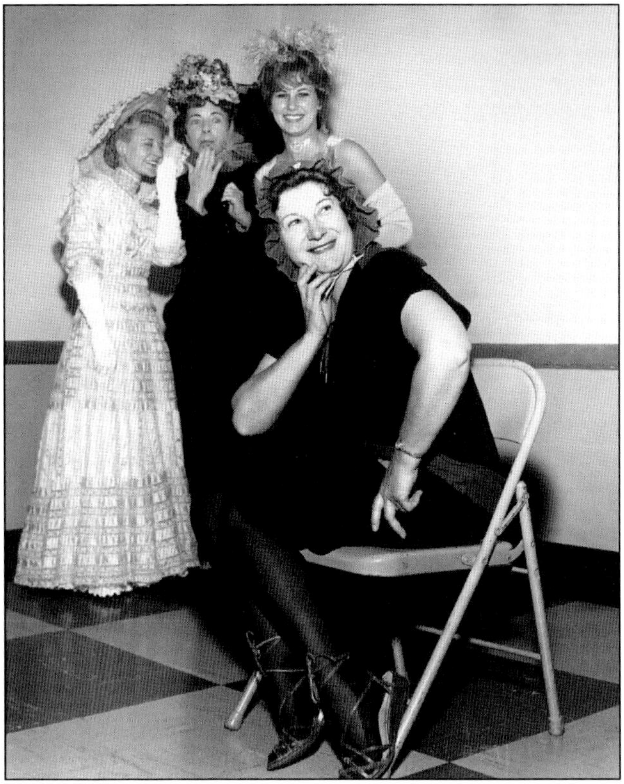

ARTS AND CRAFTS. This photograph was taken on May 29, 1961, at the Woman's Arts and Crafts Luncheon. Lucille Fields shows off her re-creation of shocking, turn-of-the-century swimwear while costumed friends look on in shock and awe.

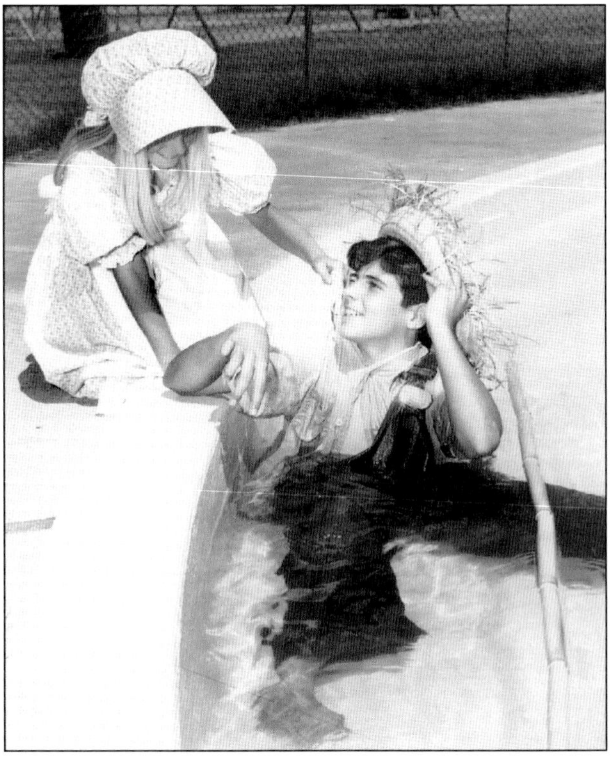

SADIE HAWKINS DAY. This photograph was taken at Municipal Park during the city's annual Sadie Hawkins Day celebration around 1960. A product of All Capps Lil Abner comic strip, Sadie Hawkins Day is the Saturday that follows November 9 each year. On this occasion, the women of "Dog Patch" pursued single men, and if caught, they had to marry. The wading pool located in the middle of the park is gone.

HUNTINGTON PARK HIGH. This *c.* 1960 photograph depicts two Huntington Park High School students with the school and classmates in the background. This image elicits visions of 1950s or 1960s family television show right down to the tennis shoes.

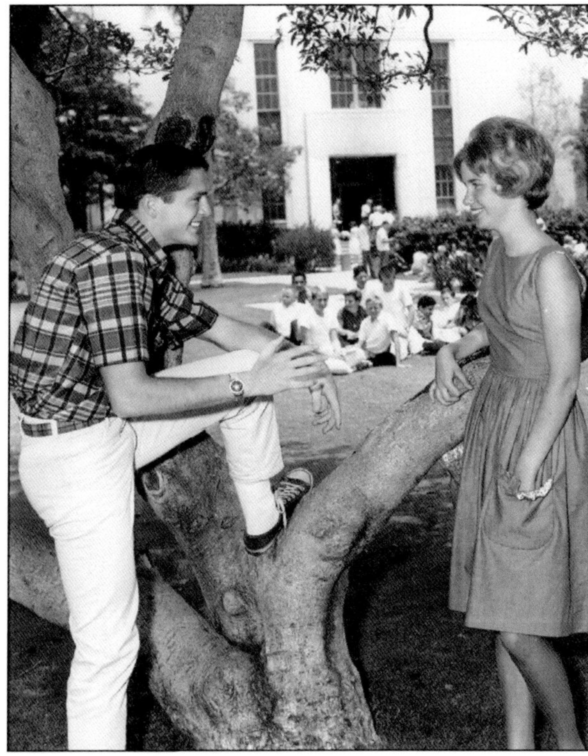

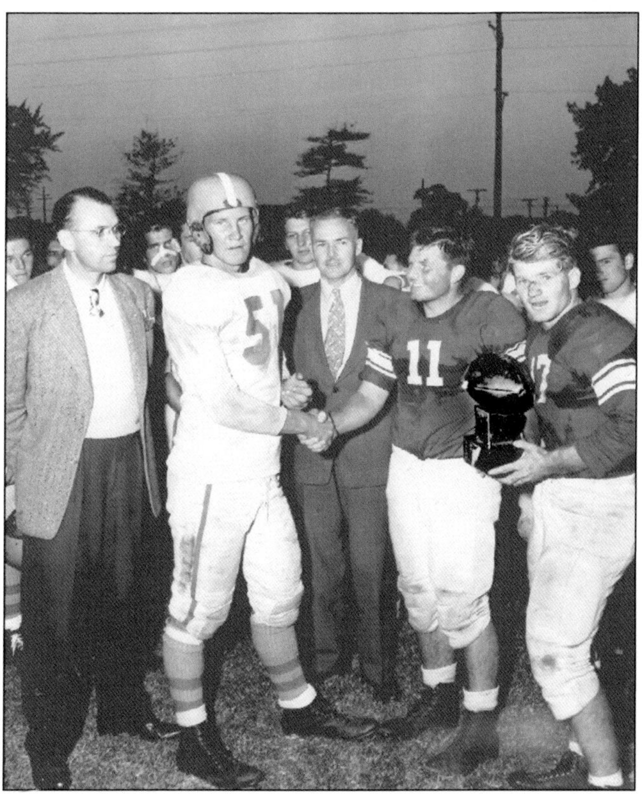

GRIDIRON RIVALRY. This photograph was taken in 1947 following the annual South Gate/Huntington Park football game. The rivalry between these two schools is among the greatest in the area. Here South Gate prepares to present the perpetual trophy to Huntington Park's No. 51, Harold Miller, seen here with Huntington Park principal Everett Chaffee (left). Huntington Park won the game 13-6. Note that there are no face guards to protect against subsequent injuries.

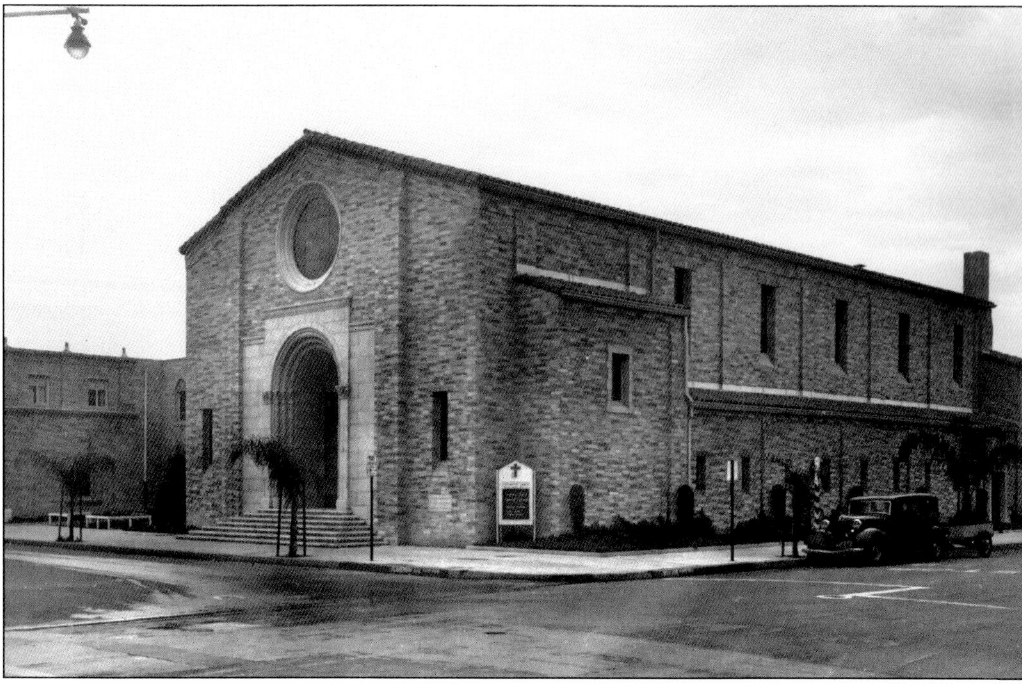

Churches Grow. As Huntington Park and its population grew, so did the size of the religious congregations. In 1937, the Baptist church, first built in 1905, was reconstructed and expanded (above) at Clarendon and Rugby Avenues. St. Mathias Catholic Church, pictured below in the 1970s, is located at Florence Avenue and Mission Place. Both churches built large adjacent schools that are still in operation, providing Huntington Park citizens with alternatives to public schools.

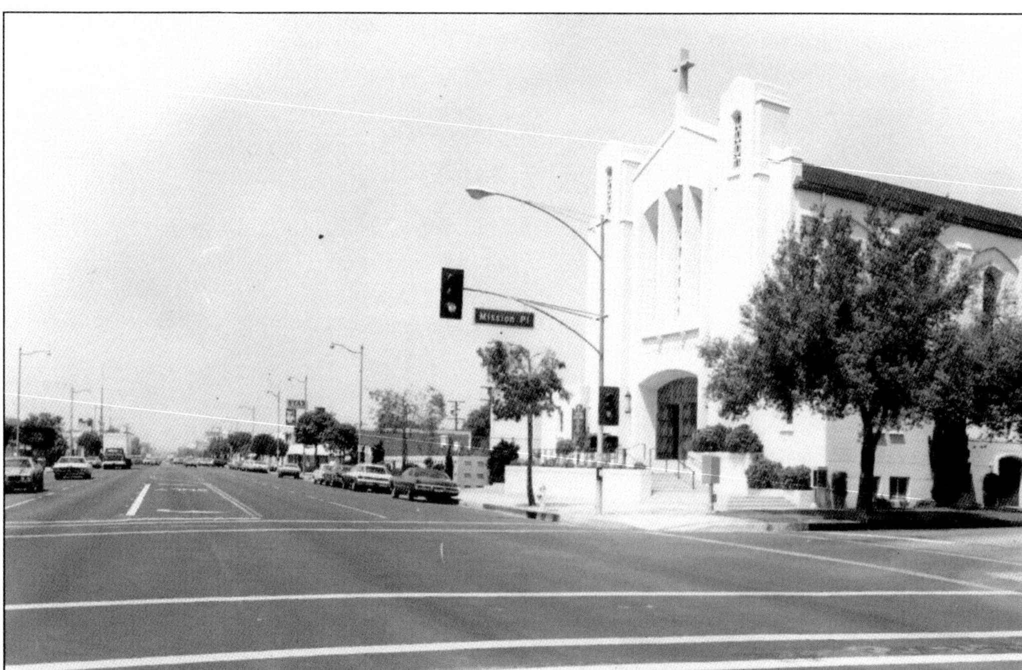

GRAND MARSHALL ERIK ESTRADA. Among the grand marshalls of the fabulous Huntington Park Christmas Parade was Erik Estrada, who took his turn in 1978. He was at the height of his American acting career at this point, starring in the television show *CHiPs*. He starred in Mexican soap operas for several years and is now in a comeback on American television.

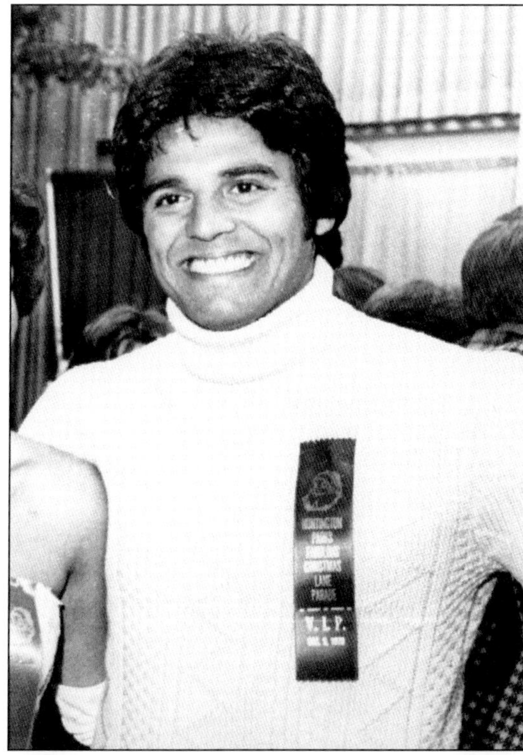

TOM BRADLEY. Huntington Park councilmen Tom Jackson (right) and Bernard Parks (left) are seen here with Los Angeles City mayor Tom Bradley at a "Hughes for Assembly" function. Tom Bradley served as mayor for five terms from 1973 to 1993 and was the second African American mayor. He was an unsuccessful candidate for governor two times.

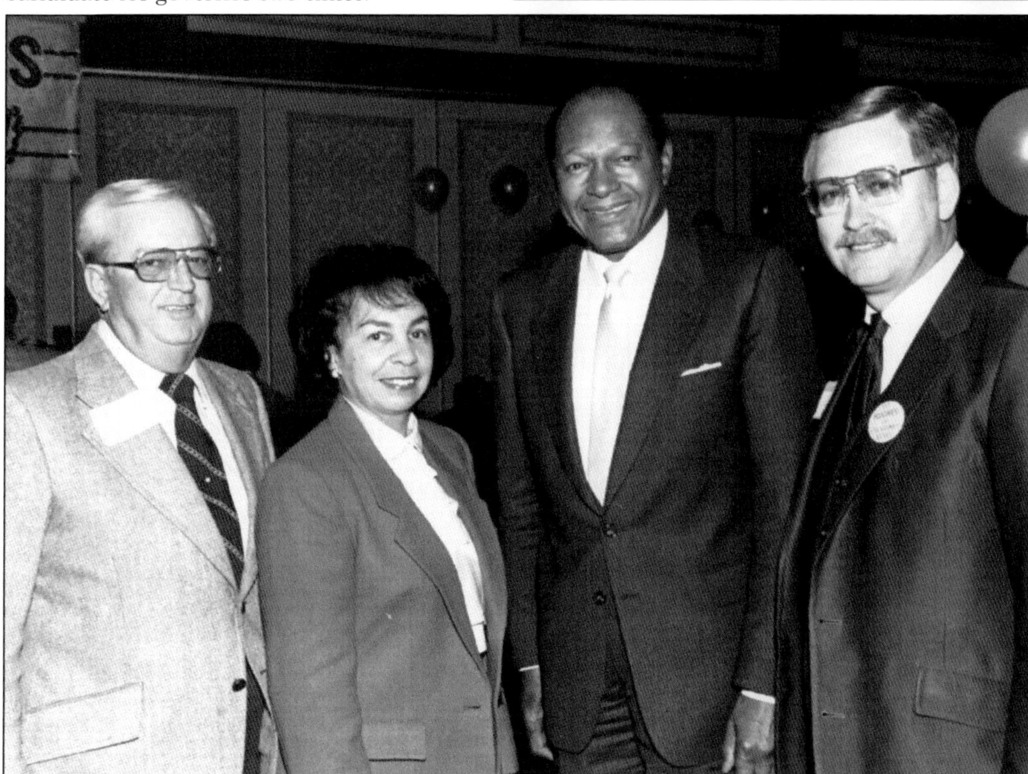

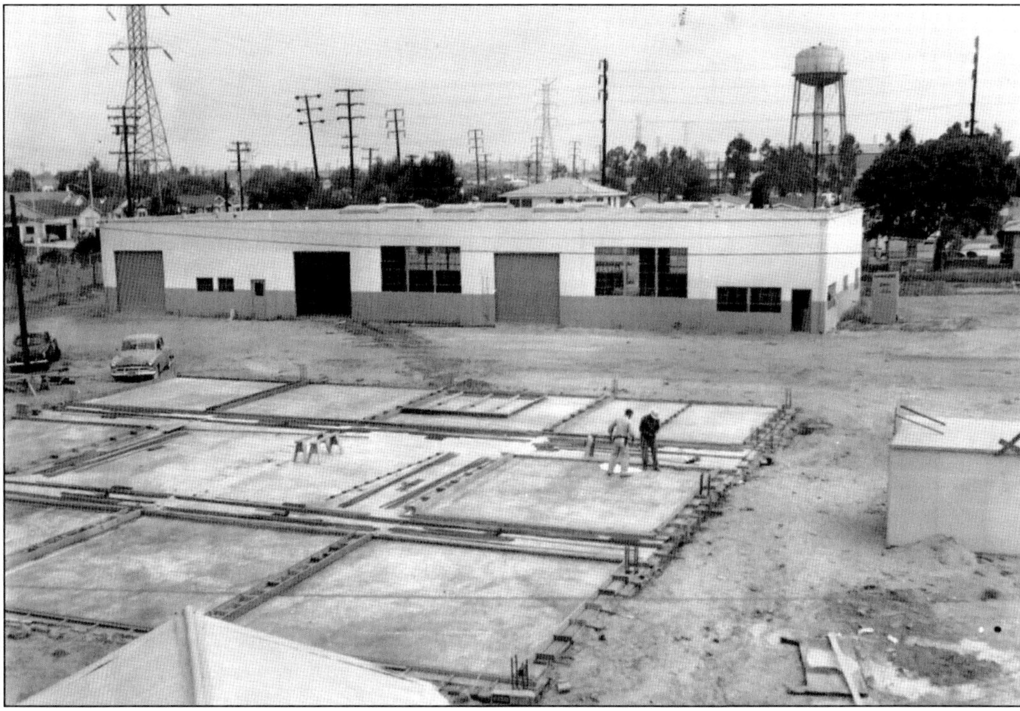

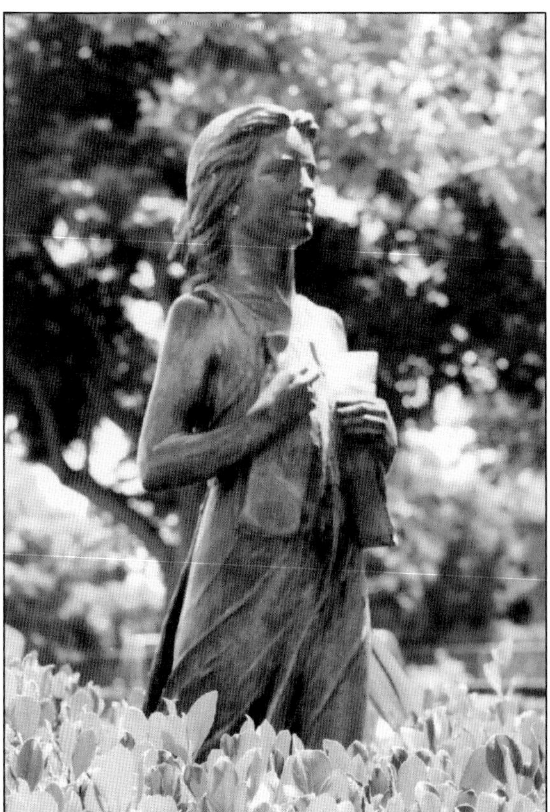

THE CITY YARDS. A growing city means a growing infrastructure. Prior to this photograph, the Public Works City Yards was mostly metal buildings. In 1957, the facility was expanded to include automotive repairs, warehouses, a water department, and administration facilities. Pictured here is the foundation of today's warehouse. Neil Poole, a 30-year city employee, is now the director of Public Works City Yards.

THE BRONZE LADY. Seemly forgotten is a beautiful bronze statue in Miles Avenue Park honoring veterans of World War I. The statue was cast in 1918 by sculptor Burt W. Johnson and was originally in front of Patriotic Hall. Dedicated in 1920 and titled *The Children's Tribute to World War One Heroes*, the child holds the caps of a sailor and a doughboy to her chest. The model for the statue was Frances Case Parker.

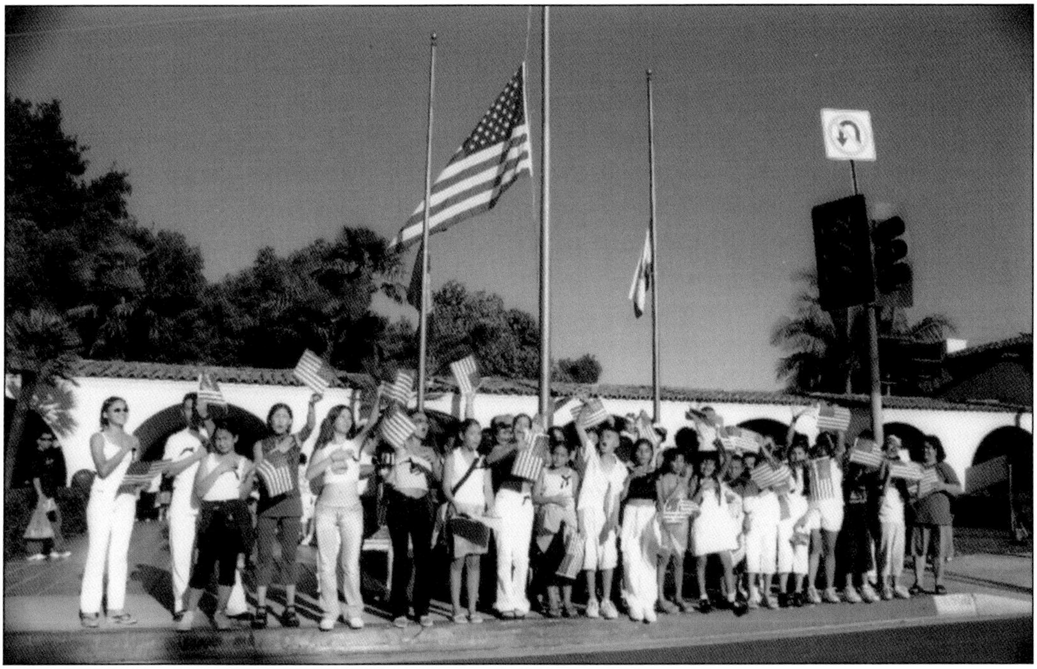

SEPTEMBER 11 TRIBUTE. This photograph was taken in front of Huntington Park City Hall on September 15, 2001, four days after the World Trade Center attack. With the flags at half-mast, and the skies free of air traffic, these Huntington Park girls show their patriotism.

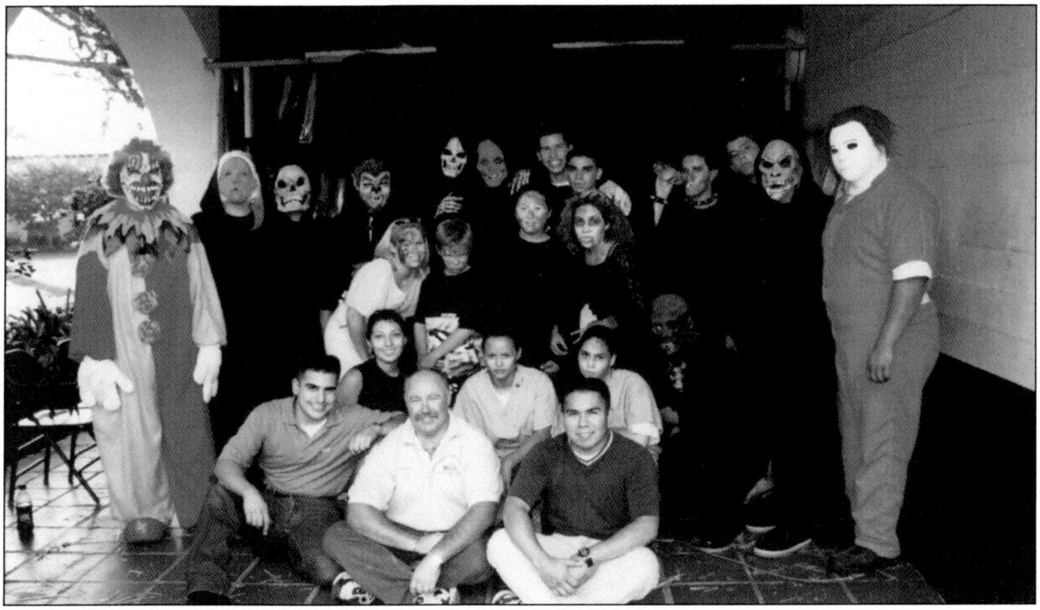

THE HAUNTED HOUSE. Each year for nearly the last 10 years, the Huntington Park Police Department and the parks and recreation department sponsor a haunted house in front of city hall. The event attracts thousands who come to be frightened. Entry is free, usually with a donated food item that is later used by the police department for their annual Christmas and food giveaways for needy local families. Officers Jose Cisneros (front left) and William Wallace (front center) are two of the founders of the event.

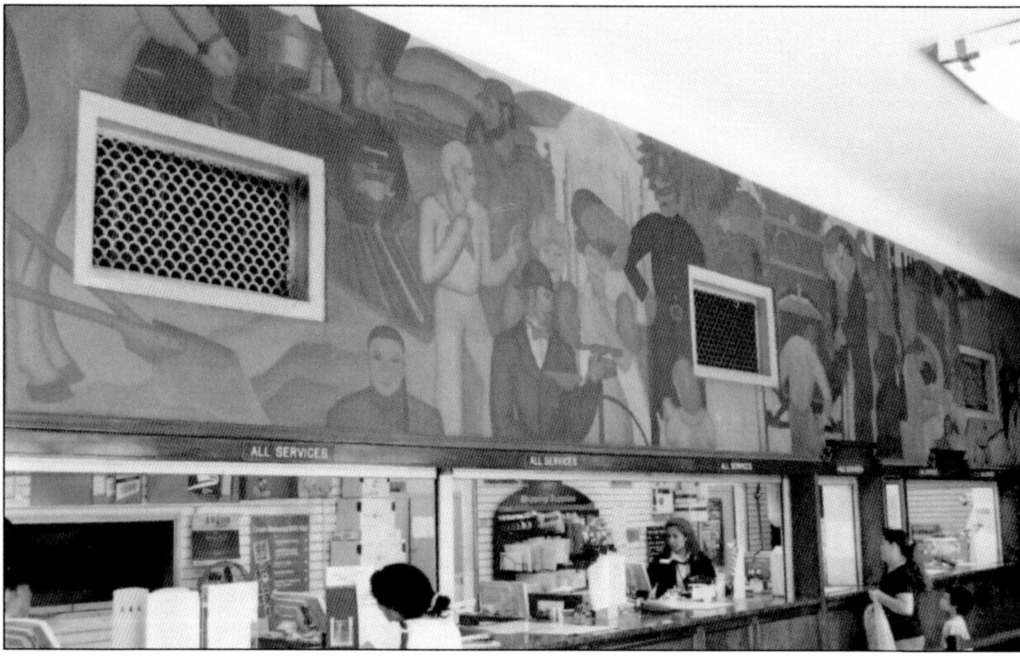

The Historic Post Office. In 1935, Huntington Park's post office was moved from Rugby Avenue to the southeast corner of Seville and Zoe Avenues. After its construction, a mural was commissioned by the Federal Art Project for its interior walls. The Federal Art Project was intended to provide employment for Depression-era artists. Painter Norman Stiles Chamberlin took two years to complete the extensive mural titled *The History of California*. The six panels feature Native Americans, Spanish friars, early settlers, and the transition into the new industrial age. Unusual for the time, people of all races, including African Americans, were shown working side by side. Efforts are underway to find help preserving the beautiful mural.

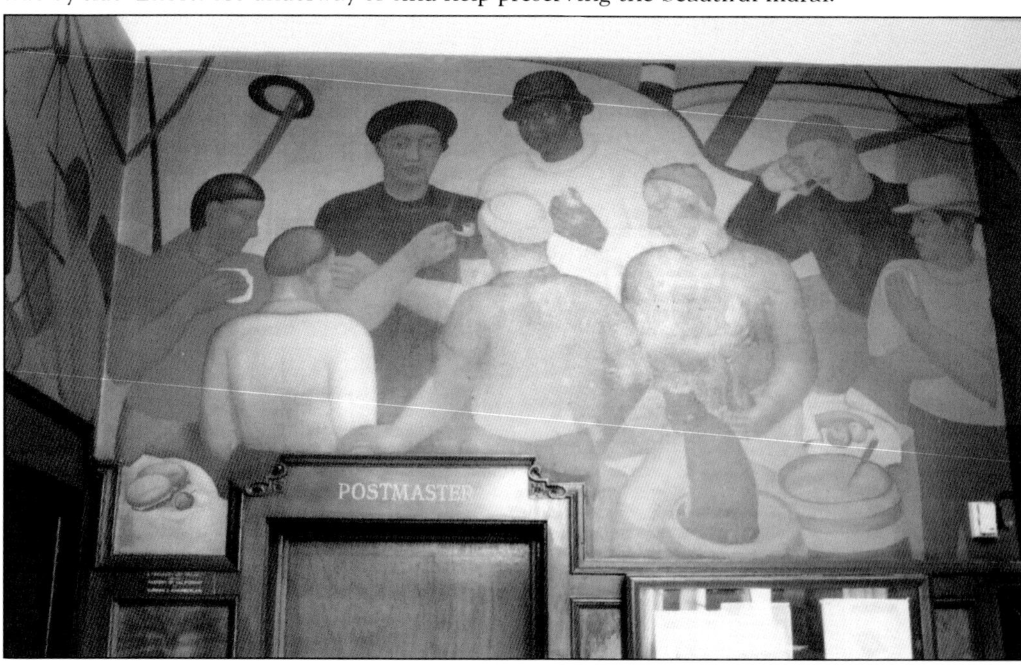

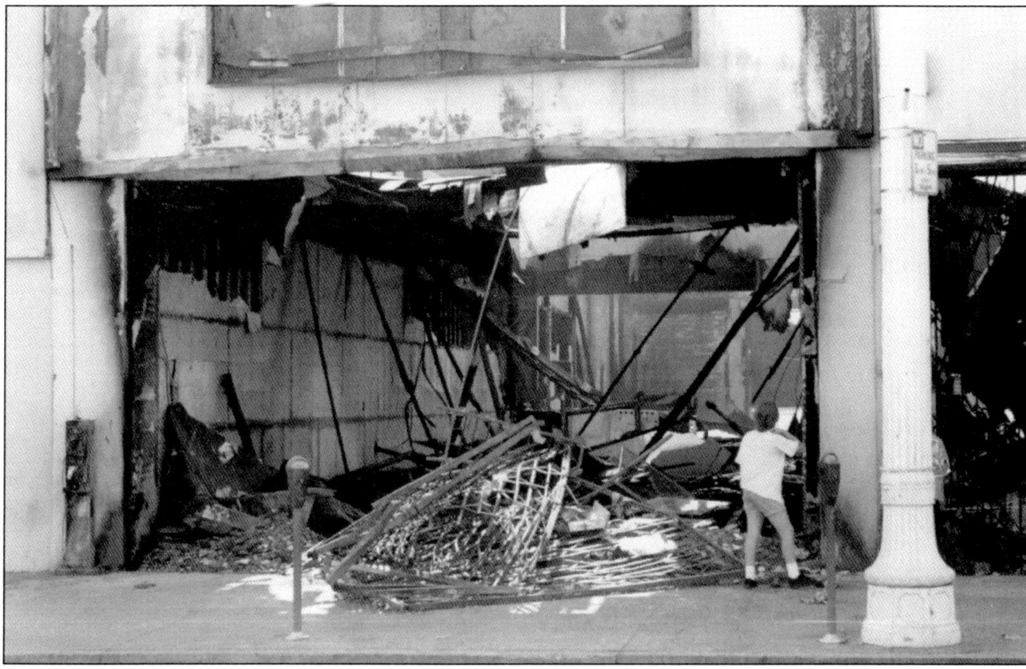

THE LOS ANGELES RIOTS. In 1992, following the not guilty verdicts of four Los Angeles Police Department officers in the videotaped arrest of Rodney King, violence broke out in Los Angeles. Some of that violence did reach Huntington Park. Although the police department defended the city valiantly, incidents of looting and arson did occur. The National Guard moved in, taking over the basement of the police department as a command post and Miles Avenue Park as a staging area. Pictured above are two businesses on Pacific Boulevard south of Clarendon Avenue that were looted and burned. The image below depicts National Guard units with their helicopter at the rear of the public library on Miles Avenue.

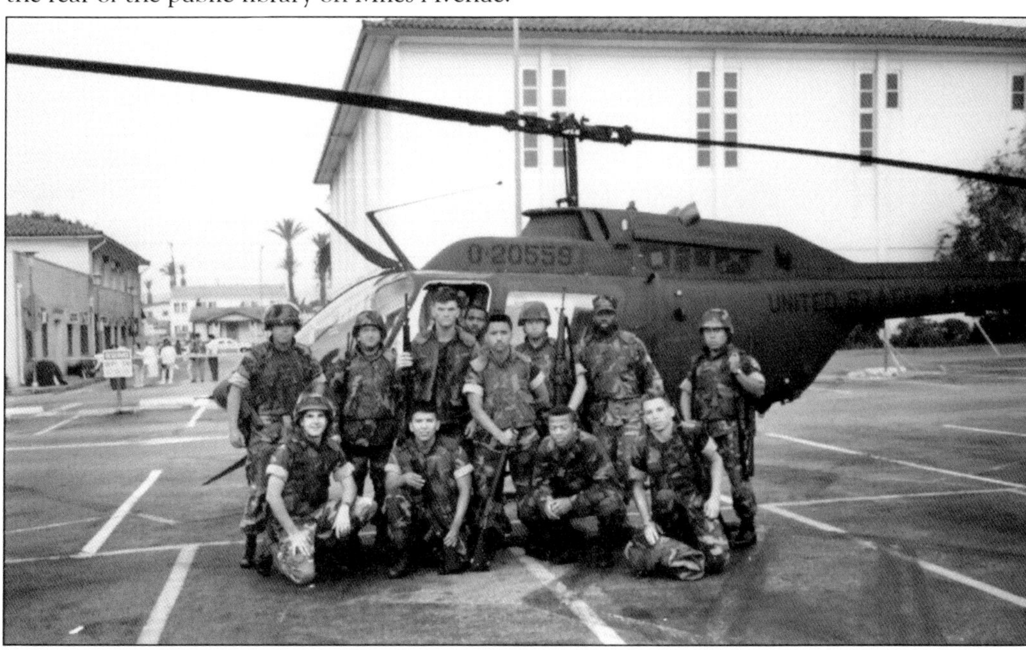

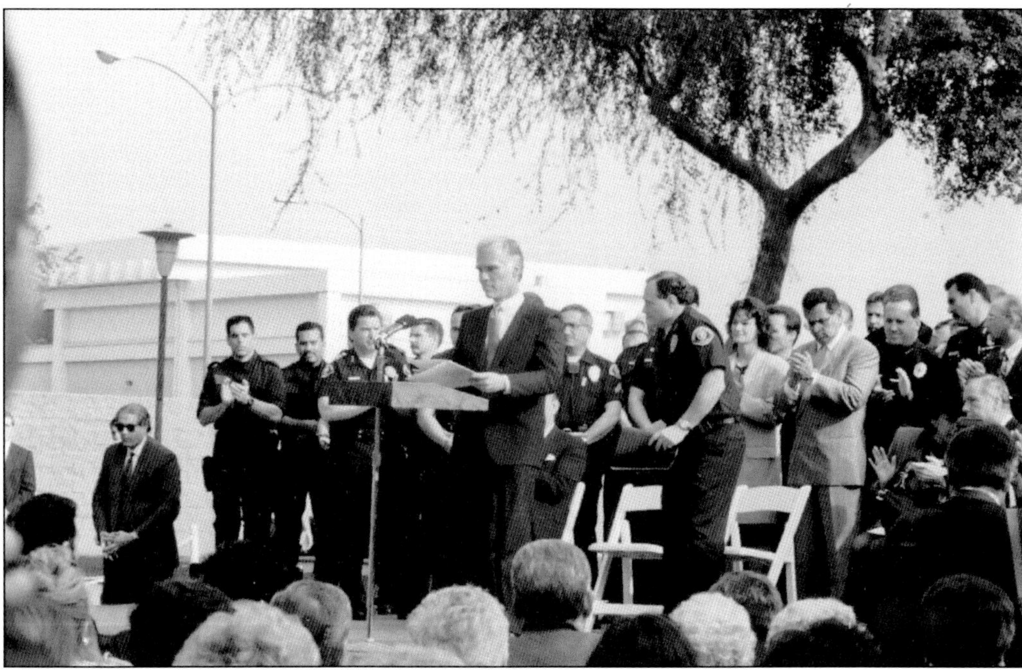

GOVERNOR'S VISIT. On January 16, 1996, California governor Pete Wilson (above) visited the city of Huntington Park. The purpose of his visit was to deliver a speech regarding gang problems in the Los Angeles area as well as all of the state of California. He is pictured here during the presentation with city and local law enforcement officials at his side. Of note, the man in the grey suit is Raul Perez, the first Latino mayor of Huntington Park. During this same time period, attorney general Dan Lungren (below) also spoke in the city decrying gang violence.

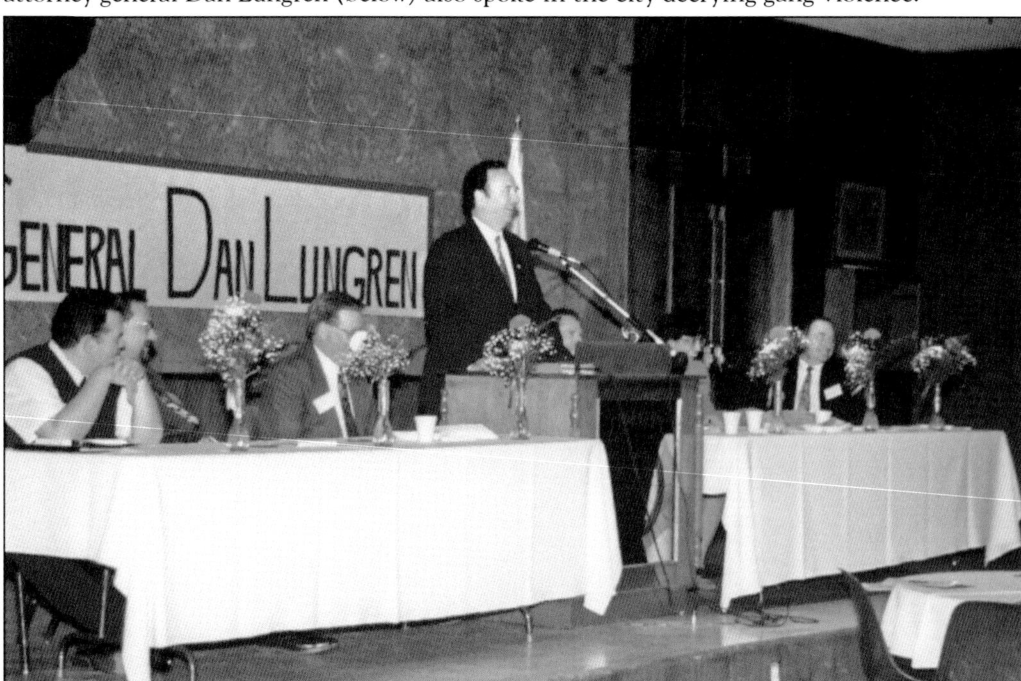

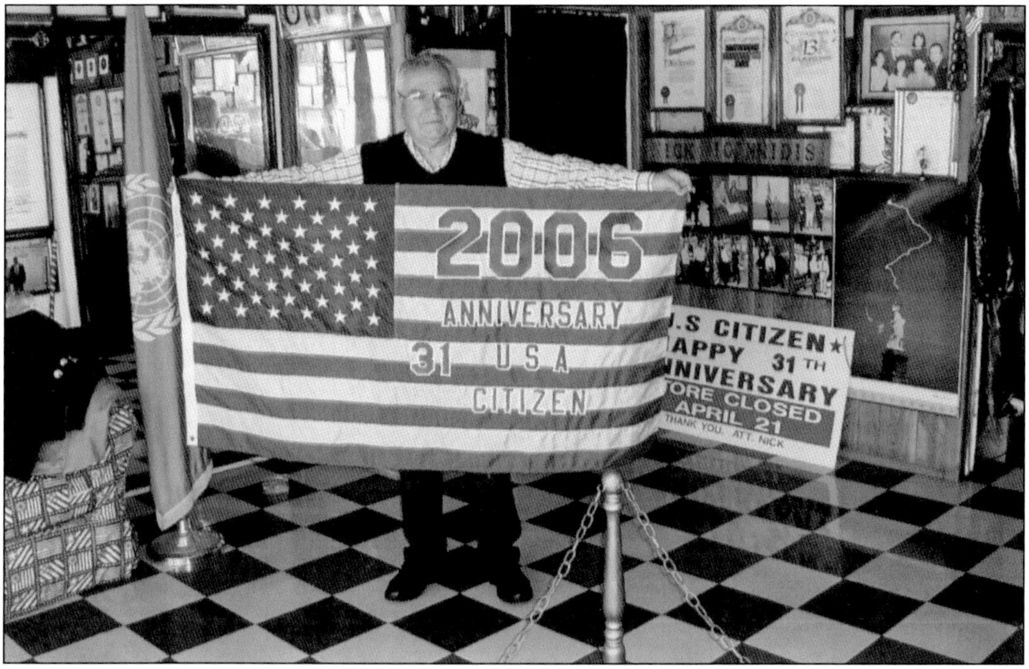

"NICK THE GREEK" IN AMERICA. Nick Ioannidis immigrated from his native Greece to the United States. He opened a small, now patriotically decorated, tailor shop at Gage and Seville Avenues and pursued the American dream. In 1965, Ioannidis, known as Nick the Greek in America, proudly became an American citizen, and he has been celebrating that honor every day since. Nick's enthusiasm is reflected in his efforts in the founding of Public Law 100-62 in 1987, proclaiming October 28 each year as National Immigrants Day. Nick makes beautiful custom men's suits.

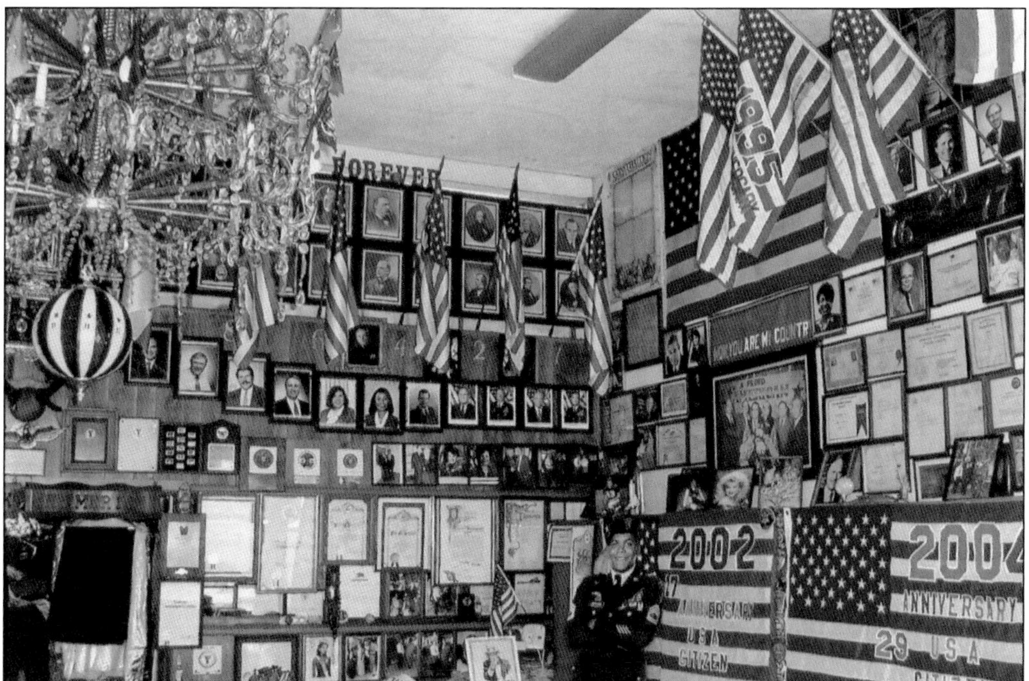

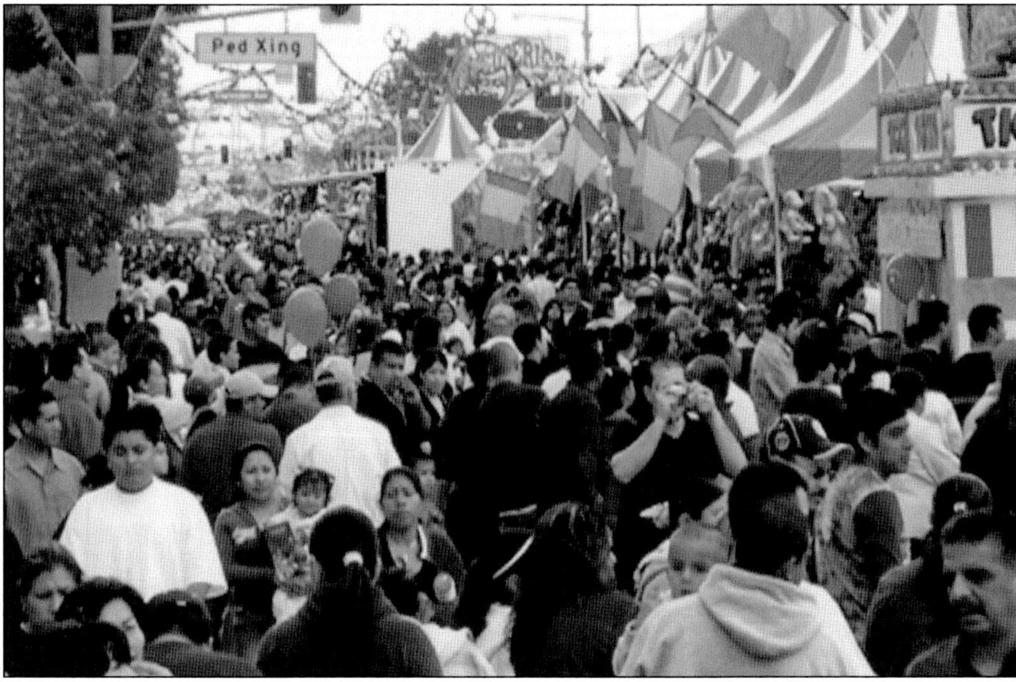

STREET FAIRS. Each year, Pacific Boulevard hosts two street fairs sponsored by the Huntington Park Chamber of Commerce. Carnival Primavera (spring carnival) is held for three days in April, where an estimated 350,000 people attend. The Sabor de Mexico (flavor of Mexico) is held for three days in September and nearly a half-million people attend. The fairs feature food, rides, and big-name Latin entertainment. They are intended to promote the central business district and are the brainchild of chamber of commerce executive director Dante D'Eramo.

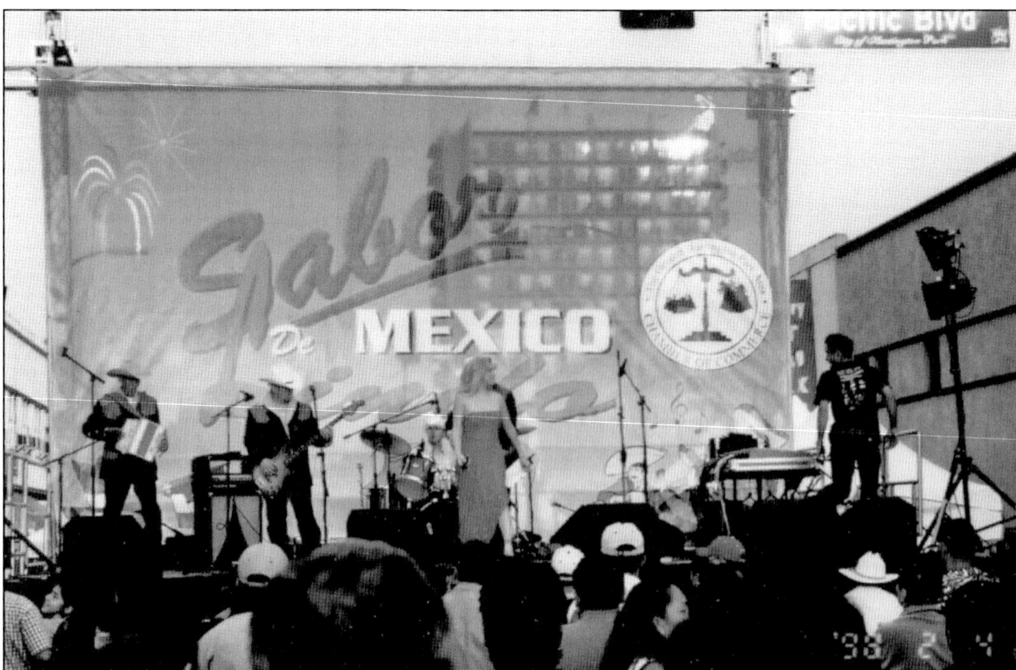

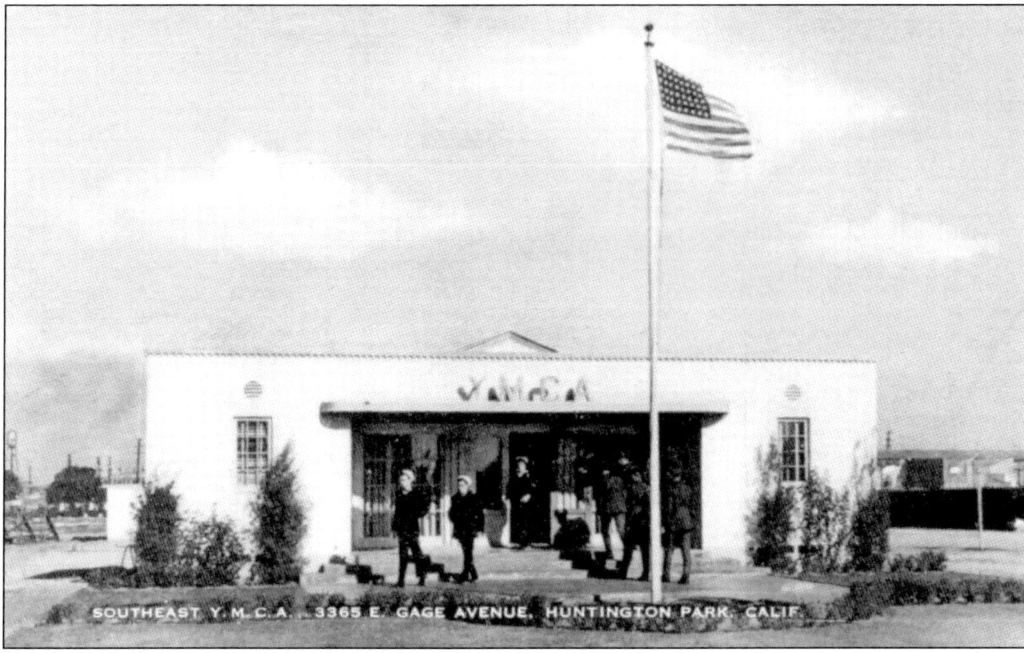

THE YMCA. The YMCA is more than 160 years old. It was first established in Huntington Park in 1928 through the high school under the guidance of George Hoyt. Local businessmen, including Maurice Sopp, and educators contributed to its growth and development. Pictured above is the Huntington Park YMCA at 3365 Gage Avenue around World War II. Generous local businessmen Nick Alexander of Alexander BMW (located on Alameda Street in the wholesale district) and Randy Sopp of Sopp Chevrolet are two of the YMCA's greatest supporters. Sopp has been chairman of the YMCA since 1990. In recent years, Alexander and Sopp created the Alexander Youth Center, pictured below, on Seville Avenue. The center provides after-school activities and day care, among other services, for the community's children.

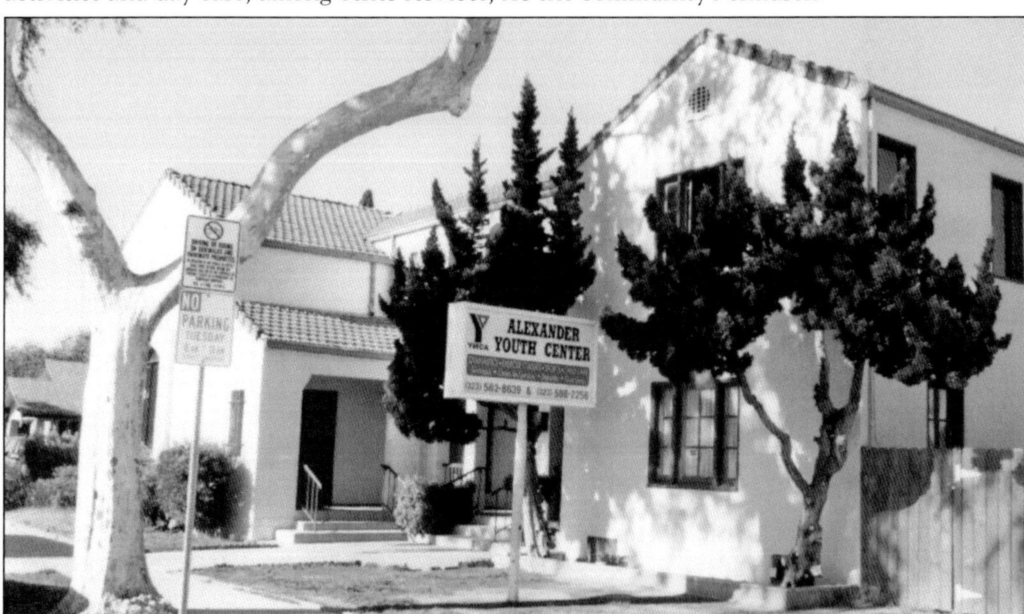

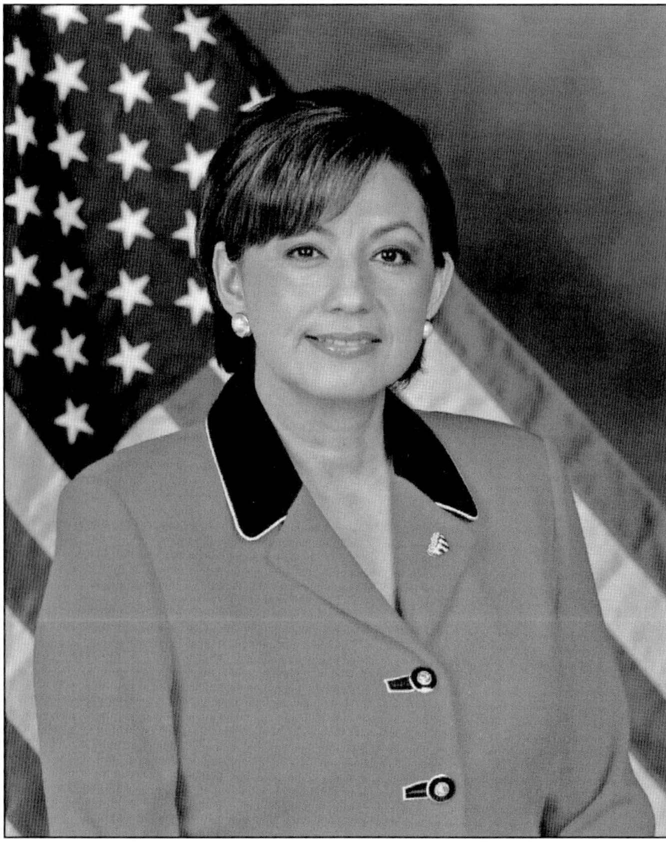

Rosario Marin. Rosario Marin (left) was the 41st treasurer of the United States from August 21, 2001, to June 30, 2003, appointed by Pres. George Bush. She graduated from Huntington Park High School in 1976. Rosario was elected to the Huntington Park City Council in 1994 and served to 2001, including a term as mayor. On January 31, 2006, Gov. Arnold Schwarzenegger appointed Marin as secretary of the State and Consumer Services Agency (below). This branch of government is responsible for civil-rights enforcement and consumer protection and licensing for various professions. In 2003, Marin cofounded the National Association of Latina Leaders, promoting the rights of Hispanic women in the United States.

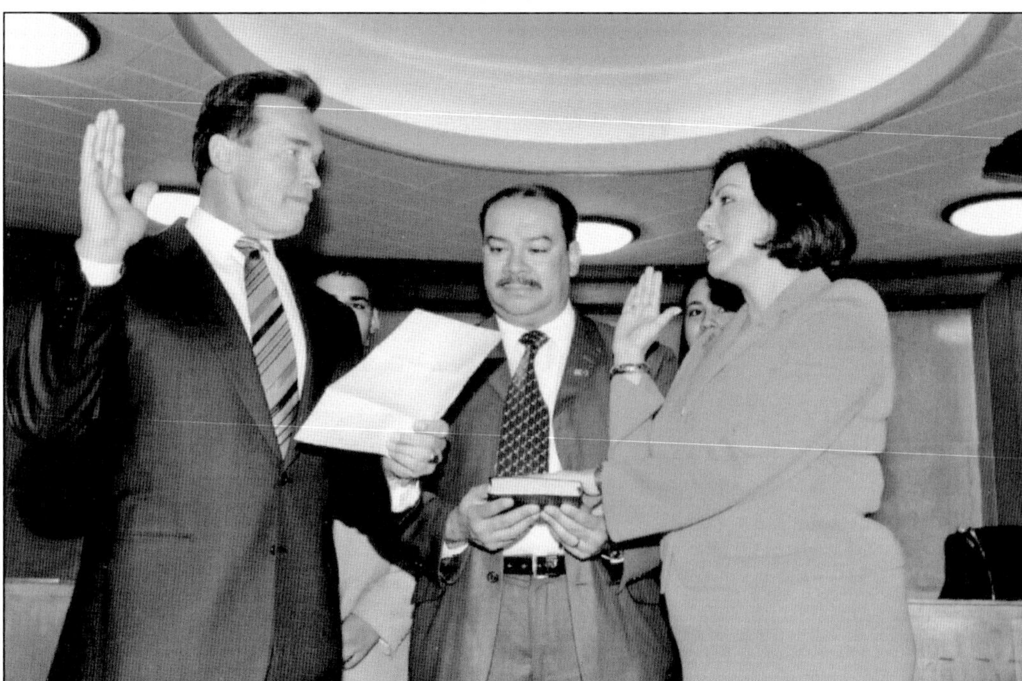

Seven

The Centennial

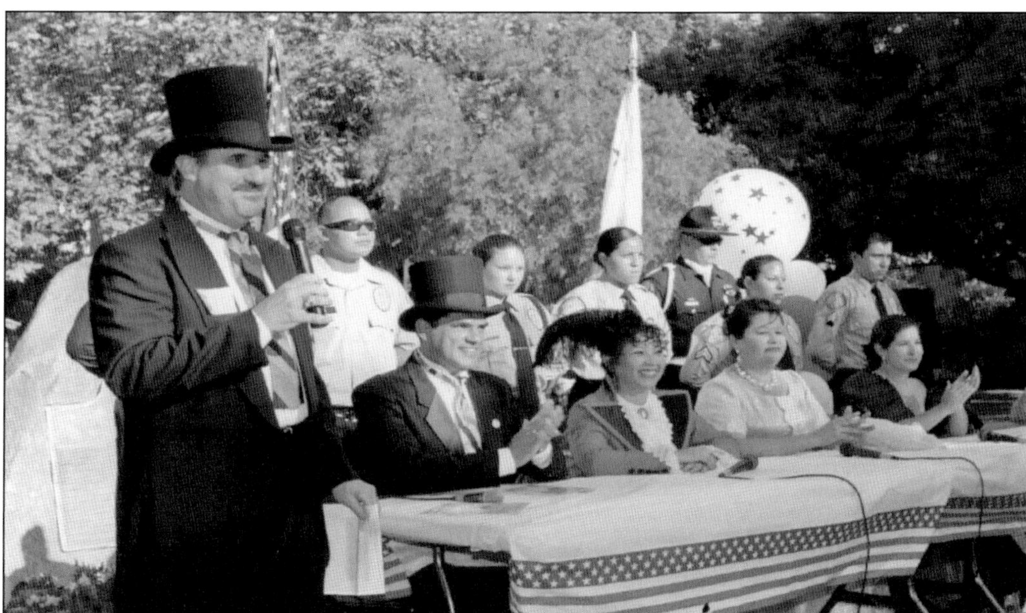

The Centennial Celebration. On September 6, 2006, the city of Huntington Park celebrated its 100th birthday. Like the golden anniversary, many events were planned for the celebration. Among the proceedings, after a horse-drawn carriage ride around the city, the city council reenacted the first council meeting. City manager Greg Korduner is dressed here in period costume, addressing the crowd that gathered to watch in the park next to city hall.

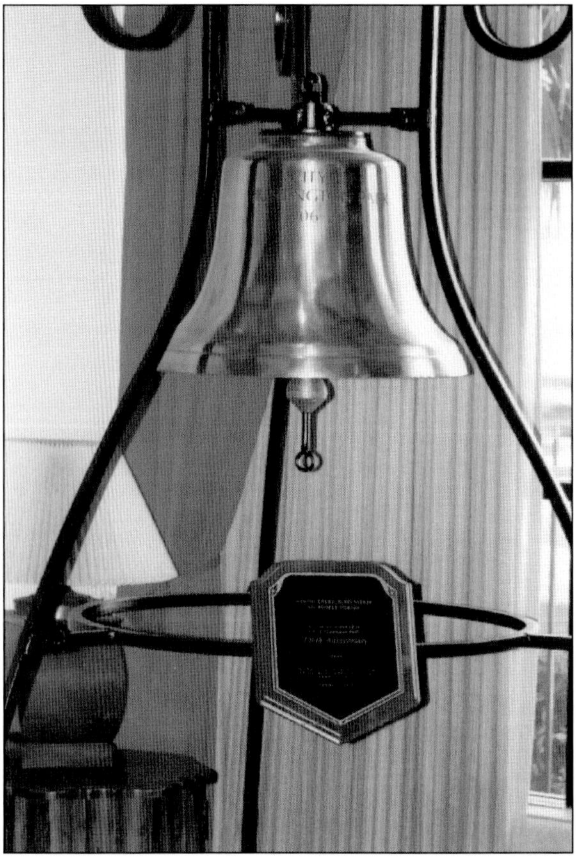

THE BELL. As part of the celebration, a brass bell was commissioned, commemorating Huntington Park's 100 years. The bell, with a plaque stating, "Where there is no Vision the People Perish," is now in the lobby of city hall for all to see. Commemorative coins, T-shirts, pins, and other promotional items were sold to raise money for centennial events. The police department also issued a special badge worn during the centennial year.

CENTENNIAL BALL. A formal ball was held at Leonardo's on Alameda Street that also celebrated the centennial. Pictured is the Huntington Park City Council and Sharon Lee, owner of the Pacific Boulevard shop Fotorama and president of the chamber of commerce. A country picnic was also held at Salt Lake Park, featuring live entertainment, games, contests, kiddie rides, and lots of food.

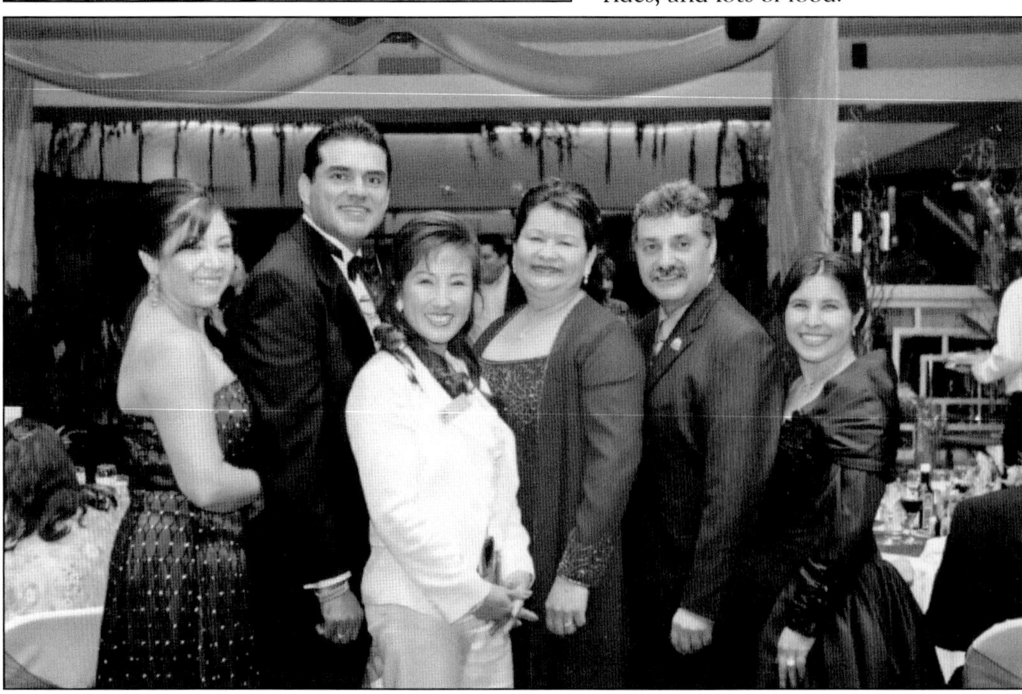

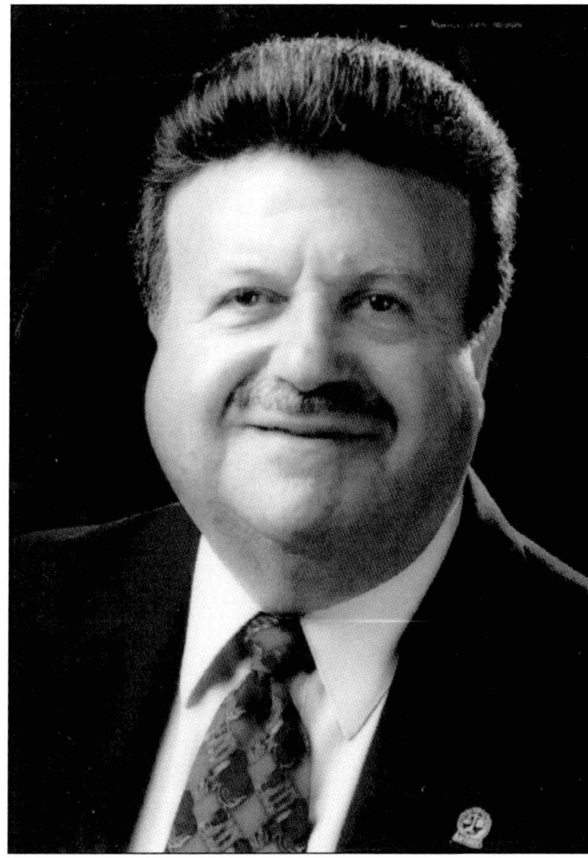

DANTE D'ERAMO. Dante D'Eramo (right) became general manager of the chamber of commerce in 1976 after working as a reporter for a local newspaper. He has actively promoted the city's businesses for 30 years and now holds the title of executive director. D'Eramo has had a direct influence on the revitalization of Pacific Boulevard and is responsible for or contributed to the success of events such as the street fairs, block watchers, fireworks shows, the parade, and sister city programs. Among his events, Dante works with the Los Angeles County Fire Department to bring the Easter Bunny (below) to schoolchildren.

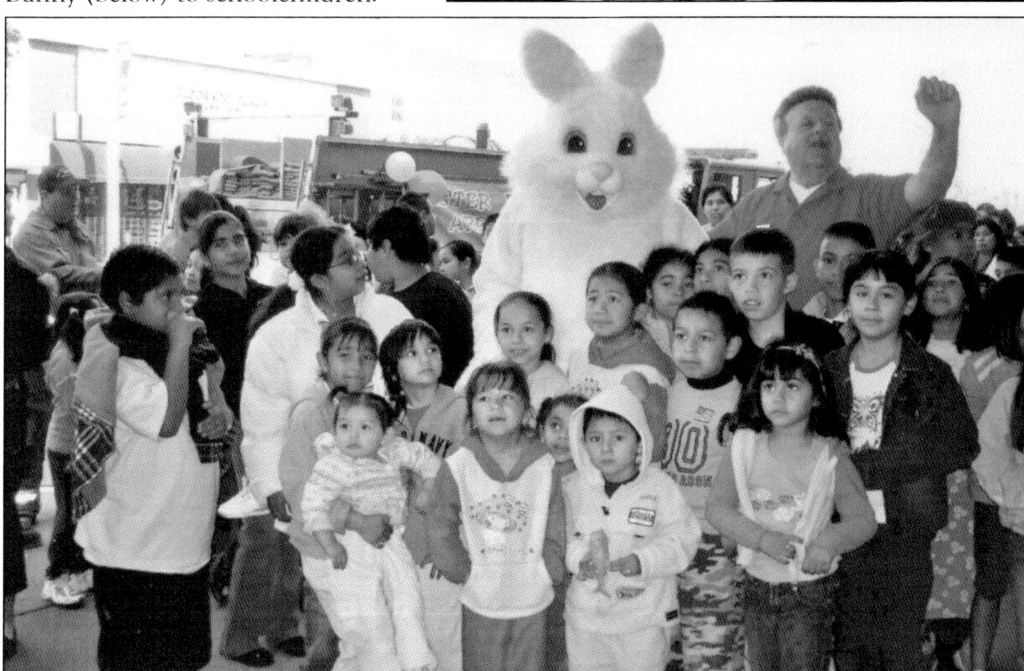

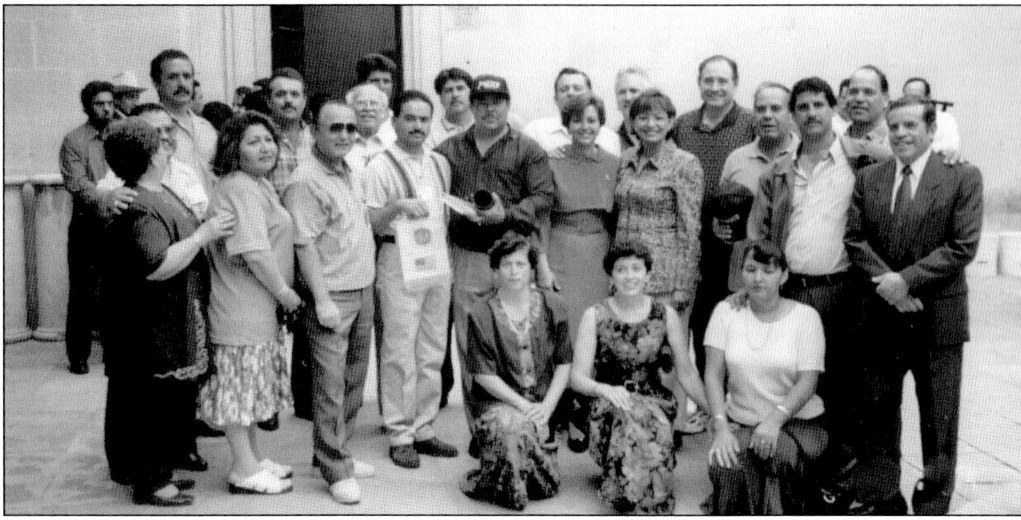

SISTER CITIES. Huntington Park has four sister cities in Mexico: San Julian, Yahualica, Puebla, and Playa de Rosarito. Sister Cities is a program for cultural exchange originated by Pres. Dwight D. Eisenhower. In this 1999 photograph, Huntington Park representatives visit San Julian, Huntington Park's first sister city. Huntington Park has donated equipment, such as police cars and computers, to its sisters to the south. The fountain in front of city hall was donated by the city of Yahualica. People such as past Huntington Park Sister Cities president and Sopp Chevrolet employee Betty Monroy and current president Andy Molina have generously donated their time to ensure the program's success.

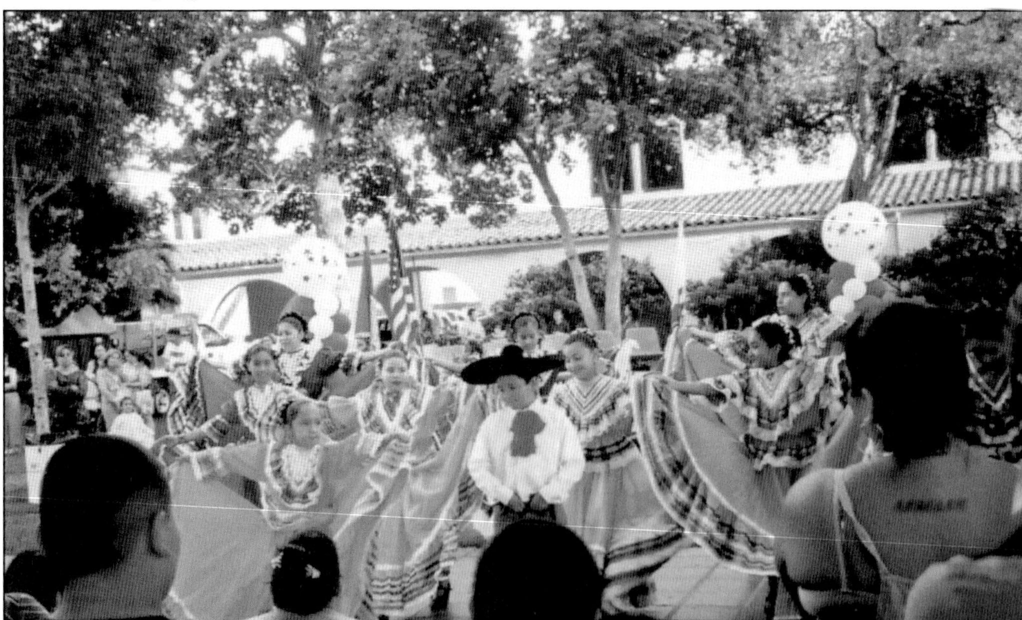

EMBRACING THE CULTURE. Pictured here during the Huntington Park 99th birthday party are Folklorico dancers sponsored by the Police Activity League. The dancers perform often at many city events. Huntington Park embraces the culture diversity of its residents. Events such as Sabor de Mexico and the El Grito allow residents to express their rich Latino culture.

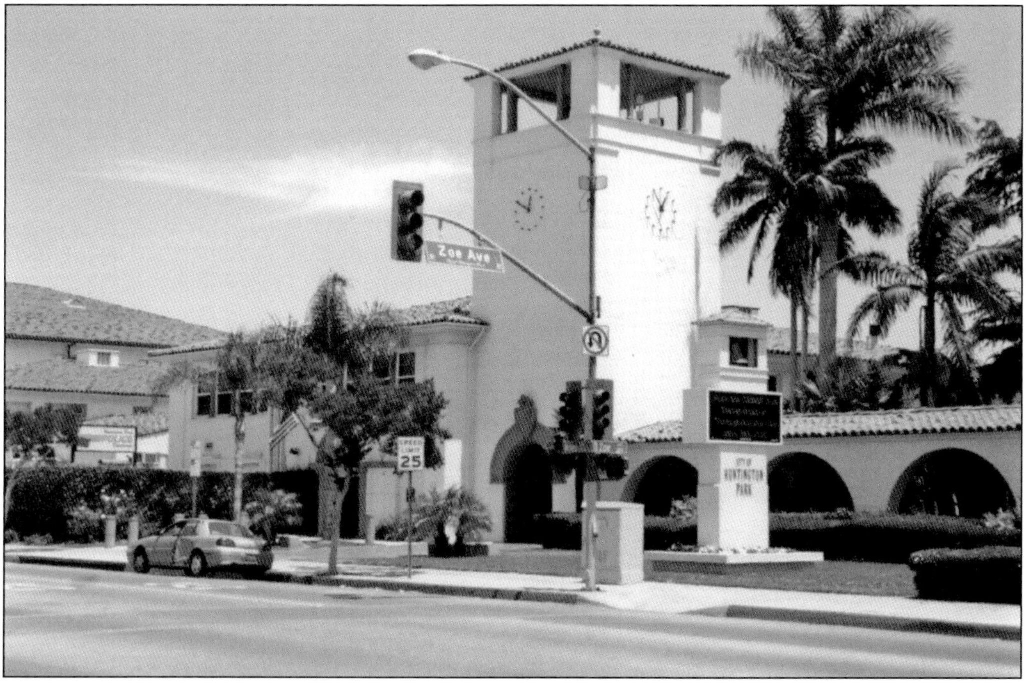

THE FUTURE OF THE POLICE DEPARTMENT. Pictured above is the front of the modern Huntington Park Police Department facility as it appears today. Chief Michael Trevis, at right dressed in a centennial celebration costume, took the helm in 2006 after being chief of police for the City of Bell for many years. Along with assistant chiefs Cosme Lozano and Paul Wadley, he will provide direction for the police department into the beginning of the next 100 years of the city's history. The Huntington Police Department continues to emphasize a partnership with its community and remains "dedicated to service through excellence in performance."

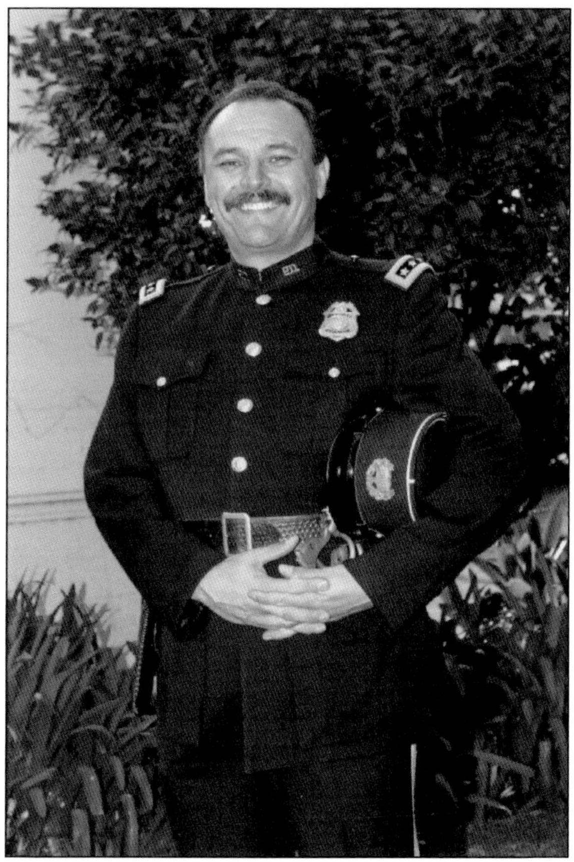

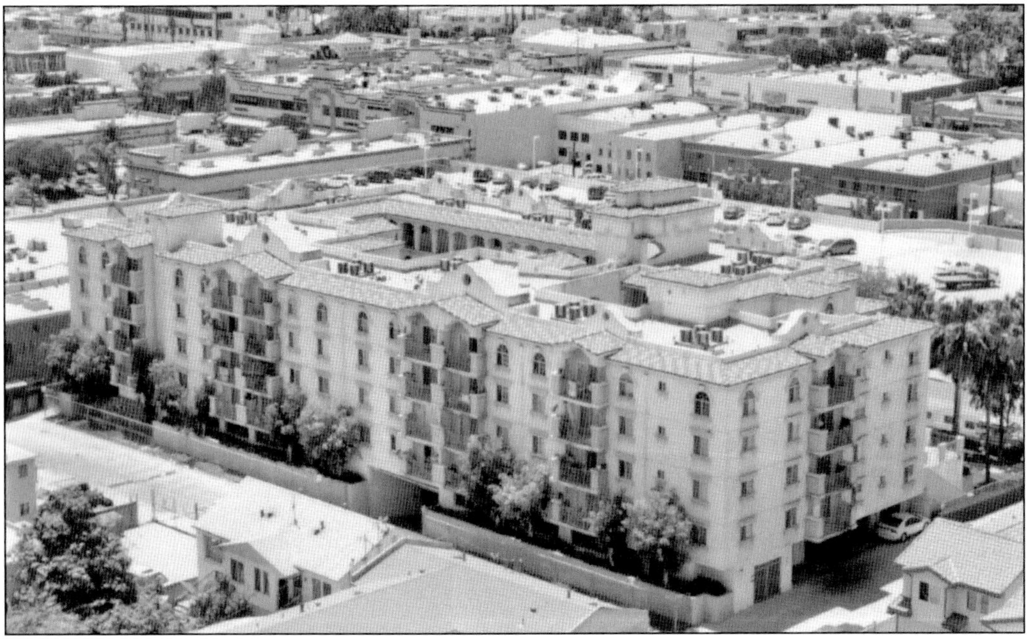

THE FUTURE OF THE CITY. The future of Huntington Park looks brighter than ever. The population currently is around 70,000, and it has become an important central hub of the Latino community in Los Angeles County. Several new elementary schools have been built in recent years, and an additional high school is planned in the west side of the city. A thriving Pacific Boulevard has returned to its preeminence as a retail sales center for the entire southeast area. As it did in its early history, Huntington Park still boasts the five good things: schools, churches, climate, public transportation, and a dedicated city government. Pictured are panoramic views of Huntington Park taken from the top of the 15-floor Concord Apartments. The modern Spanish-style condominium (above) is a good example of Huntington Park's revitalization. The beautiful Huntington Park Civic Center complex (below) can also be seen.

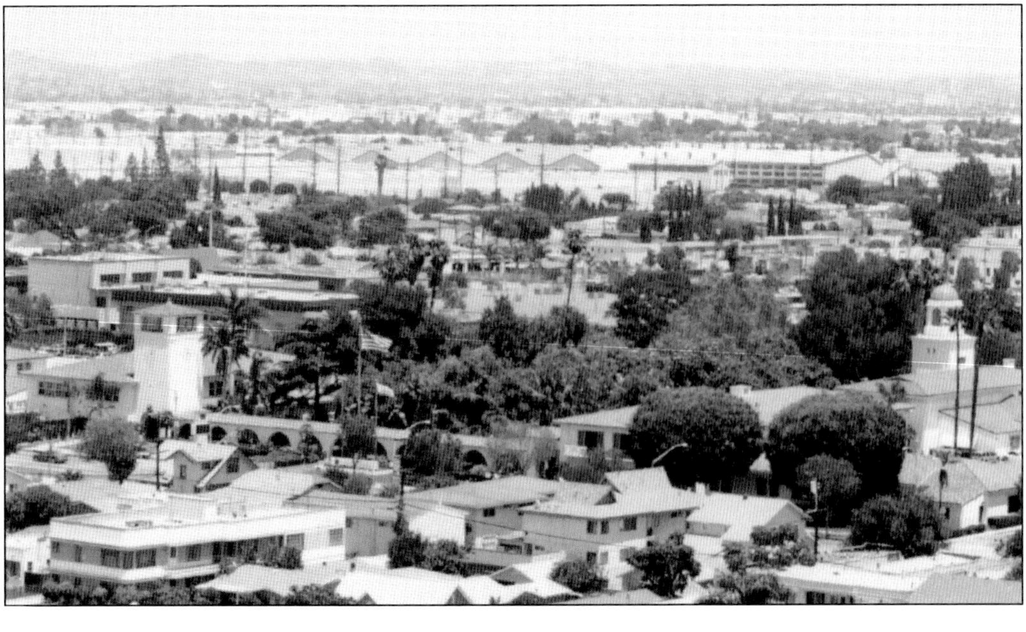

HUNTINGTON PARK CITY GOVERNMENT 2007

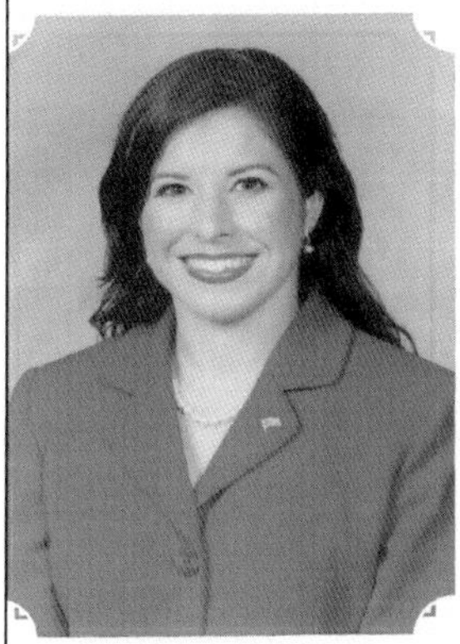

Elba Romo
City Council Member

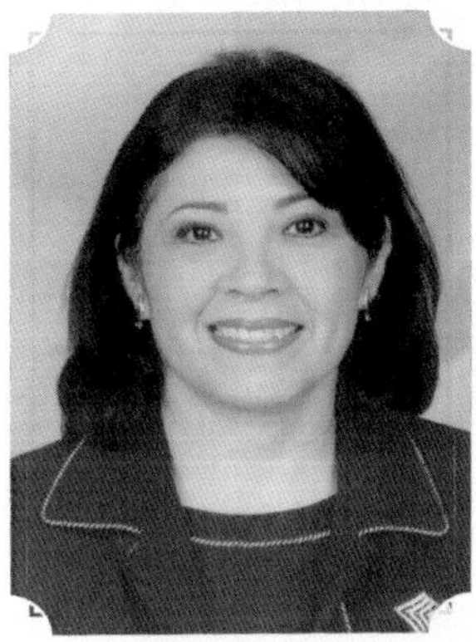

Elba Guerrero
Mayor

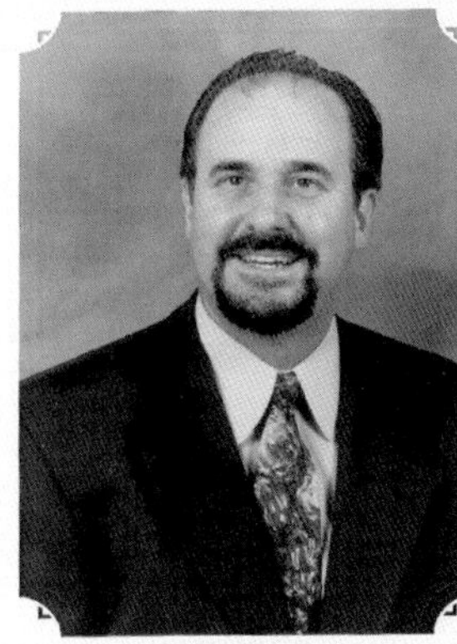

Greg Korduner
City Manager

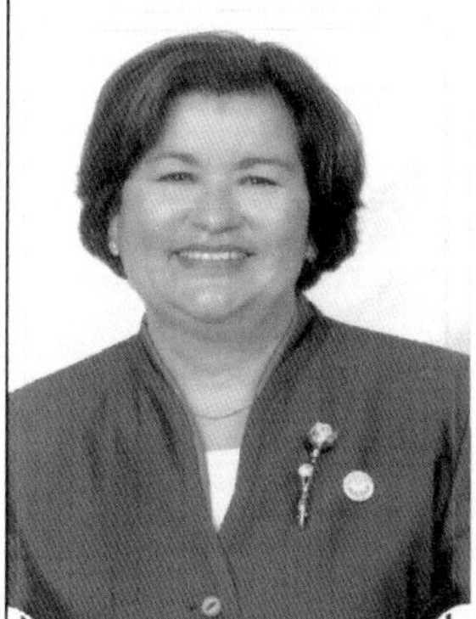

Ofelia Hernandez
City Council Member

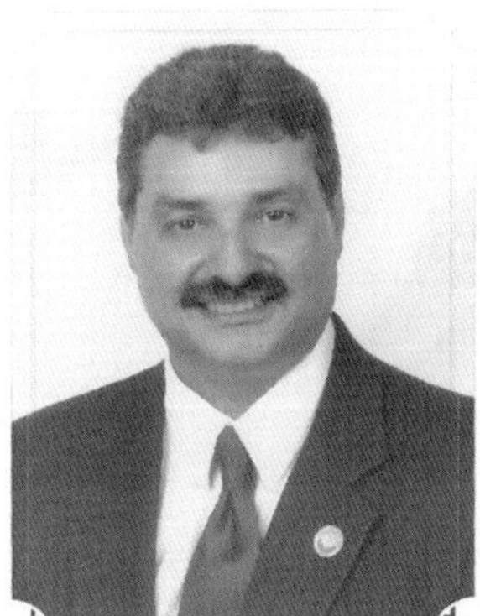

Mario Gomez
Mayor Pro-Tem

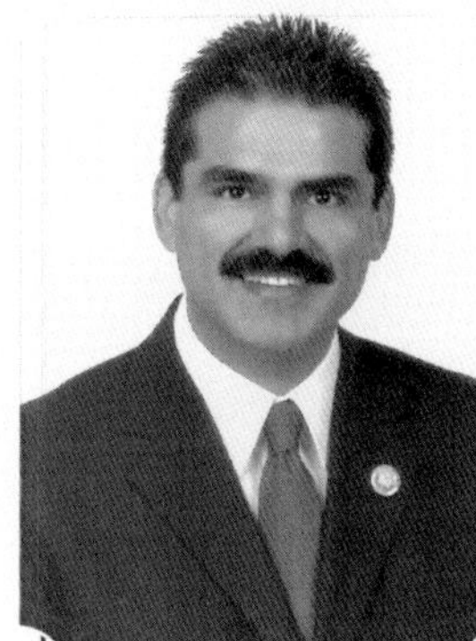

John Noguez
City Council Member

HUNTINGTON PARK CITY GOVERNMENT, 2007. Huntington Park has experienced and dedicated leadership for the new century. Like the first council members and city leadership in 1906, Mayor Elba Guerrero; mayor pro-tem Mario Gomez; council members Elba Romo, Ofelia Hernandez, and Juan Noguez; and city manager Greg Korduner are pioneers in their own right, ushering in new age in Huntington Park. All of the city council members are bilingual, with Spanish representing the demographics of the community. They serve with pride and honor.